LOOKING OUT FROM WITHIN

LIVING YOGA WITH THE SAINTS AND SAGES OF INDIA

VICTORIA MOO BRIDDELL

Copyright © Victoria Moo Briddell
All rights reserved.

No part of this publication may be reproduced, stored in a retrieval system or transmitted, in any form or by any means—electronic, mechanical, photocopying, recording or otherwise—without prior written permission from the publisher, except for the inclusion of brief quotations in a review.

For information about this title or to order other books and/or electronic media, contact the publisher.
www.linganorebooks.com.

This book is dedicated to my guru,
beloved Sri Swami Chidananda Maharaj,
of Sivananda Ashram, late President of
the Divine Life Society.

Acknowledgements

Thanks to my husband, Don, my soul mate through thick and thin. How could I have done it without you?

To our wonderful children, Matt and Christiana, and your families. To give you a little glimpse of your parents in their mid-twenties!

Thank you Max Regan of Hollowdeck Press LLC, for your great skill as a writing coach and for showing me the importance of a strong writing community.

To each of my fellow writers at Hilltoppers and Firedrake communities, I thank you for your encouragement and generosity over the years, for dispensing with disclaimers and holding each other accountable.

Thanks to Mary Dean and Sean Lemert for your careful reading of the manuscript in its early form and your helpful comments. To Bea Raydo for sharing the origins of hatha yoga practice.

To friends at Sivananda Ashram, HQ in India, for fact checking names, dates and stories.

Thanks to all the teachers and devotees who shared their wisdom and friendship with me, each one contributing in their own way to my spiritual journey.

Finally, big thanks to Joel Pitney and the team at launchmybook.com for bringing the manuscript into print and helping me to realize this project.

Contents

Prologue		1
Chapter 1	Arrival in India	9
Chapter 2	Adventures in South India	33
Chapter 3	In Nepal	55
Chapter 4	P.O. Shivanandanagar	71
Chapter 5	Swami Chidananda's Return	87
Chapter 6	The Power of Presence	121
Chapter 7	Moving Up	145
Chapter 8	Walking the Pilgrim Trail and other events	167
Chapter 9	Punjab Tour	187
Chapter 10	Summer by the Ganges	201
Chapter 11	Swami Sivananda's Disciples	219
Chapter 12	A Siren Calls	233
Chapter 13	Going Solo	241
Chapter 14	Reality gets real	257
Epilogue		277
Glossary/Dictionary		285

PROLOGUE

What is it that draws us inward, looking for meaning, for spiritual experiences, for enlightenment? What is that mysterious call that beckons us forth beyond the perspectives and cultural beliefs we were raised with to explore new ways of seeing and being? These questions have driven me for as long as I can remember; and they are questions that drove so many in my pre-boomer generation to question everything about the world we were raised in and to seek new answers, directions, and experiences. It was these questions that lead me, like so many other Western "seekers" to the East, looking for answers.

What I found was far more than I could have ever expected.

My journey began in what many consider to be the heart of the American counter cultural movement of the 1960s: San Francisco. I was a 22-year-old studying at San Francisco State University. In those days, the Haight-Ashbury, where I rented an apartment opposite the Panhandle of the Golden Gate Park, was still blossoming. People were open, welcoming, and creative. "The Haight" was more like a village then, where even if you didn't know everyone, we all shared the same sense of belonging.

That was before we became objects of curiosity for busloads of tourists to gawk at as they drove slowly down the street. It was before the media labeled us "hippies" and before word of our "free flowing" lifestyle spread across the country (and the world), opening a floodgate of young people flocking there from all across the country—runaways, those who felt rejected by society, pleasure seekers, or just the curious, all looking for answers.

Ironically, most of us were sons and daughters of the middle-class and had never known hunger or what real poverty was like, making our chosen lifestyle an enigma to our parents. Perhaps, like every new generation, we wanted to be different from our parents. We wanted something more real. The advent of psychedelics introduced us to a new reality and opened a vast gulf between us and those who had come before. I attended "be-ins" in the Park, where Timothy Leary repeated his now familiar message, "Tune in, turn on and drop out." Rock and roll music, which exploded into our lives, energized and enlivened our generation, further dividing us from our elders. We embraced nature and a back-to-the-land movement and rejected "the establishment" and everything that it stood for, which included institutions, large corporations, the military industrial complex, and "society" in general.

The war in Vietnam was going full throttle and the looming possibility of the draft for my two brothers and all my male friends scared us. People did crazy things to stay out of the war, from protesting and burning their draft card to shooting off their trigger finger. We didn't trust that our government was telling the truth and didn't really understand why the United States was involved in Vietnam. As history has proven, the government *was* lying to us and we were right to protest the war. Many of us didn't fully understand why exactly, we just intuitively knew it wasn't right, especially after the National Guard fired on the students at Kent State University. Suddenly, the war had come home and was being waged against *us*, the young people who were raising our voices in protest!

We all demanded change, and we went about it in different ways. Some moved out of the cities and back to the land and started the health-food movement. Others pursued a different reality through psychedelics. I was one of those who turned towards the philosophy and practices of Eastern spiritual disciplines. I took up the practice of "Transcendental Meditation," or TM popularized by the Beatles' Guru, Maharishi Mahesh

Yogi. I read Paramahamsa Yogananda's *Autobiography of a Yogi* and books by Sri Aurobindo. Through them I began to see that the purpose of human life on earth was to attain a higher consciousness, which the mystics called "Self-realization" or "God-realization."

My deepening interest in Eastern mysticism eventually led me to an encounter with two men who would change the course of my life forever. The first was a revered Indian holy man named Swami Chidananda, who was then president of The Divine Life Society (DLS), an international organization founded in 1936 by Swami Sivananda that was headquartered in India. I first met Swami Chidananda in May 1968 while I was visiting my family in South Africa, my country of birth. I attended a talk that he gave in Durban, the first stop on his world tour, which was to span two and a half years. I was immediately drawn in by his presence, by the feeling of holiness and humility which emanated from this extraordinary being. I had never met anyone like him in my life! Our connection was so deep that I would eventually "give up everything" to visit Swamiji at the Sivananda Ashram in India, which is the subject of this book.

The second encounter was with the man who would eventually become my husband and partner on my journey: Don Briddell, an artist from Maryland, whom I met on a ship traveling between New York and Southampton. Don and I made an immediate connection over our shared interest in metaphysics, and after going our separate ways at the end of the voyage, we stayed in touch via letters. Our relationship grew to the point that Don invited me to join him in Ecuador where he was stationed in the Peace Corps. It was during our time there that we began to study mysticism and practice meditation together. In 1969, after returning to the US, we were married.

Not long after our marriage, Don and I learned that Swami Chidananda would be visiting the Sivananda Yoga Camp in Val Morin, Canada. I very much wanted to meet him again and introduce Don to him. I hoped that Don would find Swamiji as inspiring as I did. We ended up spending the whole summer at the Yoga Camp participating in one of the first Yoga

Teacher Trainings offered in North America, under the guidance of Swami Vishnudevananda (Swami Vishnu). We, the trainees, were privileged to study with Swami Chidananda on a daily basis.

Don and Swamiji

As I had hoped, Don was duly impressed with Swami Chidananda's presence. During our stay at the Camp it became clear to us that the great *rishis* and *yogis* of the East were calling us forth to live our lives for a higher purpose. This is what we were deeply drawn to and we resolved that we would go to India to pursue this interest further.

Towards the end of the summer Swami Vishnu hosted a True World Order

Conference at the Camp and invited a number of Swami Sivananda's disciples. They were an inspiring and impressive group of swamis!

Left to right: Swamis Satchidananda, Venkatesananda, Vishnudevananda, Chidananda, Pranavananda, Sahajananda

Before we left the Camp in early September we asked Swami Chidananda if we could come to the *ashram* in India. "Yes, most welcome!" he said, and advised us to apply for student visas which could be renewed for a longer stay.

But the specter of the Vietnam War still hung over our heads, and Don had an interview with the Draft Board in the fall. We had considered immigrating to Canada, but Don decided to apply for Conscientious Objector status and make his views on the war known. When he was granted

C.O. status, we began a two-year service with the poor in Appalachia, in lieu of serving in the army. However, after three months Don took and failed his army physical, receiving a 4F, which essentially freed him from any further obligation to the U.S. government.

We were free at last to begin our journey to India! We took all our earnings from working in Ecuador and made our way to the West Coast where we sold our van and bought two passages on what turned out to be a decrepit freighter that was making its last crossing to Japan, before being scrapped. We spent the rest of the money on backpacks and travelers checks. A few friends saw us off at the docks in San Francisco and we sailed out under the Golden Gate Bridge into the Pacific Ocean. For six months we travelled through Japan, the Philippines, Malaysia, Singapore and Ceylon, eventually reaching the shores of South India in October 1970.

Our backpacks

That is where my story begins. What follows is a detailed account of that life-changing year we spent in India living among its saints and sages. It's told in the first person present tense, to give you the most intimate sense of what it was like to be Westerners encountering the beauty and spiritual depth of this exotic land.

CHAPTER 1

ARRIVAL IN INDIA

MOTHER REMA

When we reach the gate of 104 Lloyd's Road, a small boy jumps up when he sees us and runs towards the house yelling, "Americans coming! Americans coming!"

When we landed at Madras airport last evening, an Indian woman hurried up to us and asked if she could buy our liquor license. Alcohol is against the law in India and only foreigners coming in from outside are allowed to purchase it. Enterprising Indians try to buy the license for their own use. "We don't have a license. We don't drink," we told her, and she moved away disappointed to look for someone else.

We asked a taxi to take us to an inexpensive hotel. The driver took us to a place that was questionable, even by our standards, a dark building, stuffy and poorly ventilated. Since it was already evening, we decided to stay that night only, but we refused to let them keep our passports.

In the morning, we dress in our Indian clothes and hail a man pedaling a bicycle rickshaw to take us to the address on our scrap of paper. We had written to Rema from Ceylon[1] to inform her that we would be coming.

---

[1] Ceylon changes its name back to Sri Lanka when it becomes a republic in 1972.

Apparently, our letter has been received and discussed, because the little boy already knows about us as we enter the gate to the garden. He runs up the steps onto the verandah of the large old double-story house, which may have been elegant in times past, but now, the pale beige cement walls are blackened at the bottom with mildew from monsoon rains.

We walk up the front steps and are met by Prabha, one of Rema's daughters, who greets us politely and invites us to remove our shoes and come inside. In most Eastern countries it is customary to remove one's shoes by the door and put on slippers or go barefoot inside. Prabha indicates that we should take a seat with the other devotees, on a woven grass mat on the floor. "Mother is coming soon," she says.

The room is bare of furniture, except for a slab of wood hanging by chains from the ceiling in the center of the room, to form a swing. Framed pictures of saints and sages look down on us from higher up on all four walls. Presently, a short plump lady, dressed in an orange sari, enters the room from one of the side doors. She looks to be in her early fifties, with fair skin and shoulder length hair, matted into locks on the ends. Her eyes are very direct and take us in with one glance. She moves gracefully in a dignified manner, greeting all of us sitting on the floor, while she takes her seat on the swing in the center of the room.

We are at once mesmerized by the presence of Mother Rema, who swings gently forward and back. She asks us how we have come and where we are staying and when we tell her about the hotel, she looks concerned.

"You must leave there this very day," she advises. "You can move to the Madras Woodlands, near here," she says. "The manager is a devotee of mine. He will look after you."

Rema tells us about growing up as a devotee of Lord Krishna and she shows us her two-foot high black granite statue of Krishna, whom she worshipped daily as a child, by offering flowers, incense and fruits. She is from the Brahmin class and grew up well educated in the British school system, before India gained its independence in 1947. She attended University in

Madras, where she was among the first women to graduate. It was then arranged that she marry her English professor, Mr. Veeramani.

"I was still hugging my little statue of Krishna," she tells us, "not realizing what marriage meant." Apparently, her mother had not educated her on the subject of marriage, so it all came as a shock to Rema, when her husband, referring to her love of Krishna, said, "All that child's play is over now. You are married to *me*!"

Mr. Veeramani came to realize and eventually accept that he was not married to an ordinary wife. Mother Rema, as we call her, is a spiritually advanced soul. Devotees come to see her every evening after their work. Mr. Veeramani, now retired, stays quietly present in the background of their home on Lloyd's Road. He is pleasant and courteous, though somewhat asthmatic. Prabha is separated from her husband and lives with her parents in the house, along with her eight-year-old son, Ilya.

In the afternoon we move our things to the Madras Woodlands, a small, clean hotel with a pool. "Oh good," I say, "it will be nice to cool off in the pool." So, after putting our things in the room, we put on our swimming suits, wrap ourselves in hotel towels and ride the elevator down to the pool level. When the door opens with the pool right in front of us, I see it is packed with Indian men. Not one woman in sight! It is a shock for me to find that Indian women do not swim in pools together with men and that also when they take a dip in the ocean or a river, they do so fully clothed. Don is put off too, so I press the 'Close Door' button and we return to our room.

Next day, at Mother Rema's invitation, we move from the Woodlands to the flat roof of her house, where we sleep on mats under the sky. We stay with her for two weeks, learning about Indian culture first hand.

The little boy who first met us on the front steps had a dream about a lady living in Madras, who would help him study the tabla. On the strength of this dream, his father, a poor man living on the other side of India, brought his son on a long train journey to Madras. The boy took his father's hand and led him directly to Mother Rema's house. The father is staying for a few days, until his son is settled in his new environment. Mother Rema has made arrangements for tabla lessons for the boy. "He is a child prodigy," she tells us. The fact that his father brought him all the way across India to an unknown lady's home isn't considered extraordinary by anyone except us. This is a country where one's destiny can change according to a message received in a dream!

Perhaps this is because the waking and dream states are not considered as different from each other as they are in western culture. In *Vedanta* philosophy, awareness of the ultimate Reality is beyond both dreaming and the waking state. It is closer in many ways to deep sleep, where the mind retires and turns in on itself, where the thoughts subside and the true blissful Self is experienced. As the teaching says, "Just as one wakes up from a dream into the waking state, when one awakes into the true Reality, the waking state is perceived to be nothing but a dream." So, dreaming and waking are all part of the same continuum of consciousness, with varying degrees of awareness.

"What songs do you know?" Rema asks us one day. Here in India most seekers or devotees know at least one *bhajan*,[2] a spiritual song praising God in some form or other. In the company of a holy person, it is customary for a devotee to sing a *bhajan*, or lead a *kirtan*, a chant in which a line is sung to which the audience responds. "Sing us something," Rema says, encouraging us. We look at each other blankly. I grew up singing hymns from the Oxford English Hymn Book at school in South Africa and know several of them by heart. Don grew up using the Baptist Hymnal, but somehow it doesn't occur to either of us to sing a religious hymn. "Come on, sing us something," Mother Rema says again, rocking gently back and forth on her swing.

I mentally flip through my repertoire of songs. We can't really sing,

---

[2] Most Sanskrit words are italicized unless they are in common use in the English language. See the glossary at the back for their further definition.

ARRIVAL IN INDIA

"Mr. Tambourine Man," or "It's been a Hard Day's Night," and definitely not "The House of the Rising Sun." They just wouldn't make any sense to our present company.

"Well," after conferring together, "we know "Five Hundred Miles." We launch into our rendition of Peter, Paul and Mary's song, but we don't know the lyrics beyond the first verse and so we keep singing, "Lord, I'm five hundred miles from my home," before we fizzle out.

The devotees sitting around Rema stare at us with interest. They do not criticize or judge, but we feel embarrassed by such a poor representation of our country's music, especially since Rema's eldest daughter, Mira, is a classically trained singer and often performs on All India Radio. "We're going to have to learn to sing!" I say to Don later.

It's getting close to Diwali also known as Deepavali, the festival of lights. It is an important time, celebrating the return of Lord Rama to Ayodhya after his fourteen-year banishment to the forest, when everyone lights lamps and puts them in the windows of their homes. Mira has travelled from Delhi by train with her husband Raja, to spend the holiday with her parents. She and Raja sleep on the floor, in a room off the open roof where we are staying. They never close the door and I see their legs sticking out, but I don't look closely, afraid of invading their privacy. I notice that Indian women sleep in their saris and then change into fresh clothes each morning. They don't seem to have separate clothes to sleep in.

Every day with Rema we learn something new. Mira recounts a story about her Mother in which one of her devotees, living in another town, attempted to take her own life by swallowing a bottle of sleeping pills. "Mother was at home," Mira remembers, "and she began vomiting up many pills. We didn't know what was happening, but later we found out that this woman had tried to commit suicide. But when Mother vomited up the pills, the woman became perfectly alright."

"What did the woman say when she heard what had happened?" I ask.

"When she found out that Mother had vomited up all the pills, she felt very remorseful," Mira says. "She was given a second chance to live and so she has changed her life." We don't understand how these things happen, but we are getting used to the fact that the extraordinary is possible in the midst of our everyday lives. We remind ourselves this is not Biblical times. This is the 20th century! In India it is perfectly normal to have the modern world with its new technology, alongside customs and traditions that have been in place for hundreds, if not thousands of years.

Mira takes us around the house and shows us little statues of gods and goddesses that occupy niches in the wall. She explains that Rema materialized some of these objects out of thin air, and other *yogis* and *yoginis* presented some of them to her. We listen to these stories not knowing what to think. They are stretching our realm of comprehension.

"And this one," Mira says, taking a large statue of Ganesha in her hands, "this came from the ocean."

"What do you mean?" I ask. "You mean Rema found it in the ocean?"

"No," Mira says. "There is a very old *yogini* living in caves along the sea shore in Kanya Kumari, at the tip of India. Whenever Mother goes there, she visits her. One day the old *yogini* stirred the water with her hand and took this Ganesha out and gave it to Mother."

"You mean she just materialized it?" Don asks, looking suspiciously at the statue.

"Yes," Mira answers. The statue is made from gorgeous mother-of-pearl and Don inspects it carefully, with the eyes of a sculptor, looking for the seams of the mold. He can't find any. Our western belief in the reality of the physical world and how things are meant to behave in it is beginning to crumble.

When we ask Rema about it, she explains that there are three ways of materializing things. "One is just to gather the elements together, like gathering crumbs and putting them all together to form a cake. There is a vast storehouse of treasure in India, which the *yogis* know about," she explains.

ARRIVAL IN INDIA

"The second way is taking items from that storehouse and moving them from there to here. I don't do it any more. It is nothing more than stealing."

"And what is the third way?" I ask.

"The third way is actually creating something out of nothing," she explains. "Only the powerful masters can do that."

"You mean like Jesus with the loaves and the fishes?" Don asks.

"Yes, exactly," she says. "Who are we to know what these great beings can do?"

There is a large room attached to the main house serving as a temple for a life-size statue of Lord Siva and his consort, Meenakshi. Rema is an ardent devotee of Shakti, the Divine Mother. Meenakshi is the green-colored South Indian Goddess, Siva's consort, one of the many forms of the Divine Mother. Each day, Rema or her devotees dress Meenakshi in a clean silk sari and offerings are made to her. Each evening, as the sun goes down, an oil lamp is lit in her honor. One afternoon, Rema goes out and when she arrives home after dark, no one has lit the lamp.

"What is the matter with you people?" Rema is clearly annoyed. "The lamp has to be lit in the evening!"

"I'm sorry," I say.

"I am not cross with you," she replies. "You don't know. But these people are here all the time. They must do it!" For Rema, the statues in the temple room are treated like people, because to her they are alive.

"How can they be alive?" I have to ask. She doesn't take offense to my question. She knows I have a Western mind-set and don't believe these things easily.

"Everything is consciousness," Rema explains. "If you go on hitting a tennis ball against the wall, it keeps coming back to you. Like that, day after day, if you go on worshipping with sincere devotion, God responds. One evening," she continues with a story, "I put a full bowl of curd at the feet of Meenakshi and locked the door to the room." Rema lifts a fold in her sari, showing me her set of keys tied to a handkerchief, which she keeps tucked into the waistband of her petticoat. "The next morning when I unlocked the door, there was curd on Meenakshi's hand and mouth and the bowl was empty." She tilts her head and smiles at us, as our minds search frantically for a logical explanation. We either have to expand our belief system to include the possibility of what she is saying, or we have to hold what she is saying at bay and cling to our limited sense of reality.

With all her open heartedness and acceptance of us into her home, Rema is very traditional when it comes to spiritual practices. She is a firm believer in *brahmacharya*, sexual abstinence, or restraint. She has, in the way of the *yogis*, sublimated her sexual energy and transformed it into spiritual power.

One evening, we all go on an outing to the Madras beach and sit on the sand listening to the sound of the waves breaking on the shore.

"Why don't you practice *brahmacharya*?" she asks Don, trying to convince him to forgo a physical relationship for a life in the spirit.

"I like things the way they are," he says shortly. I find it interesting that many spiritual traditions advocate abstinence or restraint, to channel and sublimate sexual energy into an upward spiritual evolution. Mother Rema and Swami Sivananda agree on this point. The rules differ according to one's *dharma* and the stage of life through which one is passing. For a monk total abstinence is expected. Ordinarily, in marriage restraint is advised and fidelity to one's partner is expected. However, Mother Rema's marriage is not ordinary.

The next evening we sit together with a few other devotees to meditate. I spend the time enjoying an interior sense of peace. I am unaware of the drama unfolding behind me. Later, Don tells me about his out-of-body experience, in which he zoomed to the outer edges of the universe before re-entering his body. At one point in the meditation Rema came into the room and began stroking Don's back, up and down his spine. After some time I hear her voice say, "Stop!" This is the end of the meditation.

Later, Don tells me that when Rema began to rub his back, he lost his identity as a human being and entered into snake consciousness. He became a snake with fangs drooling with poison. "I had no sense of right and wrong, the way a normal human being has. There is no conscience in a snake. I was afraid if you moved I would bite you." I listen with a mixture of awe and horror as Don tells me how he came back to himself again. "Finally, Rema grabbed the hair on top of my head and pulled upwards. Gradually I came back to normal body consciousness."

After Don's experience, it dawns on us that we know very little about Indian culture and that their metaphysics goes far beyond our limited understanding of reality.

POWER

One thing that surprises us is that so-called spiritual power, or *siddhi*, is not necessarily paired with goodness in the way we would expect. We listen to tales of rogue *yogis* that use power as a means of controlling their disciples, of spiritual vendettas, *yogi* against *yogi*, to gain the upper hand. Mother Rema herself has had such experiences and warns us about them. She recounts one of her past lives in Tibet, where she escaped from a *yogi* who was trying to control her and chose instead to run off with her lover. This disobedience angered the *yogi* who cursed her. She explains that the lover in that birth is now her husband, which makes me wonder if is that the reason behind their rather strange relationship. While she is very loyal to him, the household revolves around her, and he takes a back seat.

It seems history repeats itself, as Rema explains her story further. "In this birth, as a young married woman, I found myself in a similar situation with a powerful *yogi*, who wanted me to be his spiritual consort and help him run his *ashram*. When I refused, this *yogi* put a curse on my two small daughters—one would lose her eyesight as she grew up and the other would remain childless. That was the curse. I knew I had to get away from him! I escaped in the middle of the night, taking one daughter in each hand and running away from the *ashram*!"

The thwarted *yogi* began to punish Rema for disobeying him by attacking her psychically and seeking to cause her bodily harm. Rema explains that if you are assaulted physically, you can take your case before a magistrate, but if you are harassed supernaturally, in the more subtle realms through invisible methods, you have to rely on making yourself strong and powerful, to ward off the evil influence. "Especially a woman on her own, without the protection of a *guru*," she says. In order to hold her own against this rogue *yogi*, Rema did months and months of intense spiritual practice, in a little hut built on the flat roof of her house. After her second daughter, Prabha, was born, she lived from then on as a celibate, observing silence and fasting for three years, taking only the water of a tender coconut once a day, no solids, fruits or juices.

"No food for three years!" I exclaim. "You must have been so thin!"

"No, very fat!" she assures me. "*Asanas* are there, *prana* is there—where is the need for food? I lived for nine years without touching anyone—neither my husband, nor my daughters," Rema tells us. "I had to protect my family against this *yogi*."

"I don't understand. How could he harm you?" I ask

"It is like being burned from within," she explains. Through her intense *sadhana*, her spiritual practice, Rema developed the same power—to burn her opponent from the inside. Apparently, she was so successful with her practices that he finally asked for a truce. However, he could not undo the curse he had already put on her children. He only agreed to leave her and her family alone from that time on.

We are too shocked to say anything. This is beyond anything we could imagine. The whole idea of *yogis* fighting with each other on the astral plane is mind boggling to us. Both Don and I, from our different backgrounds, believed that goodness and spirituality would go hand in hand, that spiritual power would naturally develop along with moral righteousness. But apparently, even in the spiritual realm there are power hungry *yogis*! Another veil has just fallen from our eyes. We conclude that power, like money, is a neutral force. It is the person wielding the power that needs to be purified. Spiritual power, like physical, mental, or political power, can be used for either good or evil in this world.

"It came to pass as he pronounced," Rema says in finishing. "First, as Prabha grew older, she began to have trouble with her eyesight, until now, she is almost blind. And then, Mira has never been able to conceive a child."

PRASAD

Because it is a holy day, there is a special *puja*, a worship to take place that evening and the young servant girl who works in the kitchen, is seated on the floor, rolling up balls of a sweet mixture and placing them on a clean tray. As we are following Rema through the kitchen, I reach down and pop one of the balls into my mouth.

"No!" comes the chorus of voices from Rema, Prabha and Mira. "They are for *prasad*!"

"Oh, I'm *sorry*!" I say, but it is too late. The sweet ball is in my mouth. I didn't realize it was for *prasad*. I know that *prasad* is specially prepared food that is offered to God during a *puja*. After the worship, the food that is now sanctified is distributed to all those present.

"The girl has had a bath and put on clean clothes so she could make the *prasad*," Rema explains. "We cannot offer food that has been eaten as *prasad*."

"I'm so sorry," I repeat, wondering whether to swallow the sweet ball still in my mouth. Spitting it out would be worse.

"You didn't know, so that's alright," Mother Rema says kindly, forgiving me. She chuckles. "You are the Egyptian Goddess who has come to try the *prasad*." Rema is teasing me about one of our conversations, in which I told her that I think I have lived one lifetime in Egypt. The servant girl has stopped making the balls and is looking up, awaiting further instructions. I popped the sweet into my mouth without thinking, like walking past a bowl of cherries and trying one. I am really sorry to have to put them all to so much extra trouble. But there is no question that the batch has been polluted and it can't be offered to God.

"You will have to take another bath and begin again," Rema tells the girl.

Indians are very clean and bathe and put on fresh clothes every day. There is a well out in the back garden of the old Lloyd's Road house and water is drawn up in a bucket on a rope and used in the little bathing stalls out back. We take "bucket baths," pouring water over our heads and bodies, soaping up and rinsing off, using one or two buckets of water. This method conserves a lot of water and the well provides enough for everyone.

"What do you use on your hair?" Rema asks.

Moo and Rema at Lloyd's Road

"Shampoo and conditioner," I answer. She chuckles.

"Here is a bottle of hair oil which I made myself," she says, giving me a bottle of green aromatic smelling liquid with a screw top. I begin to use the oil on my long hair after washing, like the Indian women, to keep the hair and the scalp healthy.

A SACRED CEREMONY

One day Rema asks to see Don's sketchbook and notices a little article he has snipped out of the paper in Malaysia, about a man who refuses to wear any clothes.

"Oh, that's just an article Don found," I say, dismissing it with a wave of my hand.

"No, no," Rema says, reading the article with interest. "There are a few great souls, called *avadhoots*, who go about without clothes. There is one such one down on the seashore in Cape Comorin. She is four-hundred years old."

"How is it possible to live so long?" I ask.

"She is a completely liberated being," Rema explains. "Very high consciousness, with absolutely no body awareness." She turns to me, smiling. "When I go there, I have to bring her down to body consciousness. I slap the water and say, 'Come. Come and play! Come and play!'" Rema pats her lap with her hand. "Then she comes and sits in the water with us. Otherwise, she roams about free as a bird."

"Is she the one who gave you the mother-of-pearl Ganesha?" Don asks. He is still trying to get his mind around it.

"She is the one," Rema confirms.

Rema tells us that there is a *yogi* living in a cave outside of Madras city, who is supported by the local government. She shows us a picture of him meditating. He never cuts his fingernails and they have grown into long, curved claws. We are fascinated by the fact that he has such long nails. It seems ridiculous to us to have hands that are useless.

"How does he pick up his food?"

"He is fed by his devotees," Rema answers.

The idea that a government values a person meditating in a cave is a new one for us. The culture of India has long since revered its saints and sages and not only gives them a high place in society, but also supports them. There are places all over India where wandering monks can get free meals. Householders are expected to share their food with a wandering *sadhu*, who might knock on their door at any time. In Indian culture the guest is considered God, and so even the very poor are willing to share whatever they have with a guest. We are certainly the fortunate recipients of this wonderful Indian hospitality, being welcomed by strangers into their homes, staying with them, sleeping on their floors and sharing their food.

It is hard to imagine how austere Rema was as a young woman, observing her now with her devotees around her, kissing the little children and holding the hands of the men and women.

She holds a little gold cup in her hand to perform a sacred ceremony, which is done once a year. She writes a *bij mantra*, a holy word, in the honey at the bottom of the cup, praying deeply and silently for a few minutes, with her eyes closed. She and the children believe that if she writes on their tongue, their school grades will improve, or their stuttering will be cured. As I sit next to her on the swing I see her roll her closed eyes upward, to the *trikuta*, the space between the eyebrows, also known as the third eye. She keeps writing with her ring finger in the honey at the bottom of the cup. Then the child in front of her sticks out his tongue and Mother Rema writes on it with the honey. Then she smears honey all around the inside of his mouth. The child sucks and swallows.

"Sometimes, if you are lucky," she says, turning to me, "a dumb one will start talking."

People sit around her all over the floor—men and women, illiterates and intellectuals. Some young university "thinkers" come in to ask her about mediation, the nature of the soul and about rebirth.

"Meditation," she says, "is like looking into the lumber yard of the mind. Some of the things inside are dirty and foul and you turn your back on them. They will die without your replenishing and feeding them. If you give your attention only to the light side of things, the dark must perish." She looks at me. "Whenever you have a moment watch the mind, what it is thinking. Soon you will see what is essential and what is unnecessary. When you realize that the unessential is crowding the mind, you will throw the garbage out."

"Jesus said, 'Watch and pray.'" She continues, "Watch the mind and clean it, purify it." She looks around the room of devotees. All faces are turned towards her. "Meditation can be done at any time, in any circumstances. Just relax the body. Don't hold it stiff and tense. It's not necessary."

Rema on her swing

JESUS, KRISHNAMURTHI AND MATTED LOCKS

Sometimes, I look at Mother Rema and see a plump, middle-aged, motherly woman with a very sweet smile and lots of love in her eyes. And then I look again and see her looking right through me and I know she knows what I'm thinking.

"Why are we so worried about our age?" she asks. "Why do we not want to admit how old we are? We want to dye the hair young again. Do we ever think about our mental age? Do we ever think about what's *inside* the head?" She looks around smiling. "If somebody tells me I don't look fifty-seven, I'm flattered!" She laughs joyfully. "After *so* many births, we're worried about our next birth! I know my past seventeen births. Anyway," she concludes, "if I must take another birth, I want it to be as a man! That's all I ask."

As a woman in India, Mother Rema has had a difficult path. Women don't have the same rights as men. She speaks to us about spiritual progress in married life.

"Sex is a thing that must be worshipped," she says, "and not done clumsily. It should be like the spontaneous mating between the peacock and the swan." I guess she is referring to a story from the Indian scriptures, because as far as I know, a peacock wouldn't mate with a swan. But, as we realize since arriving at Rema's house, the boundaries of what we think possible, keep expanding.

She laughs. "When one has been worshipping the Lord," she sighs. "He is so perfect. Men are imperfect." She tells us about her husband's gambling and drinking habits. "But," she tells me quietly, "he never went with other women."

"I wanted to learn about Christianity," she says, "so I went to a Christian school. But I never liked the confessions. Every time I went to confession, I thought, *why should I pull this man down to my level?* I was afraid I would pollute the priest's mind by raking the dirt out of my own. Then I thought, *No guru! I'll do it on my own and have a direct connection with God. Go straight to the Lord!*"

"So you don't have a *guru*?" I venture to ask.

"Have you noticed the name written on the front gate?" Rema replies.

"'Agastya' is written there. He was a Muni, a great sage of ancient India. I have a deep connection with him and he is my *guru*."

"And what is your relationship with Christ?" I ask.

"Most people talk about Christ," she says. "They don't even know what Jesus was! We aren't even one millionth of what he was! Christ didn't walk, he *moved*!" She continues, "I've had several visions—once I found Him in Egypt. Then I found Him in the Himalayas. Then again, I found Him in Egypt. In those days Egypt was a psychic country. Christ also did *sadhana* and acquired *siddhis*," she says. "That's why He made His disciples practice before they preached."

The next day Don and I take a bus to the Theosophical Society in Adhyar, outside of Madras. We are very impressed by the giant banyan tree there, which has sent roots down from the branches and spread out into a small forest. In the bookshop we find a picture of Jesus meditating in a forest. We buy it to bring back to show Rema.

"Do you like it?" I ask her. She looks at me with her piercing eyes.

"What's the use of pictures when I can see for myself?" She says, "Christ has appeared to me in pure radiant white, with a long cord around his robe and sort of a white shadow behind him. His eyes were full of infinite compassion and gentleness. When you look into His eyes, you go deep, deep, deep..."

"When I was a little girl," she tells us, "I used to play with J. Krishnamurti and sit on the lap of Annie Besant and Paramahamsa Yogananda, under the banyan tree." She continues reminiscing, "Swami Sivananda stopped at our house when he was on his India tour in 1950."

That evening, we join the other devotees to do *puja* in the temple room. While we understand the general intention of the worship, neither Don nor I understand the specific meaning of the *mantras*, nor the *mudras*, the hand gestures that go with them. I would rather be sitting in silence, especially since Rema has been called away by one of her devotees.

"He's broken his leg and is crying for me," she tells us. "I'll just go and treat him and come back." She is standing with relaxed dignity, holding a bunch of bananas, which she is taking to the devotee. Then she moves off slowly in her rubber sandals.

The next day, she tells me that she is able to cure people who have a lot of faith in her. She takes the pain into her own body and lets it work itself out, but they will still have the broken bone, until it heals normally. Her husband had been very ill with heart trouble and asthma. "He was unconscious for fourteen days," she says. "He told me I gave him new life. Unless they have faith in me, I can do nothing."

Mother Rema's hair has become partially matted at the bottom. Where it joins the head the hair looks thin, but the matting at the bottom seems like a mass. I ask her about it.

"Three years ago," she says, holding one of the strands, "all this happened within twenty-four hours. I was in a trance and some of my hair suddenly became matted." It is another instance of something we have never heard of and we can't understand what would cause the hair to do that.

Mother Rema tells us that she had a heart attack about the same time that her hair became matted. No one seems to know whether the two incidents are connected or not. Undoubtedly, she was under too much stress, although "stress" is not a word used in conversation in India. One just accepts one's *karma*, the experiences one has to undergo, and gets on with it. Rema's explanation is that the heart attack came from too much talking. Then, maybe to demonstrate that she is not alone with what happened to her hair, she shows us a picture of a *yogi* with a river of matted locks flowing down to his feet.

"Let me see how you meditate," she says to me. I am sitting in one of the few chairs and so I just close my eyes. Don is sitting across from us in another chair. I start feeling a magnetic pull in the space between the eyebrows. The talking in the room dies away and the people drift off elsewhere. It is very peaceful. Thoughts of love and gratitude flow through my mind. We sit still for perhaps half an hour or more. After some time, I feel the sensation of a full bladder and I think *I will have to get up soon*. But I don't move. Soon after that, Mother Rema stirs and says to me, "Do you want to go to the bathroom and come back?"

The next day Mother Rema gives me her orange sari, which she wore when she went into *samadhi*, a super-conscious state, for eighteen hours, sitting on a tiger skin on Vivekananda's Rock at Cape Comorin, the most southern tip of India. She instructs me, "Wear it only when you meditate." I wrap it around my shoulders for the evening meditation and again feel a drawing in of *prana* to the *ajna chakra*, the center between the eyebrows. The piece of cloth seems to be charged with spiritual vibrations and I feel so blessed receiving it.

AURAS AND CASTING OUT EVIL SPIRITS

When I find out Mother Rema can see auras around people, I ask curiously, "What color is mine?"

"Blue," she says without hesitation, "deep blue, sea blue. Do you know the blue in the rainbow? That's about one hundredth the intensity of the psychic blue."

"What does it signify?" I ask.

"Stubbornness," she says, "strong determination. You'll either *do* it, or you *won't* do it." She takes my hand and says gently, "You must be considerate of others."

"Yes." I agree. After a moment I ask, "What's Don's color?"

"Yellow," she says. "He's diplomatic. He's very deep."

I think of the blankets Don bought for us in Malaysia. We were told that since we would be traveling by train in India, it would be a good idea to have a light blanket, to fold and sit on, and to wrap up and sleep in. Don came back with two grey cotton blankets, one with a yellow stripe and one with a blue stripe. He brought them back to our room in the Sivananda Ashram at the foot of Batu Caves, on the outskirts of Kuala Lumpur and threw them on the bed. "Which one do you want?" he asked. I secretly wanted the yellow one, but gave him first choice, since he had gone out to buy them. He chose yellow, so I took the blue and grew to like it.

"Together, you're green," Mother Rema says, "the color of Meenakshi. She brought you to me."

We notice a young woman amongst the devotees, who acts very submissive to Mother Rema. She is staying somewhere in the house, with a couple of other young girls. I notice them every early morning, taking their baths out back. When I ask about her, Rema tells me that the girl was possessed and has been brought to Rema to cure her evil spirits. "She gets into fits," Rema says, "in which she kicks and bites people. Sometimes she turns around and around in circles very fast." In modern psychology I guess there would be a term for this illness. But at this time in India they still believe, as described in the New Testament of the Bible, that evil spirits can take possession of a person and that the only way to get rid of them, is to bring the possessed into the direct presence of a holy person.

"I told her parents that she must stay with me for forty-eight days," Rema explains, "but the father got impatient and came and took his daughter away."

I look at the girl sitting on the floor in the kitchen, shelling peas for the lunch meal. Her turquoise blouse and her sari are clean and fresh and her hair is combed through with oil and neatly platted into a single braid down her back. The three girls are quietly chatting together. All three look contented and happy.

"When her father took her home she became possessed again," Rema goes on. "Then the mother brought her back with her two sisters for company and said she must stay until I cast out the evil spirits."

Everything seems to happen so spontaneously around Mother Rema.

The large house is almost empty of furniture, except for a few wooden beds and one or two chairs. I wonder if the parents of the girl have come to some financial arrangement with the Veeramani family? Taking in and feeding three extra people doesn't seem to faze them. I never get the feeling that we, or the other extra people, are a burden to them. The family is not well off, but there seems to be very little talk of money for food for all these people. The central focus is remembrance and worship of God, in all forms and specifically in the form of Meenakshi and service to the devotees, who come for Mother's darshan on a daily basis.

GOD'S NAME, MANTRAS AND THE EVIL EYE

In the few days that we have spent with Mother Rema we have experienced life that is not about the acquisition of material goods, but about love and service. The spiritual vibration in India is palpable. It feels ancient here. The entire culture revolves around spiritual traditions that have come down through the generations. As an individual I try to keep open-minded and embrace the whole. Isn't this what the Holy Scriptures, the *Vedas* teach—to dissolve oneself in *Brahman*, to lose oneself in God?

In India, the name of God is everywhere and given to everything. Parents name their children after gods or goddesses; they name their businesses, houses, schools, taxis, buses, towns, mountains and rivers—everything, after different aspects of God. When Mother Rema says, "in those days," she is referring to the *Satya Yuga*, the enlightened age, the age of truth, "when a sage, a *rishi* used to sit under every tree and a *yogi* lived in every house. Every action was loaded with significance." She continues, "But how many women now-a-days know the jewels they wear in their noses are there to balance the *pranic* flow through the nostrils?"

"The external culture is still there," she says, "but the meaning behind the traditions are now known only to a few. The masses perform actions in such and such a way, because they have been doing it like that for generations, but they have forgotten why. On special days of worship, many houses will have a *tantric* form, or *yantra*, drawn in chalk outside the front steps on the pavement, or inside, on the floor in front of the altar. How many people know what these signify?" She muses, "But tradition is so strong, these practices continue even without understanding their significance."

"Is it common for all homes to have *puja* rooms?" I ask.

"Most homes do. Or, if they are very poor, just a little place set aside for a holy picture, incense and flowers; perhaps an oil lamp. If it's five lights, it symbolizes burning the five senses, if seven, lighting of the seven *chakras*. So, even in some small way, God is remembered everyday and prayers are said."

The day we come back from the Theosophical Society, we do not see Rema that evening. We are told she is "resting." The next morning she tells us that she went into a trance that afternoon and was completely dead to the world until three the next morning. She tells us that when she is in a trance state, she leaves her physical body and travels in the astral body, all over the world. Space and time do not exist in this state and she can "see" things down to the minutest detail. There was a time when her spiritual practices were done purposely, to gain certain *yogic* powers, or *siddhis*, in order to defend and protect her family. But now, she says they come to her spontaneously and during that time, she secludes herself upstairs in her room.

In South India, the culture of the "evil eye" is still prevalent and widespread. People believe in it and take steps to avoid it. It ranges from avoiding the curse by the power hungry *yogi* on Rema's children, for instance, to more mundane superstitions.

"How does it work?" I want to know.

"If you have a bowl of apples in your home and someone comes," Rema explains, "and they say, 'Oh, what lovely apples!' Soon after that, you will see one of them becoming rotten." It seems to occur especially when there is the feeling of envy, or jealousy involved. My understanding is that if you have something that someone else wants, just that envious thought can spoil or pollute what you have. Even if you have good health, or things are going well financially, you would not speak about it in public, maybe not even in private, for fear that the "evil eye" would put an end to your good fortune.

There are *mantras* for shielding and protecting oneself against negative forces, like the "evil eye." There are *mantras* for just about everything in India. Some of them are prayers to God to acquire a son, or good health. Others are said to ward off disease and accidents of all kinds. The highest use of a *mantra* or a verse of prayer from the scriptures is for the good of all, the welfare of humanity and all the creatures of the earth, for abundance, peace and harmony of the entire cosmos. Ultimately, with the purest of intentions, they are repeated for the soul's liberation from birth and death and for attaining God-realization. *Om asato ma sat gamaya, tamaso ma jyotir gamaya, mrityor ma amritam gamaya*– Lead us from untruth to the Reality, lead us from darkness to light, lead us from death to immortality of the spirit.

The function of all of the *mantras* is a way of connecting the individual soul to the Supreme. All of them involve repetition of certain sounds, many, many times. The *mantras* associated with each deity, have a specific structure and vibration. The vibration actually takes the form of the deity. So it is said, "name and form, *nama-rupa*, are one." And further it is said that the name *is* God, that there is no difference whatsoever between the *name* of God and God. Many saints have had visions of God by repeating a *mantra* encoding a name of God, hundreds and thousands of times. One such *mantra* is for Lord Rama, the embodiment of *dharma*, of righteousness—*Om Sri Ram, Jai Ram, Jai Jai Ram!*

We are still struggling to understand how practitioners with less than good intentions can become spiritually powerful. We continue to learn from Rema that apparently, anyone can gain mastery of a certain *mantra*, by repeating it over and over. They develop power, but not necessarily goodness and morality.[3]

Mother Rema has seen a good number of charlatans and does not have a very high opinion of some swamis. She can, however, recognize the genuine article when she sees it. When she met Swami Sivananda she was impressed by his simplicity and guilelessness. She also knows the father of Swami Venkatesananda, one of Swami Sivananda's foremost disciples, and pronounces him "a good man."

Our meals are taken sitting in a row on the floor, in a room adjacent to the kitchen, where the food is served on banana leaves, cut fresh from the tree out in the back garden. One day, near the end of our stay, sitting next to Rema, who is talking about reincarnation and how many births we have to take to fulfill our destiny, I say, "This can't be *your* last birth."

"Why not?" She looks at me enquiringly. According to Hindu *dharma*, one returns again and again until one is fully liberated and there is no longer any *karma* binding one to return. Even then, great souls are drawn back by the love of their devotees to help and guide them towards God.

"Because," I say, "then what would happen to people like us?"

"That's just it!" she answers.

As much as we would like to stay longer with Mother Rema, we have an itinerary to follow, and we have miles to cover before we reach Sivananda Ashram near Rishikesh, by the time Swami Chidananda is due to return before Christmas. We agree to come back to see her after visiting some *ashrams* and holy people in South India.

---

[3] This is why the moral code of ethical behavior is of utmost importance in sage Patanjali's Raja Yoga. *Yama*, that which one must observe and practice, is the first step or limb on the eightfold path. The five principles of *yama* are: *ahimsa*, non-violence; *asteya*, freedom from avarice; *satya*, truthfulness; *brahmacharya*, chastity or restraint; and *aparigraha*, freedom from desire to possess.

CHAPTER 2

ADVENTURES IN SOUTH INDIA

PONDICHERRY

We leave Madras heading south by train to Pondicherry, a French enclave on the east coast, to visit Sri Aurobindo Ashram.

On the way, the train stops in a station. I look out through the bars on the third class compartment to the tracks and the water tower on the other side and see that there are many crows waiting for scraps of food to be thrown from the train. Wherever people gather, crows are out scavenging whatever morsel they can retrieve. Some are large, black, and sleek. Others, perhaps the young, are brownish in color. When it is very hot, they open their mouths and pant and there is a constant, "Aaahhh! Aaahhh!" and sometimes, "Har, har, har!"

Besides the crow, there is the omnipresence of the sacred cow. In India, cows don't say, "moo" like they do in the West. They say, "ma, ma!" Thus they are revered, because they are forever uttering the sacred name of the Divine Mother. Cows are important also, because, like the Mother, they provide nourishment for millions. One night I see a cow sitting comfortably chewing its cud in front of a brightly lit shop window, showing off a display of paints. The two images seem so incongruous and the juxtaposition of ancient and modern, of nature and industry, make me think, *Only in India!*

Sri Aurobindo, an intellectual educated at Cambridge University in England, was one of the greatest *yogis* of the twentieth century. When he left his body in December 1950, his spiritual partner, "Mother," or "Mère" took over the running of the *ashram*. Sri Aurobindo Ashram is extensive and occupies many buildings, all over Pondicherry, to which Sri Aurobindo fled as a young man, as a revolutionary against British rule. The *ashram* is more like a large university campus with thousands of students. Everything hinges around a relationship with the Mother and if you don't have that, then it is rather superficial. Everything is clean and spotless and the food pure and *sattvic*, without chilies. Due to the French influence, it is the only place in India where we find freshly baked whole wheat bread.

I decide to clear my mind of anything negative and throw myself open to the benefit of the Mother's high vibrations. She is ninety-two now and only comes out four times a year to give public *darshan*, allowing herself to be seen by the devotees. If one is granted an interview, silent or verbal, it is regarded as a rare and priceless experience. Accounts given by those who have recently had her *darshan*, say she looks right into your soul and confusion, doubts and pretense drop away. This is not surprising, because it is what often happens to sincere seekers in the presence of a highly evolved being.

Three years ago I was told that if I sent a small picture of myself to the Aurobindo Mother I would receive spiritual help. So my friends, Stephen and Sean and I signed small pictures of ourselves and put them into a letter, which we sent off to Mère, at Aurobindo Ashram. We were told that by doing so, the Mother could focus on us and help us along the path. I didn't feel particularly connected to her and it was more like an experiment. I was willing to try anything, as I was hungry for whatever spiritual help I could get. I devoured spiritual books, went to lectures on spiritual subjects whenever I could find them. I had no preconceived ideas, was without cynicism and ready to look into everything with eagerness and an open mind.

The following year, a son, Dogen, was born to Sean and Stephen. They became involved in the Zen Center, in Sonoma. I tried hard to understand the quality of *sattva*, or purity. It was slow in coming, as I was accustomed to a very *rajasic*, restless lifestyle. In San Francisco I was embedded in a subculture where drugs were everywhere and I experimented with pot and psychedelics, in search of a deeper experience. Little by little, I became aware that certain foods have different vibrations associated with them, which affect the health of both your body and mind and that *it matters* what you eat and how you cook it. I also became aware that if spiritual evolution is a goal, it *matters* who you spend time with and the quality of your relationships.

MÈRE AND AUROVILLE

Don and I rent bicycles and ride around Pondicherry, getting familiar with Aurobindo Ashram. All day long it feels as though there is something on my head enveloping my skull, but when I put my hand up there, there is just my hair. I wonder if this is what it feels like to have Mère focus on you and pull your consciousness up? Then my bicycle gets a flat tire. Don gives me his bike and takes mine and we wheel them along, looking for a bicycle repair shop.

Suddenly, a man appears on the sidewalk with a dancing monkey, whose face is smeared with vermilion powder. The monkey dances around and attracts my attention. He does some tricks and behaves like a human. I am fascinated by his antics, but when I look up, Don and my bike are nowhere to be seen. How easily distracted I am! I suddenly see the monkey as a metaphor for *Maya*, the veiling power of the Divine Mother Shakti, who has the ability to distract the mind in an instant. All the goddesses in the Hindu pantheon have this power to veil from us seekers, the presence of the Divine, as represented by the deep meditative state of Lord Siva. They also have the power to liberate. *Yoginis* like Mother Rema have shown us that worship of the goddess, not just as a principle, but as a living reality, can bring one's consciousness up to a very high level. She has, in a sense, become an embodiment of Meenakshi, whom she adores.

The Mother of Aurobindo Ashram is very different. While still in the body at ninety-two, she is an abstract presence for us, an intellectual with a vision of the future for all humanity. She envisions Auroville, the town of the future, where people from all different countries, will come together to live in harmony and spiritual enlightenment. This future community will be a beacon light and a model for humanity to follow.

Referring to Auroville the Mother says, "We want the Truth. For most men it is what they want that they label truth. The Aurovillians must *want* the Truth, whatever it may be. Auroville is for those who want to live a life essentially divine, but who renounce all religions, whether they are ancient, modern, new or future. It is only in experience that there can be knowledge of the Truth. No one ought to speak of the Divine, unless one has had experience of the Divine. Get experience of the Divine, then alone you will have the right to speak of it."

The next day, we travel by bus out to the land where Auroville, according to the Mother's vision, will be built. It is about fifteen square miles of flat green fields and wild, scrubby vegetation, broken by deep, eroded gullies of red earth. The bus takes us along a muddy road, past half-naked Indians bending over rice paddies. We motor through a little village of huts, with palm-leaf thatched roofs, covering the outer walls all the way to the packed mud floor. Further on, in a grove of palm trees, we see a house on stilts. "That's where one of the girls lives," our guide tells us. His accent is a curious mixture of Indian and French. "This is 'Peace' area. There are also areas called 'Silence,' 'Aspiration,' 'Promise,' etcetera."

The bus stops and we sit in a loose circle of chairs in the shade of some mango trees, talking about the pros and cons of living in the future community of Auroville. Because it is just getting started, there are cultural problems and some clashes with the *ashram*. Those with a pioneering spirit, who want to move out here, are mostly Europeans from Germany, France and England, as well as a few from the U.S.A. Only a few Indians seem interested in moving out into the bush, away from civilization.

There is a sign in the dining hall in the *ashram* that reads, "Always behave as though the Mother were looking at you, because she is indeed always present." Some Westerners, misunderstanding the omnipresent quality of consciousness, feel paranoid about the sign. One young man says it reminds him of his Catholic High School, which he resented. But perhaps he hasn't looked into Sri Aurobindo's teaching very deeply. If he had, he would understand that Sri Aurobindo's interest in religions is not based on dogma at all. Aurobindo considers religions important because they are part of history and the evolution of mankind. The Mother has said that it is for that reason that they will be studied at Auroville, "not as beliefs to which one ought, or ought not to fasten, but as part of the process in the development of human consciousness, which should lead man towards his superior realization."

A Belgian girl complains that she has written to the Mother days before and has received no reply. "There's an expression in French," she explains, exasperated, "'She's playing with my feet.' I am waiting and waiting and spending all my money and she won't answer until it's all used up! I think I'll go to another *ashram*!" Sometimes it's hard to realize and accept that one needs to move on.

The bus takes us back to Pondicherry Ashram and we go into the cool basement "cave" room to meditate. It is dark except for two interlocking, neon blue triangles, one inverted—a Hindu symbol long before it became the Jewish Star of David. This symbol, representing heaven and earth, the higher Self and the lower self, also forms part of the Aurobindo Ashram logo.

On arriving back in our room, we find a note telling us to see Mr. Nolini, the secretary, the next day. We wonder if we might be granted an interview with the Mother? The next morning Mr. Nolini, tells us that Mère can't see us as her timetable is completely booked, but she will help us spiritually. As a token of that help she gives us, through Mr. Nolini, a packet of special leaves with the ashram seal on it. She also says that if we need to we can write to her and she will answer, if necessary. Given the short time we have been here, we feel fortunate even to have made indirect contact with the Mother.

BEGGARS AND SAINTS

We are travelling by train, grateful to be riding third class, with a student pass costing $30 U.S. valid for one year, courtesy of the Indian Railway Service. We are beneficiaries of part of the British legacy in India, which is a very reliable and usually punctual railway system. The trains help link India together and launch it into the modern world. The other legacy of British rule is the English language. India has about four hundred languages and dialects of its own, which made it very hard for conversation between kingdoms, ruled by the *rajas* of ancient times and even between the provinces of today. When the British colonized India two-hundred-years ago, they made English the official language. Now almost anyone with even an elementary education, except the remotest areas, can speak a little English. Since India gained its Independence in 1947, Hindi has been the official language of the government, but many mid and South Indians do not speak Hindi, so English continues to prove useful. The use of English is also an advantage as India begins to open its trade and tourism to the rest of the world.

Third class means we are travelling with the common folk, on benches made of wooden slats, with soot from the coal engine blowing into our faces through the open windows. Our folded blankets make the seats more comfortable and our backpacks go either under the seats, or above on overhead racks. We take turns going to the bathroom while the other watches the luggage. In all the miles we cover, we never have anything stolen on the train, except for a few rupees by a *chai walla*, who doesn't come back with the change.

Stainless steel squatting toilets with the pipe open to the ground below, are at either end of the carriage and also house a little sink in which to wash ones hands. The rule is that one refrains from using the toilets while the train is at a standstill in a station. One waits until the train has gathered speed, so going to the bathroom on a moving train is quite a breezy affair!

Swami Pranavananda, from the Divine Life Society in Kuala Lumpur, has given us the name of a certain Swami Gnanananda, as "a must" to visit in South India. Our train from Pondicherry to this swami's *ashram* near Thirukoilur, stops at a station along the way and a little girl, not more than seven years of age, wearing a dirty loincloth, positions herself under our open window. She begins to dance barefoot in the dust, waving her thin arms and singing along, hurriedly and persistently, with a rasping little voice. Suddenly, a slightly older girl appears by her side and starts her own song and dance. The first girl shouts at the newcomer and tries to push her away, slapping her in the face, until she realizes that all the passengers on the train are laughing at them and that she is losing time. Both the girls are now trying to out-sing and out-dance the other, with a desperation that is both humorous and turns the pit of my stomach. I try to look away, but they are impossible to ignore.

Suddenly, the train-whistle blows and the dancing stops. Both girls stretch out their arms and began chanting, "Amma, amma, amma!" in a pathetic wail. We have heard that wail before, the rehearsed wail of the beggars. I look around for something we can give them, some food at least. All we have are two bananas and we pass them out of the train window, tossing them to the little girls, who catch them in their hands. But the bananas do not please them and their wailing grows louder as the train begins to move slowly forward, grunting and blowing steam. As the train picks up speed, the little girls run faster, arms outstretched, their faces still desperate.

We have already wrestled with the question: *what do we do about the beggars? How should we respond?* We can't just ignore them as though they don't exist. It is impossible to confront poverty and have no response at all, especially coming from the Western world and travelling in the East. We know we are perceived as well off, just because we are from the West, and in some ways that is true. We are rich enough to have travelled half way around the world to come to this juncture, where we meet a couple of small beggar children, dancing under the open window of our train. In this moment, in this situation, when the train begins to leave the station, what is the right thing to do? What is our *dharma* as students and as guests in a foreign country? Moreover, what is the correct response as one human being to another?

We have come up with a policy that we will share food with anyone begging from us, but if we give money to each beggar along the way, we will never reach our destination near Rishikesh! We know that our funds are very limited and we have no way of getting more while we are in India as students. We have a certain number of American Express Travelers Checks in our hand-sewn denim money belts around our waists, which have to last us for a year. We are basically in India on faith that the cosmos will take care of us and once we reach Sivananda Ashram, we will be welcomed by Swami Chidananda, who invited us to come.

Moreover, Mother Rema told us that beggars are quite practiced in India. Some have even formed unions. She told us that some of them are professional and make quite a lot of money. But these are just children. Are we doing them a favor by not giving to them? Would we just be perpetuating a lifestyle that is degrading? Who are we to think that we can make a difference by tossing a coin? How arrogant is that? The girls have already learned the wail and the voice to be used when begging. It is turned on at will to make us feel guilty and it works, because we *do* feel guilty by not giving them money. We notice that our fellow third-class passengers don't seem to feel guilty at all. They are all too used to this begging display and look on impassively, or turn their heads and look to the inside of the train. But we have made the mistake of making eye contact and the girls will not leave our window to try somewhere else. We are their best bet.

The little girls run to keep up with the train. They run faster and faster, but finally, they can't run any more and turn back. Their disappointed faces now etched in my memory, along with the nagging feeling that we should have handled it differently. We are not used to this kind of poverty and in order to save ourselves the confusion of repeated indecision, we have tried to come up with a policy that we can fall back on. But this does not seem to work in India. Each situation is unique and different and we decide to respond in future, as each instance presents itself.

Poverty seems so complex, like an endless chain of existence, always present in some country, never really eliminated from the face of the earth. Don says of poverty, "That's what happens when a man has no initiative." I wonder if that is just what a young Western middleclass male would say? It may be true, but how can we possibly know into what life circumstances these girls have been born?

We plan to spend the night at the *ashram* of Swami Gnanananda, whose devotees claim him to be one hundred and fifty-six years old. Apparently he was born in 1814 and is said to have met Paramahamsa Ramakrishna, who left his body in 1886, and Swami Vivekananda, Ramakrishna's most renowned disciple. We are sitting in the *ashram* courtyard, wondering how we can meet with Swami Gnanananda and receive his blessing, when we are told he said he has already blessed us, without our knowing. All day long he keeps appearing and disappearing. He pops out of one door on the lower level and no sooner than we stand up, he disappears. Then sometime later, he pops out of another door on the upper verandah. He is having fun with the Westerners, playing a game of hide and seek!

Finally, in the afternoon, we are ushered into an unlit room where we bow and sit on the floor in front of him. After just a few minutes of silence he asks us, through an interpreter, if we like tea. "Tea?" It's a strange question. We wonder if we have heard him correctly. "Yes, we like tea." Immediately, he signals to his assistant to take us across the village street to the tea stall, where they offer us a cup of tea.

"What just happened?" Don asks. We look at each other and laugh, chuckling over our cups of tea. We decide it is time to leave and we go to the bus station, but the buses are full. So, we return to the *ashram* and spend the night sleeping on the concrete floor until 4 a.m., when the devotees get up to attend the *puja*, which the swami performs. We realize that we haven't a clue what is going on and that after all, we have very little connection to Swami Gnananda, who seems to be quite amused by us.

We leave after breakfast for Tiruvannamalai. On the bus I write:

> 20th Oct. 1970
> Looking out
> from within
> I see myself without the body
> but within it
> and know the body
> as the windowsill
> of the mind
> resting inside.

CLIMBING THE HOLY MOUNTAIN

Arunachala, the red mountain or the holy hill, is one of the five main important places of pilgrimage in South India for the *shaivites*, those who worship Lord Siva. The mystical mountain of Tamil Nadu, south west of Madras, rises up alone out of a flat valley of green fields and rice paddies. Geologists have found the rock formations of Arunachala to be some of the oldest on earth. Some people think it is part of the continent of Lemuria, which, as legend has it, sank into the oceans eons ago. The large, walled Tiruvannamalai Temple, with tall ascending towers, nestles right up against the foot of the mountain, with the town of Tiruvannamalai growing up around it.

Sri Ramana Maharshi is one of the most famous sages of the 20th century both in India and abroad. He is known for his saintly life, for being fully realized and for the powerful transmissions which devotees and visitors received in his presence. Even though Ramana Maharishi left his body in 1950 we want to see for ourselves the place where this holy sage lived and visit his *ashram* at the foot of Arunachala.

We read about his spontaneous awakening as a teenager and his subsequent leaving home and finding his way to Tiruvannamalai. How he spent months and months in a dark room under the temple, immersed in deep meditation, with no body consciousness whatsoever. Insects were biting him, but he felt nothing. Finally, he made his way to Arunachala and afterwards, never left the mountain. Much of his life he spent in silence. Devotees would come just to sit in the peaceful presence of *Bhagavan*, meaning God, or *guru*, as they referred to him. From the pictures we see his eyes are brimming with love.

Ramana Maharshi wandered all over the mountain for thirty years, living there in silence and union with the Absolute consciousness. One of Ramana's Western devotees, called Osborne, was exploring the mountain and found a peephole into a cave. What he saw inside seemed like simple living quarters, with an altar and deities. He concluded that the *yogis* living there were highly advanced, not needing food, living only on *prana*, life force, and some water. This was Skandashram, Ramana's first dwelling place on the mountain.

As the story goes one day Ramana, was walking around the mountain when an old lady came up to him and said, "Why do you move around so much? Can't you keep still?" He thought she must be a goddess coming to him in the form of an old woman, to give him advice. Later, Ramana's devotees brought him down to the bottom of the hill, where they built a larger ashram in which he resided until he left his body.

Some visitors once came to see Bhagavan Sri Ramana Maharshi and asked the great jnani, the proponent of the path of wisdom and self-enquiry, the best way to climb the holy mountain, Arunachala. "Just keep circling around to the right until you reach the top," he answered.

They laughed at him saying, "We are from Madras. You can't fool us with your country ways." They began climbing straight up the mountain and soon became exhausted and didn't reach the top.

We hadn't yet heard this story when we decide on our first day to climb the holy mountain. No one tells us which way to go and we set out very energetically, right after breakfast at about 7 a.m. From below it looks so easy to climb, but we should know better! After all, this is Siva's mountain, the ancient place of legends, home to *yogis* for hundreds of years. We find it very rocky, with clumps of long coarse grass growing between the rocks and gigantic boulders of what appear to be solid granite. As we climb higher over small hills and along cliffs of solid rock, we can see the green plains below us, stretching for miles all around.

Like the tourists from Madras, we make the mistake of trying to climb straight up the mountain. We can see the top of the mountain, which doesn't look that far away. However, as we clear the ridge of one hill, another always seems to rise up behind it. After climbing for two hours in the hot sun we take shelter in the shade of a huge boulder, at the foot of a sheer granite cliff. The cliff face is cool and mossy and seems to ooze water, but not enough for us to get a drink. We are very thirsty and quite exhausted. How foolish not to carry a bottle of water with us! We decide not to try to make it to the top and begin walking down a dry streambed on shaky legs. Down and down we stumble through the boulders and long scratchy grass.

Suddenly, we hear gurgling of water and we come to a place where a stream gushes out of the mountain. We drink out of the stream, wash, wallow and splash, soaking our heads, bodies and clothes. The water tastes so good! After we can't drink any more, we continue on down, until we find the path leading back to the *ashram* at the foot of the mountain. Our clothes are dry by the time we reach our room and we lie on our backs, completely still, for one hour. It's not yet noon.

We stay at Ramana's beautiful little *ashram* for a few days. Not many people are here and we are the only Western seekers. We spend our time reading about this great saint who influenced the whole world with his non-dual teachings of self-enquiry—"Who am I?"—Enquiring into the nature of the Self. He used to tell his disciples that they were all realized beings. "Not us, Bhagavan. You are."

"That is your problem," he would counter. "You don't believe it."

We spend time meditating in the very room where he used to give *darshan*. There is a life-size cut out photograph of Bhagavan reclining on the couch, just as he did while in the body. When the devotees asked him what they would do after he left his body, he replied, "I am not going anywhere. Where would I go?" He wanted them know, that with or without the body, made no difference to him. He was completely identified with the pure, Absolute Self.

Don develops a little fever while we are staying at Ramana's *ashram*. Perhaps it is due to exhaustion from attempting to climb straight up the mountain, or perhaps from different bacteria in the food or water. At this time, there is no bottled water to be had anywhere and neither do we have the facilities to boil it. We take our chances and drink whatever is offered to us.

An elderly man called Mr. R.G. comes to our room and is quite solicitous when he finds that Don is ill. He is an inmate of the *ashram* and takes the trouble to bring some medicine for Don's fever. He seems kind and caring and we are impressed by his selfless service. However, when it comes time for us to leave, we are disillusioned in our high opinion of him. Mr. R.G. asks us to give him some money above and beyond the donation we are giving to the *ashram*. That would be fine, but the fact that he tells us to do it quietly and not tell anyone else about it, shows us that he is on the make for himself, which is strictly against *ashram* regulations. It is such a small sum of money (the equivalent of U.S. $2.00) for which to compromise one's integrity!

It turns out that Mr. R.G. is the *ashram* bursar and when it comes time for us to give our donation, it is done with other people nearby, so he can't say anything. When we go out to the horse cart already loaded with our backpacks, Don says, "I am sorry we can't give you any money, because we have just enough to get to Madras." This is perfectly true. We have just enough rupees for the horse cart and the bus ride, but we also don't want to have dealings with anyone who is underhanded. We are young and idealistic and have not yet learned to be more forgiving of the shortcomings of others. Mr. R.G. follows us out to the cart and slaps Don on the back, saying, "Don't worry! Don't worry!" He is trying to save face, but he is embarrassed that we know his weakness.

THE HOLY MAN

In Mother Rema's view, the holiest man in India is the elderly Shankaracharya of Kanchipuram. She encouraged us to visit this fully enlightened being who resides in the southern *muth*, the holy *ashram* or temple, of the four directional *muths*, set up by Adi Shankaracharya of the 8th century AD. As a young sage, the original Adi Shankaracharya wandered the length and breadth of India on foot, engaging in debates with all the learned scholars and *pundits* of the country. He established the non-dual philosophy of *Advaita Vedanta*, which proclaims that all life is essentially the same in all beings; that *Atman*, the individual spirit and *Brahman*, God, are one and the same. Adi Shankara established *muths* in the north and south, east and west of India and also the ten orders of *sannyasa*, from which all the modern lineages originate. The lineage of Swami Sivananda, the Saraswati line, is directly from Adi Shankaracharya.

    The present Shankaracharya, the renowned holy man whom Mother Rema deeply reveres, is now in his nineties and has already appointed a successor. The elderly saint rarely speaks or sees anyone from outside, but we are granted an audience with his successor. It is a sunny mid-afternoon when we enter a small room and kneel on a mat laid out on the floor for us. The young Shankaracharya, now in his mid-thirties, was chosen as the successor when he was only thirteen years old. He comes into the room with his traditional walking stick and sits on a low wooden stool a few feet from us. We have brought yellow and maroon flowers and oranges on a lotus leaf as an offering, which we place at his feet. As he does not speak English, he communicates through an interpreter, asking us about our origins and our intentions. He is very jovial and friendly and wants to know whether we are finding success on the spiritual path. We smile at this question and tell him we are going to Sivananda Ashram in the north, to study with Swami Chidananda. Everyone who is anyone knows of Swami Sivananda and his disciples, some of who are also held in high esteem.

He asks us if we know of Maharishi Mahesh Yogi, who has built an ashram on the opposite bank of the Ganges from Sivananda Ashram. I wonder if he thinks we might know him because the Beatles went to visit Mahesh Yogi a year ago. Then I remember a picture of the older Shankaracharya in a Mahesh Yogi book I read and wonder if they are in the same lineage.

When he senses that we have no more questions, he falls silent and we sit drinking in his serenity, while other devotees gather quietly behind us. After some time he hands us rock candy and raisins in a little leaf-cup stitched together with grass, for *prasad*. We bow to him and take our leave. We always feel uplifted by the presence of holy people and, as if to confirm it, as we ride the bus back to Madras, we see the most glorious sunset with six or seven alternating orange and blue rays emanating from the setting sun.

We go home to Mother Rema's house and report on all our adventures during the past couple of weeks, where we went and whom we saw. We stay a few more days with her and she tells us to be aware of her special fragrance of jasmine or sandalwood and if we smell it strongly when there is no apparent reason for it, like incense burning or flowers nearby, she'll be there. If we are in tune, we might see her.

She gives us some parting advice. "Have a lot of self-confidence and don't believe everything people tell you. Go inside and ask yourself, "Who am I?" before you let someone else tell you who you are. Discover each other from moment to moment. Let love unfold between you, without imposing your opinions or beliefs on each other. Remember, consciousness is the creator of the universe, love is its savior."

We say goodbye to Mother Rema on 30th October, at the Madras Central Station and board the third-class carriage for Hyderabad.

BROTHER METHUSALAH

As we journey north towards Jabalpur through the November morning, I remember Rema asking me where we were going. "Are they *Brahmins*?" she had asked, concerned that we associate with good company. We are not very aware of and therefore not concerned with the caste system. With encouragement from one of Don's relatives, who is associated with Christian missionary work in India, we have contacted and have been invited to stay the night with a member of the mission. After a few hours by train, followed by a ride in the back of a rickshaw, we finally arrive at the home of our host, James Methusalah. His pretty young wife welcomes us warmly, with the few words of English that she knows, and later, Brother Methusalah, as he is called, arrives on his bicycle. They serve us tea and some north Indian sweets, sitting on the floor of their small, but clean house. He relates to us the story of his being saved by Jesus.

"I was a *pukka* (genuine) sinner when I first attended a revival meeting," he tells us. "I saw the light and my heart was flooded with the joy of Christ. I wept for hours." I am deeply touched by the sincerity of Brother Methusalah, but I am disturbed by fundamentalism of any kind. I have been reading Swami Vivekananda's book, "East and West," in which he stresses the need for a unity of religions. "In all the diverse forms of worshipping God, it is one God we worship and religions should accept and respect each other's beliefs. After all, there are saints of every religion."

Then along comes a man like Brother Methusalah, who believes strongly in Christ and makes no bones about preaching to others the way to salvation. He truly believes that there is no hope for those of different faiths. He tells us how much his own life has improved by becoming Christian—no liquor, smoking, movies or riches. Indeed, he and his wife live a very plain life, close to the example of the early Christians of the 1st century AD. It is a sincere and simple life, unlike those who attend church on Sunday, but don't actually try to *mold* their lives around Christ's teachings.

We accompany Brother Methusalah to the Gospel Church in the evening, where the preacher is convinced that man's soul is basically diseased and that our nature is weak and sinful. The only way out of this inherent fault, according to him, is to repent and be saved through Christ. And this is the *only* way!

I want to give our hosts something as a token of appreciation for sharing their home with us. I search through my backpack, but the only thing I can find is a silver charm bracelet, that the kind devotees in Malaysia gave me as a parting gift. It is still in its box, so it looks new. It is the only thing that even looks like a gift, so I give it to Methusalah's wife. Unfortunately, in the box is a small tag that I didn't notice which says, "with love from the Maheshwarams." I quickly remove the tag, but I think it has been seen. It is an awkward moment, but they understand the motive behind the gesture. They accept the gift graciously.

Somehow, Brother Methusalah, who is standing near my half-unpacked belongings, seems to have eagle eyes and spots a letterhead with a *Pranava*, *Om* symbol, at the top. He immediately recoils. "That is evil!" he says. He is genuinely trying to warn me to stay away from anything to do with it. I bite my tongue and keep quiet. We are guests in his house. I understand that all people are on different levels of spiritual development, be they Christian, Hindu, Muslim, Sikh, Jew or Buddhist. I have learned not to argue with others about their religious beliefs, just keep quiet and listen. Some of them, especially new converts, will preach to you and try to convert you. If you say nothing, they think they have won you over to their way of thinking. I wonder whether to stay silent, or speak out. Finally, I decide that if he wants my opinion he will ask and then I will answer honestly, as close to the truth as possible, without fear or prejudice. Otherwise, better to keep silent and save *prana*.

I am drawn to the *Vedantic* view, which says that the mistakes we make are due to the ignorance of our true nature, which is divine. What a relief! We do not have to think of ourselves as sinners! Our task is to shift our identification from the self-centered ego, to God-centeredness. Just knowing this truth intellectually, if not yet experientially, is truly liberating. *Vedanta* doesn't let us off the hook. It removes the weight of guilt and shame, allowing us to forgive ourselves and move forward. To remember our eternal connection to the infinite source we call God, is our first duty in this life. This philosophy really resonates with both Don and me. I understand this truth intuitively, that I am a child of God. I turn these ideas over and over in my mind. How would I be able to understand and experience the nature of God or Christ, if I were not of the same nature myself? If Jesus and His Father are one, then His nature must be love. It is proper to acknowledge my weaknesses, but if I am constantly reminding myself of my sinful nature and letting my thoughts dwell on that aspect, I feel weak and bogged down. I don't think this is what Jesus intended when He proclaimed we are all the children of God. I think what He meant was that we should think of His divine qualities, of His infinite love and compassion and try to emulate them.

We thank James Methusalah and his wife for their kind hospitality. They are very good people, but unfortunately we cannot share our ideas because they are so sure they are right. It is impossible to have a discussion with them. So we leave the fundamentalist view behind and head for the holy city of Benares.

BENARES

Benares, also called Varanasi or Kashi, dates back to the 11th Century BC and is known as the spiritual capital of India. We rent a room in a very inexpensive hotel, not far from the river. Down the narrow and winding lane, we make our way to the Ganges and join the throngs of devoted Hindus taking a bath, offering flowers, saying their prayers and worshipping the

holy river. It is written in the scriptures that if one dies in Benares, one's soul will be instantly liberated, so every devoted Hindu wants to die there. Smoke rises into the air from the funeral pyres on the banks, where those lucky enough to have their desire fulfilled, are cremated. One ghat has had fires burning there continuously, for over three thousand years.

We walk along the ghat, until we come to squatting washerwomen, whacking the water out of their twisted laundry on the stones. Higher on the bank, under the faded walls of ancient buildings, long colored saris are spread out to dry in the sun.

In the afternoon we decide to join some tourists on a small bus that takes us out to Bodh Gaya, the place where the Buddha attained enlightenment sitting under the Bodhi Tree. Being with a group of tourists is an unusual experience for us. We don't think of ourselves as tourists. We consider ourselves seekers of Self-realization and sightseeing on a superficial level is not really important to us. Still, we are eager, along with the others, to see the collection of rare Persian miniatures housed in a local museum. When we reach the museum, the guide hops off the bus and tries the handle of the museum front door.

"It is closed!" he informs us, pretending to be surprised. A collective groan of disappointment goes up from the tourists. We can tell the guide and the driver knew very well it was going to be closed, but in order to collect the money for the bus tour, they brought us here anyway.

That night we meet some fellow Westerners staying in the room next to ours. We spend the evening with them, drawing each other in our sketchbooks. The vibration is quite stoned and I wonder if they have been smoking pot. Was I like that three years ago? I wonder if I have changed. I perceive myself differently now, as though I am looking through the illusion of my historical self, into something vast and spacious. Yoga has introduced Don and me to something beyond our individual selves. It has given us discipline and purpose. However, they are also living quite courageously, without fear of confrontation and criticism. We all decide we are the true ambassadors from the West, ready to embrace this new culture. We are children of hope, searching for a deeper understanding and a light we know is there.

We are training ourselves to write down our dreams as meaningful events on our journey. Don has a dream that night. He is sitting in our yellow room with orange trim next to a black telephone. He is there for hours waiting and waiting for the telephone to ring. Finally, the phone rings and he wakes up. It is the alarm clock ringing and he is surprised that it is not a telephone. He wonders if the dream, which seemed to take all night, actually happened in the last second before the alarm rang? That gets us to thinking about the nature of time and of the different dimensions we live in. We get dressed and go in search of the *ashram* of Ananda Mayee Ma.

Sri Ananda Mayee Ma, the blissful Mother, is the greatest female saint in India in the 20th century. She was born in Bengal in 1896 and grew up virtually illiterate in the simplicity of village life. She is revered by Gurudev Sivananda and Swami Chidananda and indeed by everyone in India, including Prime Minister Indira Gandhi, who is one of her devotees. Ananda Mayee Ma, also called Sri Ma Anandamayi, has been completely free and enlightened from birth. She was never under the illusion that she is a separate self.

We have heard that she has an *ashram* in Benares and after some enquiries we find it. We enter a large spacious room with very high ceilings and lots of light pouring in through the open archways on one side. There is a group of people dressed in white seated on the floor across the room. Some of them turn and look at us. We ask if Ananda Mayee Ma is here and are informed that she has gone elsewhere, to a place called Kankhal, near Haridwar. She moves about frequently, never staying long in one place. We trust if it is meant to be, we will meet the blissful mother at another time.

CHAPTER 3

IN NEPAL

KATMANDU

We know that Swami Chidananda is not due back to Sivananda Ashram until sometime before Christmas, and not wishing to get there too far in advance of his arrival, we still have about five weeks in which to explore this part of the world. We take a train from Benares north to Patna, in Bihar state. It is the dry season and no rain is expected until the next monsoon, six months from now. We decide that rather than taking another train and then a long overnight bus ride on very windy roads (guaranteed to make me car sick), we will splurge and use some of our travelers checks to buy tickets on an Indian Airlines flight from Patna to Katmandu.

As the propellers whir to life, the engine roars and we charge down the runway and lift into the sky, heading north towards the highest mountains in the world. When we get up to several thousand feet to our cruising speed, the flight attendant comes down the aisle towards us. He takes me by surprise when he asks me, "Would you like to go up to the cockpit and see Mount Everest?"

"Yes, *please!*" I immediately unbuckle my seatbelt. We are so surprised at the invitation, as even then, people have already started hijacking planes. God bless Indian Airlines for giving us an unforgettable gift—the aerial view of the approach to the Himalayas! The pale, dry plains far below, give way to dark green as we approach the lowlands, covered with thick forests. Then suddenly, we are over the first range of mountains, large green giants with light-green, jewel-like paddy fields, studding the top of every ridge. The unearthly view looks like an astral vision from a dream. The pilot points to the horizon, where Mount Everest and the other peaks of the grand Himalayan range, gleam white in the morning sun. "There they are!" he says, proudly. It is such a thrilling sight! Strung out across the horizon, dazzling white and jagged against the deep blue of the sky.

"Which one is Everest?" Don asks.

"Straight ahead," the pilot says pointing through the cockpit window. These mountains are so magnificent that they lift our hearts and take our breath away. Soon, we must return to our seats, as the plane hums over the first range of foothills and begins descending into the Katmandu Valley.

Compared to India, Katmandu looks *really* old. I feel as if we have gone back in time to the 12th or 13th century. The buildings are mostly made of wood, with elaborately carved doors and trim. The Star of David and the *swastika* are prominent motifs in the woodwork. This star form appears in India, Pakistan, Afghanistan, Tibet and Israel. Hitler appropriated the *swastika*, which has been used by Buddhist, Jain and Hindu cultures for centuries as a symbol for wellbeing and auspiciousness. While the star, made of interlocking triangles is a stable form, a closed system, the *swastika* is open and dynamic, often appearing in Tibetan culture with little feet on it, symbolizing perpetual motion, or the continuous cycle of life. Unfortunately, the Nazis have forever tainted it in Western eyes as a symbol of aggressive superiority and genocide.

We rent a small room in a two-story wooden hotel in the center of town. Since we are in such close proximity to each other all day long, we implement the "no talking rule" in the mornings. We agree not to talk to each other until noon, so that we have the morning free to meditate, read and study or write and draw in our sketchbooks. We buy a big piece of ginger root in the market place and boil slices in our small blue pot, on our one-burner, kerosene pump stove. Fortunately, ginger and tea are inexpensive. Milk is harder to come by and is mostly from buffalo or yak. The first night we are there I get diarrhea and what we call "the purple burps" caused by some foreign bacteria that create stomach gas, which smells like sulfur. We are familiar with it from living in Ecuador.

Carved wooden window.

The Peace Corps is very good about looking after former volunteers and their spouses, traveling in different parts of the world and we get free gamma globulin shots to prevent hepatitis, from the local center. From the first day I feel like my whole metabolism has speeded up, due perhaps to the altitude, or the atmosphere, both physical and mental. There are lots of young, hip gringos here, mostly all smoking pot, which is legal, and large chunks of hashish, which I'm not sure is legal. Then there are the black market moneychangers, who have a better exchange rate than the bank. I find myself talking more and expending energy for our daily needs. As soon as I get too caught up in the day-to-day activities, all I have to do is look at the backdrop of the gigantic mountains and feel their stillness. They remind me that we are part of something much bigger than ourselves.

Prayer wheels are everywhere. The town is mostly Buddhist and is full of Tibetan refugees, dressed in their traditional costumes of hand-woven deep red or black dresses, wrapped and tied at the back, over colorful blouses. We take a bus out of town to a Tibetan Refugee Camp and find a hall full of men and women weaving rugs and carpets. Many Tibetans have fled from their country, which the Chinese now claim, and have escaped across the borders into Nepal and India. The weavers are chanting *mantras* in layers of overlapping nasal sounds, interspersed with the clack of the shuttle shooting back and forth in between the threads, and the smack of the wooden looms. In a little gift shop at the Refugee Camp, we purchase a small statue of a Tibetan monk with a begging bowl in one hand and the other hand over his mouth, in a gesture of silence.

From our hotel room we can go up some wooden stairs and onto an open flat area with walls on two sides. There is no actual running water in our hotel and we are allotted one bucket of hot water each per day, which is carried up to us by the *pani-wallah*, the water carrier, who earns his living by delivering buckets of water to customers in town. We are a little higher than the nearby buildings, so no one can see me up there, but I hang a cotton shawl from a clothesline, to give myself more privacy. There is only one fancy hotel in town that looks relatively modern, where tourists and visiting dignitaries might stay, but we assume it is way out of our price range, so we don't even go there to look.

The Nepalese, like Indians, are all up early, doing what they call "morning ablutions"—brushing their teeth and gargling with salt water, clearing their throats and spitting. There is a man nearby, whom we can't see, down in one of the narrow alleys, adjacent to our building, performing all these cleansing rituals with such vigor, it sounds like he's going to choke or gag on his own tongue. We hear him every morning as smoke rises from hundreds of little cooking fires, casting a haze over the town.

"This must have been what London was like in the sixteen hundreds," I say to Don, as we gaze out over the valley. "So much smoke!"

"It's a wonder the place hasn't burnt down!" he says, surveying the scene. "All these wooden buildings, with a cooking fire in each one."

But by mid-morning the smoke has cleared and the November air is crisp and clean again. I take my bucket of hot water into the corner, where the two walls come together and the sun is at its warmest. I remove my outer clothes and hang them on the line behind me and keep my underwear in a little pile by the bucket. Then I dip the top of my head into the bucket until my long hair is thoroughly soaked, squatting and shampooing my hair and the rest of my body. I scoop clean water over my head with a smaller plastic container and wash my underwear in the water that remains. It is amazing to me, how much I can actually clean with one bucket of water!

We eat in a little hole-in-the-wall place, where the food is cheap and delicious. After three meals there, we happen to peer through the doorway, into the courtyard where the food is being cooked in pots over an open fire. A stack of the large crisp *poppadums* that we have enjoyed with our meals these last few days, are lying on the dirt floor and the brass plates are being scoured with mud and then put out to dry in the sun. "No wonder I've got diarrhea!" I exclaim. "We're not eating here anymore!"

We find one of the warm cafés where all the Westerners hang out around wooden tables drinking hot yak butter tea. In a casual conversation we meet two guys who want to trek in the mountains, which is what we'd like to do too! Frank is a tall, blond Peace Corps Volunteer who was stationed in Ceylon, but now his tour is up. Ilan is from Israel. We also meet a young Nepalese man, Chota Re, who offers to be our guide. He speaks some English and his father is a lama in a monastery at the base of Mount Everest. Chota Re tells us it will take about ten days to hike in and ten days back. We are excited about having the monastery as our destination and meeting a real lama. He also advises us on the provisions we will need for such a trek.

I make a list in the back of my sketchbook: Sugar, 5 *darneys* (a Nepalese measurement), 5 tins of butter, 10 packets of milk powder, 2 bottles of lemon juice, chocolate, dried coconut, dahl, dates, 4 kilos of rice, tea, coffee, chili powder, salt, pots, plates, soup powder, biscuits and porridge. Chota Re locates a Sherpa called Lamsang, to carry the provisions and we agree on the price. We will do this whole trek for one hundred dollars, including the food! We shop in the market and little shops for the provisions and each of us takes a portion in our backpacks, so Lamsang will not have to carry it all.

Early next morning the six of us leave by bus, which will take us up to a town where the trail starts. When we get off the bus four hours later, we see Chinese guards carrying rifles, patrolling the area where Nepal shares a border with Tibet. They scowl and cross over to the other side of the street. They glower at us from their side of the street and we realize, with an odd feeling that in their eyes, we are the enemy.

We follow Chota Re to a steep trail and begin walking up rough steps and then a well-traveled walking path. We walk in single file, all up hill. I am walking behind Lamsang, who is carrying an enormous load. He is a short man with a large chest, from breathing at such high altitudes. His legs, bare from the knees down, are strong and sinewy. His calf muscles look as hard as rock and he is walking barefoot! I have my head down and watch every step he takes, trying to put my own feet exactly where he steps. I am wearing the only shoes I have, besides sandals, navy blue canvas shoes with rubber soles, which I bought in Tokyo, six months before.[4] Lamsung's feet are very wide and his soles are so calloused that it almost seems he has some kind of shoe on. He doesn't seem to feel the rocks and pebbles and keeps up his steady pace for about an hour.

---

[4] "Sneakers" as such, have not yet been invented. Canvas shoes with rubber soles are called 'tennis shoes.'

CLIMBING TO 13,000 FEET

We climb up and up and eventually turn and look down on the town far below us. As the sun sinks lower and we get up higher, we can finally see the snow clad peak of Mount Everest. We have a long walk ahead of us. My REI backpack, which was too big for me when I bought it in San Francisco, but foolishly took it anyway, thinking, *bigger is better*, is now feeling heavy and uncomfortable. When we get to the place where we are to spend the night, I am glad to set it down on the ground. The overnight stopping place consists of a couple of thatched huts, open on one side, with adobe benches to sleep on. There is a wooden table, shared by other travelers going the same way, or on their way back to Katmandu. A few young men and women, huddled around the table drinking tea, swap stories of their trekking adventures. These are not professional climbers, nor even well equipped trekkers. They are just travelers, like ourselves, who want to walk in the mountains. There is no special hiking gear with moisture wicking materials, or sturdy hiking boots in this crowd, which include some local Nepalese. But I figure if a Sherpa can walk barefoot, then surely my rubber-soled shoes will be fine!

While Lamsang begins cooking some dahl for our supper, Don and I walk to the edge of the ridge and sit down looking over the vast space before us. We are now at over twelve thousand feet. On the other side of the valley a range of massive giants whose outlines crisscross each other forming range upon range of mountains, one behind the other, fill the space between us and the grand Himalayan peaks. A young man from another party comes up behind us to look at the view. We smile when we overhear him mutter, "You could freeze to death up there!"

We have other troubles. Perhaps because of the long bus ride, or the strenuous uphill climb, or the altitude, Don's old Peace Corps injury has reappeared. Bleeding kidneys are turning his urine red with blood. We lie down on the adobe benches, with all our clothes on and decide to deal with this problem in the morning. Masterdon was Don's nickname in the Peace Corps. A little prayer goes through my mind before I fall asleep.

> *Moon rising over mountain*
> *With Jesus in my mind,*
> *Oh, heal, heal, Himalaya!*
> *Heal your ailing son,*
> *Heal cosmic forces,*
> *Heal the Masterdon!*

Everyone is awake at sunrise and we have hot tea and porridge. We confer with our little group and tell them of Don's medical condition.

"There is a Swiss Hospital in Pokhara," Chota Re informs us.

"How far away is it? How many days?" Don asks, spreading his small map out on the table in the sun.

"Three days," Chota Re says, pointing out the route.

"Do you think you can make it?" Frank asks. Clearly, Frank and Ilan want us to continue. They are worried that the expedition will fizzle out with only the two of them. We are concerned that Chota Re will be stranded if we have to drop out and they don't go on.

"Three days..." Don hesitates. "I am afraid if I keep walking that long, something might bust loose. It could get worse."

I am very disappointed, but Don's health obviously comes first.

"You could probably make it," I say, more for the others than for Don, "but then we might be stuck there, in Pokhara. The only way out is by helicopter."

"It would be better to see the Peace Corps doctor in Katmandu," Don decides, knowing they will not turn him away. Frank and Ilan reluctantly agree. Chota Re furrows his brow, but nods his head. Lamsang stands by listening. I don't know how much of our conversation he understands.

So, just as easily as this wonderful trek came together, this once-in-a-lifetime opportunity, which fell into our laps, now slips through our fingers.

IN NEPAL

We take whatever provisions we were carrying and give them to the others to stuff into their packs. We wave goodbye to them and wish them well. Then we breathe in for one last time the magnificent view of the mountains, knowing we will never get to Mount Everest, not in this lifetime and head back down the trail.

Mount Everest

Life can crumble away so easily when we put our faith in temporal things. They give us a false sense of security. Swami Sivananda says to "detach and attach"—detach yourself from the love of passing things and attach it to God, to the eternal. But the eternal seems so vast and unknown. I feel that to come close to God is the purpose of my life, but I know I am not brave enough to leap into the unknown. I am afraid I will find myself dangling out in space without any roots or wings! At times when I feel lonely, I find myself longing for a nice cozy home. I shake these ideas out of my mind. Right now, the only sense of home comes from the relationship that exists between Don and myself. Wherever we are, that's where home is.

HOSPITAL AND PEACE CORPS

Don has his kidneys x-rayed at the Shanta Bhawan Hospital in Katmandu on 25th November. I sit outside on the lawn and paint a picture of the hospital building in my sketchbook. It is a small private local hospital. I take off my shoes and paint my feet into the foreground of the picture. The doctor has cabled the Peace Corps in Washington DC to see if they will take financial responsibility for Don's case. He says Don needs a cystectomy—pictures of the kidneys taken via a tube through the penis. But nothing can be done until they hear from Washington. The doctor advises Don not to travel and so we have to wait in Katmandu.

There was another time about three years ago, when we were stuck in Cochabamba, a small Bolivian town, for a week. It was the week of Carnival and we were unable to get a connecting flight or a seat on any plane to Rio. We did not accept the circumstances gracefully and ended up disliking everything, including each other. This time, *yogic* discipline is our saving grace. We structure our day from morning to night and decide to make use of this time as our own 'Sadhana Week,' using it for spiritual practice. We agree to watch our minds closely and if any desires or leanings towards doing, saying, or even thinking something which our conscience knows is not aligned with the truth, we are to write it down. We believe this will help purify our consciousness, as it learns to discriminate between finer and finer distinctions.

Our days go like this: waking up at 6 am for prayers and meditation in silence. We are both so tired today from our trek, that we fall asleep again until 9 o'clock. It is so cold in the unheated room that it is hard to get out from under the covers! After the meditation, we continue to observe silence and I go up on the roof to take my bucket bath and do *asanas*. Then we eat our breakfast in our room: hot chocolate or tea, toast, butter, cheese or boiled eggs and papaya. After breakfast we do whatever each of us wants to do—painting, drawing, reading, or letter writing.

At noon the silence is broken with prayers for world peace and individual and general enlightenment, prayers for the consciousness of the world, for political leaders and spiritual leaders. We offer thanks and prostrations to all those who have assisted us along our journey. The prayers are spontaneous and whatever is felt is said by each of us. There is no set pattern or rule, though we often repeat a few *mantras* and chants, the Lord's Prayer and Swami Sivananda's Universal Prayer. After noon we break the silence if we wish, but try to keep out all unnecessary chatter. A little later we go out for a walk, to buy fruit and vegetables for the evening meal, and maybe a tea snack of chocolate, gingerbread, or apple pie.

On one of these outings, we stop by the post office to mail some letters home. We line up at the window to purchase stamps. It is a small window with an iron grid, behind which the postal clerk is trying his best to serve customers. Apparently, it is not part of the Nepalese culture, to form a queue and take turns, one at a time. The small crowd of people just pushes towards the front hoping to be the next to be served. The postal clerk's face is tense with stress as arms shoot towards him from all sides holding money and shouting voices demand stamps. It is unnecessary chaos. I feel sorry for him, but he is part of the problem. He could insist that everyone behave and take their turn. Instead, a Western man appears at the back of the crowd and begins making people get one behind the other. He raises his voice in an authoritative way, determined to get them into a "civilized" queue. People quiet down and actually listen to him, perhaps intimidated by this foreigner. I guess by his accent he is Australian. I am thankful he isn't a bossy American, imposing his will on another culture! We stick stamps on our letters and get out of there as fast as we can!

Back in the room we are free to continue what we were doing earlier in the day, until 6 pm. Don is reading Henry David Thoreau's *On Walden Pond* and writing down his own theory of how a democracy could really work. I am reading *Christ in India* by Dom Bede Griffith. The book is about how, for the Christian, the 'space' between man and God must always be maintained. Bede Griffith is a *bhakti yogi*, approaching God through devotion, believing that the individual soul is distinct from God, although they're of the same essence. *Vedanta* philosophy states that because we are of the same essence, the individual soul can merge into and become one with God. *Bhaktis*, both Hindu and Christian, don't want to lose their individuality, because they love to worship God.

At 6 pm we have an evening meditation. Then we fire up our one burner kerosene pump stove and cook our dinner in our small blue enamel pot. We have a short prayer before bed at 10:30 pm. We are more than ready to leave Katmandu, but we are waiting for the all clear from the doctor. This daily schedule, while sounding rigid, saves us and makes our enforced stay worthwhile. We continue to write down our dreams everyday, which are quite detailed and vivid. Some of them seem more meaningful than others.

Don is back in the hospital and Frank, who has cut his trek short and is back in Katmandu, wants me to go to a movie with him. The movie is in the American Embassy theatre, which allows only Nepal Peace Corps volunteers and Embassy personnel to attend. Frank really wants to go to the movie and thinks we can bluff our way in. "Okay," I agree, "but you do the talking, 'cause I'm not a good liar."

As we walk across town I ask Frank, "So, what happened to you guys after we left? How far did you get?"

"We walked on as far as Pokhara, another three days."

"That's where the hospital is, right?" I ask looking at him as we make our way down a narrow street. "Where we might have taken Don?"

"Yes. It's very beautiful there, with lakes. A real jewel of a place," Frank says, slowing his pace a little.

"So what happened to the trek? Why didn't you go on to Namche Bazaar, as far as Everest?"

"Well, after you guys left, it got really cold. I wasn't warm enough, my feet hurt and I just got tired of walking. So I came back."

"And Ilan?" I ask.

"Ilan went on with Chota Re, who was going to see his father anyway." Frank says.

"That's good. They kept each other company."

"Lamsang took half the provisions and went home," Frank goes on. "He was near his village outside of Pokhara, so he was happy."

"I'm glad it all worked out," I say. Then, I add, "We were very lucky, you know. To think we had everything we needed!"

"Except good health," Frank says, with a twist of irony in his voice.

"Yes, well, that's the way it goes." I lapse into silence.

When we get to the Embassy Theatre the Nepalese gentleman at the door knows very well we are not part of the Nepal Peace Corps, but Frank keeps insisting that we are. I am standing off to one side trying not to smile, embarrassed at being part of our pathetic attempt to gatecrash the movie. The man asks Frank something in Nepalese, which Frank can't answer. The game is up! We have been caught out lying and Frank sheepishly admits he is, or was, in the Peace Corps in Ceylon. Then, very patiently and courteously, the man invites us in. He is so nice about it, that we feel even more foolish. I realize that just because I didn't do the lying, I am guilty by association and I inwardly renew my vow to speak the truth.

The film we see is called "The Fixer," appropriately about a man who insists on telling the truth whatever the personal cost. The story is about his struggle with his conscience, which won't let him compromise his integrity under the severest of circumstances. When a man shows this kind of strength he's victorious, even if he appears to lose outwardly, because he sticks to the truth at all costs.

The next day, Don is released from hospital and we begin making preparations to leave Nepal. In the streets of Katmandu we stop and stand with the town's people, who are watching a second-story window with rapt attention and anticipation. Suddenly, a little girl, dressed like a goddess, appears. She is the youngest member of the Nepalese royal family and is revered as a manifestation of the Divine Mother. She can be seen at the window everyday at three o'clock in the afternoon, to give the common folk *darshan*, a glimpse of holiness. I wonder what kind of life she will have, growing up as a princess in this culture. I imagine it will be very restricted.

We make our way to Ruby's Restaurant, where we have eaten several times since coming to Katmandu. While we are ordering our tea, we meet a Kashmiri swami who immediately brings to my mind Mother Rema's warning about certain so-called holy men. "Most of them are frivolous hypocrites," was her description. Fortunately, we have only come into contact with Swami Sivananda's disciples, who, as we know them, are sincere, selfless workers. But this Kashmiri swami fits Mother Rema's description to a T. He is tall, with well-combed, oiled hair and soon finds out we are going to Rishikesh.

"What do you hope to learn in six months, to a year?" he asks with a cynical snicker. He tells us proudly that he is "quite independent of any *ashram*." Don is wearing his *japa mala* around his neck and the swami catches hold of it and says sarcastically, "Oh! You purchased one of *these*!" We sip our tea and don't react to this man. He doesn't have a good vibration.

When we go to the American Express office for our last mail pickup, we notice the same swami there with a young Western man, who seems to be quite infatuated with him. We greet the swami and tell him we are leaving for India tomorrow. Later, outside, we pass the two of them on the pavement. The young Westerner doubles back and runs after us. "Do you have any dollars for Indian currency?" he asks, looking back at the swami, as if they have cooked up a plan.

"No. I just cashed some at the bank," I say.

"The *bank*!" he exclaims. "Why?"

"We don't like dealing on the black market."

"Oh," he says, frowning and I can see him thinking, *you guys just don't know how things really work!* Then he rejoins the Kashmiri swami and they walk away, chuckling loudly.

In the story of "Siddhartha" by Hermann Hesse, one of the things the prince has to learn is how to wait. In Nepal we have learned how to wait. We have waited for the Peace Corps in Washington DC to send Don's medical records to the Peace Corps doctor in Nepal; we have waited at the Shanta Bhavan hospital for Don to get better; we have waited for the bus to take us to the airport and now we are waiting for the plane to take us back to India. While we wait we watch a test pilot for Nepalese Airlines fly his Convair around and around the valley, landing and taking off, then landing and taking off again, like an endless cycle of birth and death.

I scribble these words in the Indian Airlines office:

> Leaving the mountains, the valley and the cold water freezing our brains,
> through fever heat and kidney pains.
> Little blue pot boiling over flooding and filling our stomachs again and again.
> We look at each other across plastic bowls of dahl and beans and it seems quite foolish, this meandering through dreams, believing what we're doing has to be done.

Paramahamsa Ramakrishna had a vision of God in which he saw two interlocking triangles, one inverted over the other. From the vibrations generated by these two forms, the entire cosmos was created. While we are waiting for the plane, I take a triangular shaped rubber stamp lettered on each side of the triangle, "Tribhuban Airport, Immigration Section, Katmandu Nepal" and stamp it both ways to form interlocking triangles.

Finally, our flight comes and takes us to the Patna airport. While waiting for the luggage, I write: Back into India, 9th December 1970. Leaning against the rail in the sun, I look down at my shoes. Around my feet are little black ants running busily here and there. It's good to be back where ants are warm enough to run around!

CHAPTER 4

P.O. SHIVANANDANAGAR

ARRIVAL IN RISHIKESH

We take a train northwest all day and night and the next morning we arrive in Haridwar, or Hardwar, an ancient town and important Hindu pilgrimage site, where the River Ganges exits the Himalayan foothills.

We climb into a *tonga*, a light, two-wheeled horse-drawn carriage, to take us to Ananda Mayee Ma's Ashram in nearby Khankal. But she has gone elsewhere and we have missed her again!

We ask the *tonga* driver to take us to the outskirts of Haridwar, to visit our friends, the two brothers from Pennsylvania. John and David have come to India with their teacher, Alice Christensen, to practice yoga in the small ashram of her *guru*, Swami Rama. We have tea with them and are thinking of spending the night, until they tell us that our destination, Sivananda Ashram, is less than an hour further up the Ganges by bus or taxi. We are eager to get there before dark, so we bid them farewell and pay a few rupees, to share a taxi to Rishikesh.

The narrow road follows the Ganga for some time and then branches off through dense scrub forest and jungle. The only vehicles we pass are *tongas*, buffalo carts and bicycles. There is so little traffic on the road between

Haridwar and Rishikesh that men sometimes lie down in the middle of the tarmac, where it is dry, and fall asleep. Taxis just drive around them. A few people walk along the road, which crosses the railway tracks and presently comes to the outskirts of Rishikesh, where gypsies with wooden carts display their goods. We are coming off the plains and entering the foothills of the Himalayas, a range of forested hills stretching out towards Dehra Dun in the west and ahead of us, to the north and east, the high Himalayan mountain ranges. This is as area designated by the Indian government as a national sacred district, due to the fact that seekers of God, *sadhus*, *yogis* and *sannyasins* have lived here for hundreds of years, doing *sadhana* for the attainment of God-realization. *Ahimsa* is strictly practiced here—no killing of animals, no fishing in the holy rivers, no meat or egg consumption is allowed.

Rishikesh is a very small town with two streets intersecting a third, bordered by the Ganges on the southeastern side. Most of the people in the streets are *sadhus*, or swamis dressed in the orange cloth. Some of the passengers get out here and we ask the driver to take us a couple of miles farther, across the bridge over a stony river bed, up to Muni-ki-Reti, Beach of the Sages, where the Sivananda Ashram buildings sprawl at the base of the forested hills. At the bottom of the narrow valley the Ganges flows pristine, a pale turquoise color, between the mountains rising on both sides. It is early evening on the 10th December, and we can see the full moon rising between the mountains above the river. How auspicious! This is our first view of our spiritual home. Such a thrilling sight!

At the bottom of a flight of steps leading down from the road and then up another flight is a small building with "Reception" painted over the door. We enter and are greeted by the swami sitting behind a large wooden desk.

"Hari Om!" He takes our passports and copies in his careful handwriting, the relevant information into his large ledger. "Don and Moo Briddell," he says, handing the passports back to us, "we have been expecting you." We are surprised. "Swami Chidananda has sent a letter," he explains.

"After you go to your room, you may go up and see Swami Krishnananda in his *kutir*." He points up the steps and to the left.

We are shown to our room in Gujarat Bhavan, a double-story building adjacent to the lower road by the river. It is a large upstairs room overlooking a central courtyard, where towels hang on a line. The windows have bars and wooden shutters, with no glass and are bolted from the inside, as are the double wooden doors. The room is furnished with two mattresses on the floor and a low table against the wall. There are two sets of cement shelves built into the wall, which is painted with a pale green whitewash. We unpack, folding our few clothes on the shelves and stashing our backpacks on the bottom.

Then we head up the main steps and turn left to a long building with a rounded front overlooking the road and the river. When we knock, a swami opens the door. He is about my height, 5' 7", a little stout around the middle, a shaven head and piercing black eyes.

"Hello. We are looking for Swami Krishnananda."

"I am Swami Krishnananda," he replies gruffly. "Take off your shoes."

We slip our sandals off and follow him inside. Swami Krishnananda is the General Secretary of the Divine Life Society and is in charge of the daily running of the *ashram*, which is home to about two hundred and fifty monks, who refer to themselves as "inmates," and several visitors, both foreign and Indian. "Inmate" is a term referring to a permanent resident of the *ashram* and not, as in the worldly sense, to someone who is being held against his or her will.

We come to love and admire Swami Krishnananda who, even though he is not our *guru*, is one of Sivananda's most brilliant disciples. We feel honored to meet him. We begin to study *Vedanta* under the auspices of the Yoga Vedanta Forest Academy, the philosophy department of the *ashram*, where Swami Krishnananda is a senior teacher. He is a Sanskrit scholar and well versed in the *Vedas* and the *Upanishads*. He knows the esoteric meaning of the scriptures and he lectures with clarity on any particular subject bringing out the hidden meaning of the ancient texts, although sometimes I don't have the spiritual or life experience to fully grasp what he is saying. He gives us much to contemplate. I can't help thinking that if he were in the Western world and had become a professor instead of a monk, he would have been teaching at one of the top universities of the USA or the UK. As it is, we, the students of the Yoga Vedanta Forest Academy are the fortunate recipients of all of his wisdom.

Swami Krishnananda

He appears to be quite gruff, but somehow takes a liking to us and whenever Swami Chidananda is away from the *ashram*, Swami Krishnananda takes us under his wing. Since Swami Chidananda has not yet returned from his world tour, we spend time sitting with Swami Krishnananda and getting to know the *ashram* routine. We have been given special permission to stay as students for six months to a year. Without prior permission, visitors or aspirants are usually allowed to stay in the *ashram* for up to three days, if there is room. For longer stays, Swami Krishnananda screens applicants carefully, purposely making it difficult for some people.

One day I am in his reception room when a young Western man enters and asks if he can stay in the ashram. "Why do you want to come here?" Swami Krishnananda questions sternly. "What for?" He keeps shooting the young man with questions to see how and what he will answer. At first I feel sorry for the man, but I soon realize that this grilling is Swami Krishnananda's way of finding out whether he is a genuine aspirant, or just out for a free ride. The *ashram* does not charge anything for room and board and runs purely on donations by devotees. It is part of Swami Krishnananda's job to make sure it is not used as a free hotel.

The inmates and guests are expected to make use of the facilities provided to do *sadhana*. Even though the daily schedule is not mandatory, we are definitely encouraged to participate in as much of it as we can. What I love about Sivananda Ashram is that ultimately, what we do with our time here is up to us, which is a good metaphor for life. The daily practices are not rigidly enforced and we find that it is perfectly all right for each person to sincerely work on their own form of *sadhana*.

In his wisdom, Swami Sivananda realized that people have different characters and so each is encouraged to follow the path that best suits his or her temperament—either through *Bhakti Yoga* (devotional), *Jnana Yoga* (intellectual), *Karma Yoga* (selfless service), or *Raja Yoga* (the path of meditation). Swami Sivananda's teachings include the yoga of synthesis, which combines all four. He taught that no matter which path one chooses to follow, they all ultimately lead to God. None is better than another, but it is good to develop a multifaceted approach, so as *sadhaks*, as spiritual seekers, we stay emotionally balanced and sane and don't go off the deep end. But within this more lenient and all-embracing scheme, we are expected to be self-disciplined and put forth full effort. All the disciples, especially Swami Chidananda and Swami Krishnananda uphold Gurudev's teachings and follow them in letter and spirit.

MORNING PRAYERS

The *ashram* wakes up in the predawn hours, which is the best time for meditation according to the *yogis*. It is called *Brahmamuhurta*, God's time. The world is still asleep and the *yogis* are awake. Anywhere between the hours of 3 a.m. and 6 a.m. is considered ideal for meditation, because the world has not yet woken up and all the busy minds have not yet started filling the atmosphere with busy thoughts. We get up at 4:30 a.m. and wash in the common bathroom downstairs. Next, we fire up our little stove and make a cup of tea. The Bhajan Hall, where the early morning prayers and meditation take place, is at the top of the long flight of steps above the road. We wrap our blankets around our shoulders and heads, against the brisk breeze blowing down from the foothills. It is winter now and the Himalayan ranges at higher elevations are covered with snow. The walk up the hill helps to get the blood flowing and wakes us up. We can hear bells from Gita Bhavan and other *ashrams* across the river, and sometimes voices of monks reciting *mantras* drift across the water. This sacred area between Rishikesh downriver and Tapovan upstream, with Shivanandanagar between the two, is greeting another day. Only one or two lights show against the black mountain across the river, silhouetted by stars and the waning moon making its way towards the western horizon.

Sanskrit prayers start at five—*guru stotras*, offering thanks and praise to the *guru* and all teachers; *shanti mantras*, for the welfare of all beings on the planet, *May auspiciousness be unto all, peace be unto all, may all be free from suffering and disease*; and the morning hymn, invoking and glorifying the great *rishis* of the past and present, and the goal of Self-realization. When we first arrive at the *ashram*, I just concentrate on the sounds and the rhythm of the chanting and learn everything off by heart, without knowing its meaning. I love the sound of the Sanskrit language, which has an elevating effect on me. It drones and makes the bones in my face hum, until everything is buzzing. I feel like I've done all this before and I'm just picking up where I left off.

It's dark in the hall, with only the light that is given off by the two oil lamps on the altars. There is some chanting of *Vedic mantras* and a simple *bhajan* by a one of the young *brahmacharis*, a young monk in training. Then starts a period of silent meditation, which lasts between twenty to thirty minutes. All is quiet outside. Even though the external conditions are wonderfully conducive to meditation, in the beginning, the thirty minutes seem to drag on, because we are relative beginners. Perhaps some of the serious practitioners, who sit for two and three hours at a stretch, are still in their rooms. I wonder why there are so few ashramites attending the morning program. I imagine that the time dedicated to meditation is not long enough for adepts. They may want longer periods of silence and stillness. Or perhaps some of them are still fast asleep. All these thoughts spin through my mind, as I sit in the darkened hall. It is about now that sleepiness starts to overtake me and it is a struggle to stay awake.

Some days later I hear Swami Krishnapriyananda Mataji, who makes it a point to attend every morning, asking Swami Chidananda, "Swamiji, why not *insist* that everyone attend morning meditation?"

"If they don't attend, who are the losers?" Swamiji replies. In some things he is very lenient and wants people to do *sadhana* because they love to do it, to attend the morning program because they feel it is the best thing for their progress, not because it is forced on them from outside. Sometimes, Swamiji comes to the morning meditation unannounced and then everyone who isn't there regrets that they missed it.[5]

Outside the folding doors, a length of iron railway track hangs suspended from a hook. Every hour on the hour of the day and night, a monk strikes the track with an iron rod. This is the "clock" that can be heard

---

[5] Many years later, when Swamiji has moved his rooms down to Guru Nivas, overlooking the Ganga, he makes a promise, that whenever he is physically present in the ashram, he will attend the morning gathering and give a little message from six o'clock until ten past six. Even when his body is older and frailer, he is brought up the hill in the ashram car and arrives just before 6 a.m. That insures that everyone attends, because nobody wants to miss a chance to be in Swamiji's presence.

throughout the ashram. After what seems like an age, I hear the rod striking—*one-two, three-four, five-six.*

After morning prayers are over, we walk outside by the Sivananda Pillar in the courtyard and look up at the brightening sky. The pillar is a four-sided, white marble obelisk, inaugurated by Swami Sivananda in 1958, with the doctrines of the main religions of the world inscribed on one side. The heart of religion, as Sivananda sees it, is written underneath: "God is love. The only true religion is the religion of love or the religion of the heart." And then engraved at the bottom in black letters—"SEEK FIND ENTER REST IN GOD." On the second side are Gurudev's Twenty Instructions, of how to live a spiritual life, with his "BE GOOD DO GOOD" underneath. His Universal Prayer[6] on the third side, followed by "BE KIND BE COMPASSIONATE." The disciples of Swami Sivananda have inscribed the fourth side of the pillar with his short biographical sketch, "as a token of reverence, infinite gratitude and eternal love to the beloved Master, the blessed saint of Ananda Kutir." Under that are the four words, which describe Sivananda's vision and purpose of life, which also appear on the Divine Life Society crest, "SERVE LOVE MEDITATE REALIZE."

SETTLING IN

Swami Tejomayananda, our *Vedanta* teacher, says that starting the day with the right sort of vibrations, charges your battery for the whole day. I'm sure it's true, but it's going to take a while to get used to an eighteen-hour day, with just six hours of sleep.

After the prayers are over at six, tea is served from large metal teakettles, carried by kitchen staff around to strategic points in the *ashram*. Inmates appear from their rooms with their own mugs or cups and hold them out for the *chai walla* to fill them with the hot steaming sweetened

---

[6] See back of book for Universal Prayer

milky tea. Along with the others, we look forward to this cup of hot tea, which is also served in the afternoon in the same manner.

During our first days at Shivanandanagar, until we get used to the schedule, we come back from early morning prayers to the room and have another little nap until breakfast. Eventually, as we become more aligned with the vibration of the place, we no longer feel sleep deprived and are able to get up very early and stay up for evening *satsang*, which sometimes goes on until ten at night.

From the flat area where the *tonga wallas* wait with their horses for customers, up to the beach beyond Sivananda Ghat, is a section of road for foot traffic. On the river side of this short road is the Ayurvedic Pharmacy with a pump house on one end and the police station on the other. In between the two is Ananda Kutir, also known as Gurudev's Kutir. This is the original cement building where Swami Sivananda lived when he started the Ashram in 1936, on a parcel of land given to him by the Maharaja of Narendranagar.

Sivananda Ashram from the opposite bank of the Ganges

Originally an abandoned cowshed, the *kutir* is comprised of one long narrow room with shuttered windows and double wooden doors, overlooking the Ganga. There is a passageway with a desk where Gurudev wrote in pen and ink, many books on all aspects of yoga. A couple of steps lead through a doorway into his small bedroom and an even smaller *puja* room, where a large picture of Lord Krishna is still worshipped on a daily basis. In the back is a bathroom with a Western toilet and a bucket for the bath water. In India one bathes by dipping clean water from the bucket, pouring it over oneself and allowing it to flow down a drain in the floor. From the front room, a flight of steps leads from the double doors down to the river's edge, where two large cement seats have been erected. This is where Swami Sivananda used to sit and gaze at his beloved Ganga.

In Hindu mythology, there is a story about how the sage Bhagirathi was in charge of pouring Ganga down to the earth. In order to prevent a flood, Siva caught the river in his hair, turning her into many rivulets until it was safe to release her to the earth. In monsoon season, the water often rises up to the top of the flight of steps and sometimes even floods into Gurudev's Kutir.

There are very few bathrooms in the *ashram*, because most people go to the *ghat* steps and take a daily dip in the Ganga. Since the *ashram* is mostly for monks, women go farther upstream along the beach, towards the black rocks and take a dip there. Western women sometimes wear swimming suits, but Indian women, being very modest about showing their legs, unwrap their saris and take a dip wearing their long cotton petticoats and blouses. The water is icy cold. I don't immerse myself in the Ganga for another couple of months.

Above the pedestrian road are a number of buildings, including the one where we stay, Gujarat Bhavan, so named because the devotees from Gujarat provided the funds for its construction. The *ashram* has its own post office, P.O. Shivanandanagar, which comprises a small suite of rooms, usually full of workers packing up parcels of Sivananda literature, to be shipped out to devotees around India and abroad. Books are wrapped in brown paper and tied with string. Large parcels are wrapped in cloth and sewn up on the sides. The address is written in indelible ink. In the years when Swami Sivananda was training his disciples, from approximately 1940 to his *maha samadhi* in 1963, he wrote over three hundred books on all aspects of yoga. He used a hand-cranked wheel printing press in the early days and was famous for distributing his literature free of charge to everyone who came to visit him.

Being a doctor by profession, before he renounced the world to become a *sannyasin* Swami Sivananda was very keen on being of service to the sick and suffering poor of the area. He opened a dispensary and cared for the sick using Ayurvedic herbs and tonics. Later, allopathic medicines were added.

Near the post office steps opposite Gurudev's Kutir on the upper side of the walkway, there are several little windowless rooms, tucked into the hillside. Some of these are monks' *kutirs* and one of them is designated as the small kitchen, where breakfast and supper are served to us "foreigners." "Foreigner" is a designation for anyone who is obviously from outside of India. The inmates eat in the dining hall at the back of the post office.

Wooden doorways at the front of these small rooms open east, towards the river. The little kitchen has a bare electric bulb hanging in the back room. In the morning, sunlight falls through the doorway across two narrow tables, where we sit on wooden benches and wait for the unpasteurized milk to be heated enough to kill the germs. Breakfast and supper are usually the same, a cup of hot milk and two or three rusks from the bakery in Rishikesh. We dunk our rusks in the hot milk and eat them, watching Purushottama, a short man with shoulder-length hair, dressed in a white T-shirt and *dhoti*, slowly stirring the heating milk in a large pot. One evening, as we wait for our cups to be filled, I notice a strange, dark spot on the wall separating the front from the back room. I nudge Don with my elbow and gesture at the wall. We realize the dark splotch has feelers and legs. It's a cluster of large cockroaches keeping warm and no doubt, waiting for some crumbs to be left on the table. Purushottama, unperturbed by the cockroaches, continues stirring slowly and methodically, taking care not to let the milk boil over.

One of the first principles of yoga is *ahimsa*—respect for all living things and avoidance of violence towards others. The *ashram yogis* live side by side with cows, dogs, monkeys, scorpions, roaches, rats and snakes. No one thinks of harming them and if they do, they don't act upon it. Sometimes the wooden bed frames are sprayed with a contraption that looks like a bicycle pump attached to a can of Flit, which is supposed to discourage roaches and bedbugs.

I remember a story Swami Chidananda told us from the time when he was a young *sannyasin* and was in charge of accompanying some visitors across the road. He didn't want the monkeys to frighten the visitors, so he picked up a stone, with no intention of throwing it, "just for show." But Gurudev saw what he was doing and scolded him. "A *sannyasin* should not even *think* of harming any creature," he said. "A *sannyasin* should never be a cause for fear in anyone."

Including ourselves, there are about nine foreign visitors in the *ashram* and the cooks try their best to accommodate us. For a few days they begin preparing special food for our lunch, like grated raw carrots and beetroots, because someone has informed them that Westerners like eating salads. But supplies are scanty and soon we are back to usual *ashram* fare—*dhal*, *subji*, rice and *roti*.

Since Christmas is just two weeks away, we Westerners, including three Germans, one African from Ghana, one French, one English, one Swede, one Venezuelan and four Americans, are meeting once a day for Christmas carol practice. We are meeting with Swami Nadabrahmananda, in charge of music at the *ashram*. He is a short plump man with light brown skin and a smooth shaven head. We are told he is one of the few remaining *Nada Yogis* in the world. Before he became a *sannyasin*, Swami Nadabrahmananda was the court musician in the palace of a *raja*. He is a master musician and can play several instruments. He can "sing" through his hands, chest, nose, ears and top of his head, the crown *chakra*. He demonstrates for us one day by putting the palm of his hand first over one of Don's ears and then mine. He is able to transfer the sound through his arm to his palm, which acts like a speaker! On another day, he shows me an album with photographs and newspaper clippings of scientific research that was done on him. The scientists sealed him in a box with a monkey and a burning candle. They hooked him up to a polygraph and other electronic devices, so they could monitor him playing the *tabla* while holding his breath. In five minutes the candle went out. Then after a few more minutes, the monkey lost consciousness. The article reported Swami Nadabrahmananda didn't take a breath for half an hour and played the *tabla* all the while!

MONKEYS AND DOGS

Water is heated with a fire under a large tank of water for the morning showers in our building, Gujarat Bhavan, which is built around a courtyard on three sides with a high retaining wall up against the hill below the road, on the fourth side. The bathrooms and clothes washing area are separated through a gap in the buildings. The courtyard between the buildings is strung with clotheslines where visitors hang their wet towels and articles of clothing to dry. One morning, one of the Indian visitors after drying his back with a side-to-side motion, hangs his towel over the line. In an instant, one of the monkeys jumps down and snatches the towel and carries it up to the flat roof, where he begins toweling his back in a perfect imitation of the man.

Bhagavan, our building caretaker, a short rotund man, always wearing a white *dhoti* and shirt, yells at the monkey in Hindi and the towel owner joins in, shouting for the monkey to bring his towel back. We watch this hilarious scene from the upstairs verandah. The monkey stays out of reach enjoying his superior position. It is very funny to see the monkey copying the man, but we are advised to steer clear of them, as they are sometimes vicious.

One day, I am carrying a bag with some fruit and biscuits hidden under my shawl and a big monkey jumps out of the bushes like a highway robber and bares his teeth at me. "Here, take the whole thing!" I yell, slinging the bag in his direction. It is better than risk being bitten.

We are told monkeys knock on the door, begging for food. Occasionally we hear a knock on our door, but when we open it there is no one there. One morning Don and I are reading in our room and a large monkey bursts through the double doors, which we have forgotten to bolt from the inside. Don is reading a spiritual magazine called *The Plain Truth*, and as the monkey grabs the bananas off the shelf and runs for the door, Don whacks his disappearing behind with the magazine. He is too quick for us and manages to get away with the whole bunch. "He got the bananas, but I got him with *The Plain Truth!*" Don says and we have a good laugh.

There are several dogs in the *ashram* who are enemies of the monkeys, both of them scrounging food wherever they can get it. Often a fight will break out during a *puja* or prayer, with a lot of barking and shrieking, which seems incongruous, but the ashramites take it in their stride. After all, the monkeys were here first. There are two tribes of monkeys; the grey ones with the pink faces that run over the *ashram* roofs and the wild ones with black faces, that live in the surrounding forest and don't appreciate human company. Everyone in the *ashram* refers to the biggest male monkey of the pink-faced clan as "the President." The animals live in our midst, but nobody treats them as pets. They belong to no one.

Unfortunately, most of the dogs have a serious case of mange. Westerners have a different mind-set regarding animals. We believe in keeping animals healthy, but we also kill them for food. Here, cows are permitted to wander freely and find food wherever they can, but most are hungry and unhealthy. One day, down by the Ganges, I observe a cow that is so sick her bones just give away and she can no longer stand up. This is an extreme case and I don't stay around to see what becomes of her. The *ashram* keeps its own small herd of milk cows on its dairy farm, just south of Rishikesh. They are well fed and cared for and provide all the daily milk for the *ashram*.

Margot, a lady from Europe living in our building, takes pity on one of the mangy puppies. "What can we do for him?" she asks. "Is there a vet in Rishikesh?"

"I don't know of any vet," I answer. "People don't have pets here. They are too busy trying to survive."

"I have heard that if you rub old engine oil on the skin it will cure the mange," says Jean, an English girl. Somewhere, Margot gets hold of some old black engine oil and rubs the puppy's skin with it. But her good intentions backfire and the puppy doesn't like it at all! He runs around the upstairs verandah, rubbing his little body against the white walls, leaving streaks of black engine oil about a foot high, around the base of every wall. Bhagavan is not happy! Complaining bitterly in Hindi, he waves his hands in dismay, pointing to the streaks. I only know a few words of Hindi, but I understand his frustration.

"Yes, Bhagavan, it is a mess," I agree, "but she was trying to save the dog." Bhagavan is still distressed and goes off muttering to himself. I am sure we foreigners are nothing but a nuisance to him.

Hridayananda Mataji, a doctor disciple of Swami Sivananda, tells us that there was once a dog that was so sick that a visitor decided to put him out of his misery and gave him a small dose of arsenic. It must have been just the right amount to kill everything but the dog himself. In a few days the dog recovered and from then on was perfectly healthy and mange free.

CHAPTER 5

SWAMI CHIDANANDA'S RETURN

THE WELCOME

There is a palpable sense of excitement in the *ashram* as word spreads quickly that Swami Chidananda will be arriving on 22nd December in the evening. He has been away from the *ashram* on a world tour for two and a half years and everyone is longing for his *darshan*. The *ashram* is swept clean and strings of marigolds are hung at the top of the steps by the Vishwanath Mandir entrance. Finally, the evening of the 22nd arrives and a crowd gathers at the bottom of the steps by the road. There is no gate at the bottom of the steps and some tree branches with green leaves have been tied together to form an archway under which Swamiji will pass. Don stands on the wall to the side of the steps waiting to take a picture with his camera.

At twilight, a car comes up the road from the Rishikesh direction. Swami Krishnananda is waiting on the road with a garland, ready to greet Swami Chidananda, the returning President. As Swamiji steps out of the car, joyous cries of, "Jai ho!" and "Swami Chidananda Maharaja ki Jai!" arise spontaneously from the crowd. Swami Krishnananda garlands Swami

Chidananda, who prostrates at his feet. A plate with burning camphor appears and Swami Krishnananda performs *arati*, waving the light in front of Swami Chidananda's slender figure. Then he hands the lamp to an attendant and prostrates on the road before Swamiji. This is the traditional greeting between two of Swami Sivananda's foremost disciples and we count ourselves extremely blessed to witness the love and respect they have for each other. Soon, these two great souls make their way through the crowd towards the steps.

The Ashram Steps

Swami Chidananda climbs slowly, because so many people want to bow down and greet him. Swami Krishnananda reaches the top of the steps first and sees one of the sweepers smoking a cigarette. He gestures to the sweeper to put it out. There is no smoking allowed in the *ashram*.

Together, they climb the steps to the Vishwanath Mandir to greet the deities and then to the Samadhi Shrine, to prostrate in the place where the body of Swami Sivananda is interred. Usually, when a *sannyasin* dies, the body is put in a burlap bag, weighted with stones and carried by boat into the middle of the river. After prayers and *mantras* are recited, the body is consigned to the Ganges. But Swami Sivananda, at the time of his *maha samadhi* on 14th July 1963, had hundreds and thousands of devotees all over the world. Devotees will come to this *ashram* for decades to visit the place where Swami Sivananda's body is buried and offer their prayers, bowing their heads to the white marble slab that covers the top of the crypt. Every morning and evening, monks wipe the place clean and do *puja*, offering flowers and leaves, bathing the little *lingam* sitting on top of the crypt with milk, honey and Ganges water. No one doubts that Gurudev Sivananda's spirit is merged with the infinite consciousness pervading the entire cosmos, but still, the place where his earthly remains reside is a holy place, made more so by all the prayers of the devotees.

In 1970, the approach to the Samadhi Shrine is an open-sided hall[7] with a corrugated tin roof covering its whole length, which runs alongside the Sivananda Press building. Evening *satsangs* are held under this roof in the summertime, or in the open air by the Sivananda pillar.

As Swami Krishnananda and Swami Chidananda come out of the shrine, Swami Chidananda spies us standing on the sidelines amidst many devotees, and smiles.

"Ah, you have come," he says. "Are you finding everything alright?"

"Yes, thank you Swamiji," we answer with palms together in the traditional *pranam* greeting, grateful that he knows we are here.

Everyone is full of smiles, happy that Swamiji is back. We all move towards the Bhajan Hall where Swamiji invokes God and Gurudev and addresses all the ashramites, reminding them of their good fortune that in of all the places in the world they live in a most holy spot, in the sacred land of Bharatavarsha.[8] Swamiji leads a few *kirtans* and all join in, filling

---

[7] In 1987 to commemorate Gurudev's Birth Centennial celebration, a large Samadhi Hall is built, with the Samadhi Shrine enclosed at the end of the hall.

[8] This is the ancient name for India.

the hall with joyful energy. Then, he retires to his rooms and we don't see him again until Christmas Eve.

ASHRAM CHRISTMAS

Somehow, the job of the Christmas program has fallen to us, despite the fact that neither of us is good at singing or music. Luckily, everyone knows some Christmas carols and I write a little song about Swami Chidananda's travels to the tune of, "God Rest Ye Merry Gentlemen," which I hope does not sound too irreverent. We plan to sing it for Swamiji as part of the Christmas Eve celebrations, with Swami Nadabrahmananda playing the harmonium for musical backup.

Many paper streamers and simple decorations are purchased and we are to decorate the Bhajan Hall, where the Christmas Eve celebration will take place. With the help of the other Western visitors we climb on chairs and hang the streamers this way and that, crisscrossing the hall and making it look festive. We even hang streamers around the two altars at the end of the room, flanking the larger than life statue of Saraswati. After finishing the job, Don finds one short piece of streamer lying on the floor. Not wanting to waste it, he flings it up toward the ceiling and it catches on the decorations above us. We stand back and admire what we have done. It looks colorful and festive in an overdone sort of way.

Just then, as if on queue, Swami Chidananda arrives to inspect the preparations. He often carries a walking stick to accompany him around the ashram. He takes in the whole room at a glance and nods approvingly. Then he looks up and spots Don's little piece of streamer that has been thrown flippantly aloft. "What's this?" Swamiji asks, pointing with his walking stick. He has spotted the only thing that was done carelessly!

We learn very quickly that Swami Chidananda does not operate in the same way as the majority of us, what we would call "ordinary" human beings. We only think we know what is going on around us, but because we gather our knowledge through our mind and senses it is limited to the sensory and mental input. We cannot understand how Swamiji operates, because his awareness rests in consciousness, which is not limited by the mind. He is always more aware than we guess, knowing things that seem out of reach for most of us.

When he spotted the only streamer that was flung up just to find it a place, it was because the motive behind the action was careless and not done with the correct intention. Swamiji always seems to zero in on the motive behind the action, more than just the action itself. He does not approve of carelessness, because by definition, "yoga is skill in action." He uses every opportunity to make us aware that we must start paying attention to what we are doing. No matter how small and insignificant we think our actions are, they carry weight; they add up to form our character and ultimately our destiny. He does all this in a natural way. He points things out, often with humor. It is up to us to grasp the lesson and correct ourselves.

Our "Christmas Program" in 1970 is anything but polished. We sing the song I have written, which is quite corny and even the senior swamis laugh. Then our friend from Ghana proceeds to do his "magic show," which entails pulling handkerchiefs out of a hat and hanging them on a wire, which he has strung between the two pillars holding up the little dome on the small altar to Lord Kartikeya. We all keep waiting for the magic, but it never appears. It is like a joke without the punch line! Perhaps the handkerchiefs themselves are supposed to be the trick? The senior swamis, seated on the floor, heads turned towards the magic show, look with interest and some amusement towards the altar, as our friend from Ghana begins to disappear behind the white handkerchiefs.

Because Swami Sivananda encouraged everyone to find their own way and express their own talent, ideas are not dismissed until proven dysfunctional or useless. Even though the monks are Hindu *sannyasins*, all religions here are recognized as equally valid paths to God. So the atmosphere at the *ashram* is very tolerant and accepting of different religious ideas. They give us Westerners free rein to run the show on Christmas Eve, as we blunder along with our version of a gospel song, some readings from the Bible of the birth of Christ and finally, the Christmas carols.[9]

At about 11 p.m. a French lady, Mother Yvonne Lemoine, arrives fresh off the plane and the long taxi ride from Delhi. She is a bit unsteady on her feet and Swami Chidananda welcomes her as she finds a place on the floor to sit. Half of Rishikesh has come to the Christmas *satsang*, crammed into the Bhajan Hall, all squeezed together and seated on the coarse, sisal carpet. Indians do not have the same sense of 'private space' as we have. There is a saying in India, "If an elephant enters a crowded room, it will always find space." Older ladies think nothing of squeezing into a six-inch floor space in front of you and plopping most of themselves in your lap!

Towards midnight we sing "Silent Night," and everyone who knows the words joins in. Despite our mediocre offering and what appears to be disorganized chaos, we realize we are in the presence of great souls, who by their very nature infuse the evening with holiness.

Suddenly, fruitcakes in tins appear, just the right number for each of the Western visitors. They are carried up to the front and placed in front of Swamiji, who calls each of us up to the front to receive one from him. There is even one for Yvonne and I say to Don, "She just arrived! How could they know?"

Swamiji overhears me and says quietly, "Yes, everything is arranged."

Then, special Christmas *prasad* of cookies and sweets for everyone is brought out on trays and after offering it to God, each person comes up and prostrates before Swamiji, who puts it into their hands. Usually, the right hand is cupped on top the left to receive *prasad*. There are some Western folks in line who must be coming from other *ashrams* and Swamiji's attendant informs him that they are going to the back of the line and receiving *prasad* two and three times. "What does it matter?" Swamiji replies. "It is Christmas and they are far from their homes and must be missing their families. Let them come." We understand now it is mainly

---

[9] In later years the Christmas program will include a Christmas tree and a full-fledged choir with many rehearsals before the final performance.

for this special *prasad* that people have walked all the way from Rishikesh. Treats like these are rare and everyone wants to have a taste. We feel guilty with a whole fruitcake each and cut them up the next day to share with the others living in our building.

It is after midnight when Swami Chidananda stands up to indicate that the *satsang* is over. The other senior Swamis, Krishnananda, Hridayananda Mataji, Premananda and Tejomayananda follow his example and we follow them outside into the cold, starry night. We all carry flashlights, called torches here, to see our way around at night, as there are no electric lights outside the buildings. Power shortages are almost a daily occurrence and if they happen at night, we get by with torches, candles and oil lamps.

Suddenly, there is a commotion inside the Bhajan Hall and Don and I go back to see what it is all about. The local people from Rishikesh are tearing down the streamers and decorations, scavenging everything they can carry away. At first we are shocked at this kind of looting behavior, but the ashramites take the attitude that the decorations are also a kind of *prasad* for the townspeople. The celebration is over anyway after midnight. On Christmas day the *ashram* resumes its regular schedule.

MORNING DARSHAN

For the first four months we have no private interview with Swami Chidananda, but we see him every day at 11 a.m. in the Bhajan Hall, where he comes to give *darshan* and meet visitors from India and abroad. When Swamiji enters the room, often murmuring, "Narayan, Narayan, Narayan," (God, God, God), sunlight streams through the two sets of double doors, which are left open unless it's raining. On the outside is a set of screen doors to keep out the cows, dogs and monkeys. Tall and slender, Swamiji walks carefully down the aisle which people have left clear, towards a large flat cushion with a wooden backrest against the pale green wall. He crosses his feet, sitting in half lotus, one ankle resting on his folded leg. He brings his hands together and offers *pranam* to those gathered around him.

Above him, hanging all around the room, are different sized pictures of saints and sages, enlightened beings from the past and present, from Asia and the Middle East. There are renderings of the Buddha, Jesus Christ, and many Indian *yogis* and swamis of different lineages. Swamiji always looks bright and fresh in his pale orange *dhoti* and folded upper cloth draped over one shoulder. In winter, he wears a woolen shawl, until the sun comes over the mountain and the cool air begins to warm up. To the right side of Swamiji is a set of dark green double wooden doors leading into the back room, where the hall caretaker sleeps. On the wall to the left of Swamiji's seat hangs a framed painting of the *pranava*, the Sanskrit symbol for *Om*. It is a watercolor by Swami Vedantananda, a Polish lady who joined the *ashram* in Gurudev's time. She lives upstairs in Lakshmi Kutir, the building reserved for permanent women residents.

People come from all around the world just to sit in Swamiji's presence. He appears completely relaxed and if no one has any questions, we sit in an easy silence. I don't wonder why people come from near and far to sit in the presence of a realized saint. It seems so natural and obvious to me and I imagine that we are all having a similar uplifting experience. Often, what I think is an urgent question dissolves, so that I can't recall it at all. Thoughts disappear and consciousness lifts and expands. It is said that most things in this world can be purchased, but not *satsang*. We cannot purchase the company of the wise and holy. That can only come through God's grace and from the yearning of the soul for something higher. Sitting with Swamiji allows us to vibrate at a higher frequency, if only for the time being.

All *yogic* practices are to purify the mind, like weeding out the unnecessary thoughts, so that higher awareness can reveal itself. Swamiji addresses us as, "Radiant Immortal *Atman*, blessed children of the Divine!" It is not just a figure of speech. They are words emanating from a being who himself is immersed in God-consciousness and he uses every opportunity to remind us that our nature is divine. *Vedanta* explains this truth and while we intellectually know it is so, it takes a purified mind to actually experience it.

Much of the time we are caught in our own sense of who we think we are, limited by our background and personality. Our minds, with all their busy thoughts, will not let us believe it.

Swamiji's morning darshan

Over the first few months, Swamiji meets with us each morning and many aspects of yoga are explained as he patiently answers visitors' questions. One day Swamiji shows us how to hold the japa mala and roll the beads. Traditionally, one is supposed to turn around at the Meru (named after Mt. Meru in the Himalayas), the bead with the knot and tassel, but Swamiji says he keeps on going, using the tasseled bead to keep track of how many rounds. By showing the use of a mala for *mantra* repetition, Swamiji brings our attention to the use of an external aid to draw the mind inward and make it one-pointed, as a preparation for meditation. I like the fact that he acknowledges the rules are there to support the practice, and sometimes it's okay to bend them.

I find myself in a dilemma, because Swamiji's *darshan* always begins at

11 a.m., which is the same time that lunch begins. I try to eat my meal of rice, *dhal*, and *chapatti* very fast and then after washing my plate under the tap, run as fast as I can from the dining hall up the many steps to the Bhajan Hall. When I arrive panting, Swamiji asks, "Where have you been?"

"I just ran up the hill, Swamiji," I say, sitting down, not elaborating on an explanation. Swamiji does not always give a comment. Sometimes he just acknowledges things with an almost imperceptible nod. I don't like to come in to the *darshan* late, so sometimes I choose to miss lunch so I can sit with Swamiji. But I find I can't do that very often, because lunch is the only daily meal served and I am usually always hungry. I find out later, that some inmates have *tiffin* carriers, stacking metal containers inside a hinged frame fastened by a clasp, with which they pick up the food from the dining hall and eat it later in their rooms. We don't know about this possibility and, as guests of the *ashram*, we feel we have no right to ask for special privileges. Swami Sivananda teaches, "Adapt, adjust, accommodate."

Other than the *ashram* kitchen there are only two places that serve food in the area—the Madras Café at the bottom of the hill on the lower road and Choti Walla's, which is a ferryboat ride away across the Ganga.

Swamiji doing japa

However, neither of them is available to us, as money is very scarce and we cannot afford to buy food in a restaurant. There are other *ashrams* in the area, but we wouldn't dream of turning up there looking for a meal. Eventually, a second lunch sitting is added at noon, which I am able to attend after Swamiji's morning *darshan*.

On the way to the Bhajan Hall one morning, Don finds an enormous Luna moth lying motionless on the path. We presume it is dead, because it doesn't move, even when lightly prodded. He picks it up and carries it carefully to Swamiji, who takes it ever so gently and allows it to rest on his hand for several minutes. Swamiji admires the distinctive markings on the moth's wings, looking down at it with such love and tenderness. All of a sudden, the moth comes alive and flies out of the Bhajan Hall. It really seems as though Swamiji breathed life into it!

On another day an Indian *Mataji* comes and pours her grief out before Swamiji. She has just lost her son and she is overcome with sorrow. Her speech is punctuated by deep sobs of grief, which brings tears to many of us. Swamiji listens to all that comes from her heart and when she is finished talking, he allows the silence to settle. Then touching his chest, says to her, "You see, I am your son and you are my mother." Coming from anyone else, this might seem inappropriate, audacious even, but she accepts it from Swamiji, with his deep compassion and understanding. The concept lifts her into a place where she can accept her loss and regain her composure. Swamiji's love is so great it can absorb even the most intense sorrow.

Ahimsa, non-injury, the first injunction of Patanjali's eightfold path, is a noble concept meant to guide the aspirant towards purity in action and also introduce the idea that refraining from harming one thing is protecting the whole. I want to know how to put this concept into practice in a practical way so I ask Swamiji how to sweep the floor without killing the ants. Does it mean we are supposed to take it literally and not harm *any*thing? How strict are we to be regarding small insects? When Swamiji answers, "I don't like to sweep the floor. I take a soft cloth and wipe it from one side to the other," he shows me how far I am from his understanding and how much patience it will take to actually put this *ahimsa* into practice! By treating even ants with reverence Swamiji shows that from his *swabhava*, his inner nature, flow only thoughts of compassion, kindness, sympathy, brotherly-unity and cosmic love.

One day Swamiji begins talking of Badrinath Temple, a holy place of pilgrimage high in the Himalayan region. Krishnapriya Mataji says, "When Swamiji next goes to Badrinath, can't you take some of us with you?" Swamiji looks over at her, making no comment. "Just a *few* of us, Swamiji," she pleads, "just a *small* group."

After a few moments he replies, "When I next go to Badrinath, I will not even take Swami Chidananda with me!" Swamiji is pointing out that his name "Swami Chidananda" is not, in the deeper sense, his identity! We are all familiar with Gurudev's teaching put into a song, "We are not this body, not this mind. Immortal Self we are!" All the *yogic* practices point us towards our deeper Self, beyond our personality and beyond our name. We all laugh, because we understand that Swamiji wants to leave all that behind and rest only in the silence of the Self. Swamiji is making a joke, but actually we do not realize how much he has given up to be here with us.[10]

---

[10] Swami Chidananda's wish and natural inclination was to live a life of seclusion in the high Himalayan region. After his first trip to the West from November 1959 – end of December 1961, Swamiji lived incognito for two years in various parts of India. He was on his way into the mountains when Gurudev's will drew him back to the ashram. When Gurudev fell ill, Swamiji postponed his trip to the mountains and stayed on in the ashram. On 14th July 1963 Swami Sivananda left his body, attaining Mahasamadhi. The

SWAMI CHIDANANDA'S RETURN

Akhanda kirtan, or unbroken singing of the *mahamantra*, has been going on continuously since the inauguration of the Bhajan Hall on 3rd December 1943. World War II was raging in England and Europe and because, at that time, India was part of the British Empire, the Indians felt they must do what they could to help in some way. The chanting was started by Swami Sivananda himself to promote world peace and has been going on ever since. There has been and always will be a swami sitting by the door chanting, "*Hare Rama Hare Rama, Rama Rama Hare Hare, Hare Krishna, Hare Krishna, Krishna, Krishna, Hare Hare,*"—either out loud if the hall is empty, or, if the hall is occupied for some function, he will chant quietly under his breath. Visitors are encouraged to take a turn and chant for an hour once in a while.

We are told that the continuous chanting of this *mahamantra* creates a very strong vibration to counteract the negative forces in the world. Furthermore, it is the firm belief of Swami Sivananda's disciples that the powerful, positive vibrations generated by the *yogis* meditating in the Himalayas, are keeping the forces of darkness in the world from getting the upper hand. Many people think that *yogis* meditating in caves are selfishly pursuing their own search for God. But here, it is believed that the collective positive currents generated by the *yogis* nullify much of the world's turmoil. Why shouldn't this be true, when we all find such peace just sitting in Swamiji's presence?

An elderly German couple, Mr. and Mrs. Hans Franke, are spending some time at the *ashram*. They became acquainted with Swami Sivananda's literature after World War II and become sincere devotees of Gurudev and Swami Chidanandaji. One morning, Mrs. Franke comes into the morning darshan carrying a tiny bunch of blue wild flowers, that she has picked to

---

following month Swami Chidananda was elected President of the Divine Life Society and in obedience to his *guru*, he gave up his idea of seclusion, sacrificing his own wishes and surrendering completely to his *guru*. He dedicated the rest of his life to Gurudev's mission.

A relaxed moment with Swamiji

offer Swamiji. She kneels with some difficulty on the floor in front of him, to offer the little bouquet. Swamiji says, "Thank you! Thank you!" and carefully receives the flowers from her. He looks at them smiling and asks, "Do you have flowers like this in Germany?"

"Ah," she says, nodding her grey head. She seems to understand Swamiji, but her English isn't good enough to reply. Or perhaps she is just too overwhelmed by all of Swamiji's attention on her.

"Something similar," her husband answers for her. Then he begins to relate a story to Swamiji. All of us listen attentively. "I was sitting in my office at home," he says. "It was evening and my wife was in the living room, knitting. She called to me to come and see what she was knitting. 'Come here. Come and see what I am doing.' But I was busy and I said, 'Let me finish paying these bills and then I will come.' Then I heard Gurudev's voice calling me from the living room! Immediately, I got up to follow the sound of his voice. As soon as I stood up and began walking to the other room, a big piece of the ceiling came crashing down onto my desk, just where I had been working!" At this point Herr Franke's voice becomes choked with emotion and he his wife also begins to cry. We are all touched by the story.

"Yes, yes! Gurudev is watching out for his devotees," Swamiji assures them.

A BABY LIVES

In the early months of 1971 a baby is brought to Sivananda Ashram in the arms of a young British woman, Eleanor, who is not his mother. For many days, Eleanor had been staying in a hotel room in downtown Delhi across the hall from the baby and its mother. According to Eleanor, the baby was always crying and hungry. For many nights she heard the door slam and the mother leaving the crying infant in the dark room, while she went out onto the streets to look for clients. Finally, Eleanor thought she must do something, or the baby was going to die! She brought the baby to Rishikesh and she was directed to Sivananda Ashram.

Even I, who know nothing about tiny babies, can see that this baby isn't healthy. His face is pale and drawn and his little arms and legs are thin and undernourished. Eleanor holds him with such care, her face constricted with anxiety and worry. First, she wonders will she be allowed to stay in the *ashram* with a baby and secondly, what should she do with it? How will she feed it?

"Let's go and ask Swami Krishnananda if you can stay," I say. "He is in charge of running the *ashram*. If he says you can stay, it will be alright."

She picks up the swaddled baby and walks with me to the room where Swami Krishnananda receives visitors in the morning, while simultaneously conducting *ashram* business. We enter the room and take a seat on the floor on one side, waiting for him to finish signing some bills and important looking papers.

"How are you getting along?" he asks me, when at last he looks up from his business. He doesn't see the baby right away, as Eleanor has him wrapped in a small blanket. "I am well, thank you Swamiji," I say, gesturing to the little bundle, "but this baby needs your help."

Swami Krishnananda looks surprised. "What is it? Are you the mother?" he asks Eleanor.

"No, sir," Eleanor speaks up. "The mother left him abandoned in a room all alone," she says.

"What?" Swami Krishnananda asks. "Where is the mother?"

"She is a street walker," Eleanor says, wondering how to explain that the mother is a prostitute.

"What do you say?" Swami Krishnananda is a bit impatient and likes people to be precise with their words.

"The mother is a woman of the streets," one of Swami Krishnananda's attendants explains to him in a loud whisper, using an old-fashioned term.

"She was using drugs," Eleanor elaborates. "I was afraid the baby was going to die of starvation, left in the room day after day. I just couldn't leave him there alone."

"Ah!" says, Swami Krishnananda, finally getting the picture. "What nationality is the mother?"

"She is Swedish," Eleanor says.

"Then we must contact the Swedish Embassy in Delhi," Swami Krishnananda signals to his attendant. "In the mean time," he turns back to Eleanor, "go to Dr. Kutty and she will help you with food for the baby."

"Does she have permission to stay here?" I ask to make sure it is official.

"Yes, yes," Swami Krishnananda waves his hand in a gesture of dismissal.

Dr. Kutty is an OBGYN doctor, who, as a young woman, visited the *ashram* with her parents when they were on a pilgrimage to the high mountain temples of Badrinath and Kedarnath. When she met Swami Sivananda, she fell in love with his magnanimous personality and became his ardent devotee. He said to her, "Come here. This is your *ashram*." So, when she finished her medical training in Lucknow, she came and settled at the *ashram*. She now has a very busy practice caring for the poor women of the area, who come down out of the surrounding mountains to attend her clinic. For them she is a Godsend.

Dr. Kutty organizes some kind of food for the baby and slowly it begins to get some color back and gain a little weight. I admire Eleanor for rescuing the baby and finding a safe haven for them to stay, until something can be sorted out. I don't know what I would have done in her place—to take the baby or leave it? I would not have known what to do.

One evening Mother Yvonne watches the baby so that Eleanor can attend the *satsang*. When we arrive back at our building, the baby has been fussing and crying the whole time. Mother Yvonne's nerves are on end and she is worried the baby is getting hysterical. She is happy to hand him back to Eleanor. I stand by feeling useless, with no natural instinct to know how to comfort a baby.

After a couple of weeks a tall, thin, Swedish man arrives from Delhi. He will accompany Eleanor and the baby back to Delhi, where the baby will be sent back to Sweden and cared for by the next of kin. The embassy has been able to trace the identity of the mother, but she has disappeared onto the streets of the crowded city.

I stand on the road as they get into the taxi to take them to Delhi. Eleanor is holding the baby in her arms in the back seat. She waves with her one free hand. I wave back and then bring my hands into the prayer position. I watch the car moving down the hill toward the bridge.

DISCIPLINES AND RELATIONSHIPS

Even though we are not seeing Swami Chidananda privately, we feel as though we are being watched over by him. When Swami Chidananda is in the *ashram* most everyone appears more light-hearted. When he leaves to go on tour to various branches of the Divine Life Society (DLS) in India, the inmates feel his absence. An intangible presence is missing. When we know Swamiji is in residence, even if we don't see him, it lifts the consciousness of the devotees and we feel his protective presence.

His presence seems to infuse everything with meaning and purpose. Watching him interact with people is an eye-opener for us. In any gathering, all eyes are riveted on Swamiji, who deals with situations in a simple, direct way. He addresses all with respect and no question is too trivial for him. While Swami Krishnananda, deals with the everyday running of the *ashram*, building expansion, budgets and bills, Swamiji answers personal inquiries, remembers the names of family members, enquires into their welfare and guides hundreds of devotees, on different levels of spiritual development. He will know just the right thing to say to each one of us, often addressing issues that have never been voiced. If he chooses to, he can read our thoughts. I find out early on that he knows each one of his devotees better than we know ourselves.

Control of the tongue is one of the important *yogic* disciplines; firstly through conserving speech and secondly by restricting taste. We decide to fast without eating for a week. We drink lots of water and get hungry. After the first couple of days the hunger pangs subside and then we start using up what the body has stored, which isn't much, since both of us are quite thin. I learn that fasting breaks the habit of eating in an automatic, unconscious way and gives me a new, more detached perspective on food. It helps clear the mind for concentration and meditation comes more easily. However, as we begin to lose energy we feel physically tired. So, we decide we will break the fast on the eighth day. We know that eating a heavy meal on a stomach that has been fasting can be detrimental. It should be done carefully, introducing a little at a time, starting with easy to digest foods, like fruit or fruit juice.

"What shall we eat?" I wonder out loud.

"What about fruit?" Don says. "Let's walk down by the Ganges and see if there is any fruit for sale?"

Just then, there is a knock at the door and we open it to find the young messenger boy, who serves Swami Chidananda, holding a plate of peeled pieces of papaya. He is also holding a cloth bag slung over one arm. On the plate is a little note in Swamiji's handwriting, saying he thought we would like this fruit. The boy hands us the plate of papaya and then takes a book out of the bag. It is a hardback volume entitled, *Light Fountain*, written by Swamiji, when he was a young *sadhak* in his late twenties, his observations and insights into the daily life of Gurudev. We thank the boy and take the plate of papaya and the book into the room.

"How does Swamiji know exactly what we need?" Don asks.

"I don't know, but I have wanted to read this book. Look, it is printed in South Africa!" It is a new edition printed at the Reservoir Hills DLS, near Durban. Swamiji has been sent some copies by book post and has given one of them to us. Not only has Swamiji blessed us with the book, but he has also sent us the food we need to break our fast. This is just a simple example of the way Swamiji operates, with right action and perfect timing. It happens many times and we know it is not co-incidence. We don't understand how he does it, but somehow he knows what we need, on all levels, physical, mental and spiritual.

I begin to develop a deep trust in Swamiji, realizing that he has only our ultimate good in mind and our long-term welfare at heart. In the traditional *guru*-disciple relationship, one is encouraged to observe the *guru* for some time—how he lives, how he acts in different circumstances and conditions, allowing the disciple time to make up his or her mind whether this is the right spiritual teacher for them. Once the mind is made up, there should be no room for doubt.

In the *yogic* tradition, seeking a spiritual teacher is an important step that happens only when the individual is ready, when they are prompted from within. Finding a *guru*, especially a realized master, is one's greatest good fortune in life.

I observe that Swamiji does nothing lightly. It is my understanding that once the *guru* takes on a disciple he is responsible for the spiritual guidance of that person. The relationship is usually formalized when the *guru* gives the disciple *mantra diksha*, or *mantra* initiation. When I think of our different backgrounds, Don's from the Eastern Shore of the Chesapeake Bay and mine from the East coast of Southern Africa, encountering a saint like Swami Chidananda, seems like a real miracle. Swamiji says, "It is only when grace is there that when the call comes, one responds." We have been blessed in spite of ourselves.

INTENSIVES: WHO AM I?

Peter and Galina, another young couple, are living in the *ashram* when we first arrive. Together we help put on the Christmas program. Peter is tall with a beard and a ponytail and Galina is slender with shoulder length brown hair, which she sometimes wears in two braids. She is from Russian-speaking parents and grew up poor in New York City. "When I was growing up," Galina tells me, "My mother told me when I was hungry I could cut pictures of food out of magazines and pretend to eat them. I couldn't understand why it never helped."

Galina studied with a man who originated the *Enlightenment Intensive* format and she encourages us to try it. As a spiritual practice, it requires several days of intensive self-inquiry, all day long, until it is time to retire at night. Other than the intensive self-inquiry, no other talking is allowed. Two other young men in our building want to join us in the practice. There is David, whose wife decided to go back to Delhi and left him a day or two earlier. I can't quite understand their disagreement, but relationships are very tenuous, especially under the stress of traveling in a foreign country. The other person, Carlos, is from Columbia, South America. Carlos is very slender with almost a pretty face for a man. He has long hair, which he wears in two braids wound on top of his head like a crown.

The plan is that this intensive will continue for three days with no interruptions, so we arrange ahead of time to have our meals brought to the room. We eat fruit and yoghurt and once a day we go to the dining hall and come straight back without talking to anyone else. We inform Swami Hridayananda Mataji what we are doing, in case we are missed in evening satsang. As long as we are engaged in a spiritual practice, it is allowed and encouraged at Sivananda Ashram.

The first day of the intensive, we drag an extra mattress in from Peter and Galina's room, so that three sets of partners can sit facing each other for the practice. Seated about four feet apart, one partner says to the other, "Tell me who you are." Then that person listens in silence for half and hour, while the other continues to identify themselves in ever-deepening layers of reality. We quickly get through names and superficial ways of identifying ourselves and begin to look deeper. Basically, the practice makes you ask the question to yourself, "Who am I?" and then follow it as far down as it will go. If you are the listener, you keep your eyes on the face of your partner, giving them your full attention.

When the half hour is up, we switch and the erstwhile talker, preparing to listen, says, "Tell me who you are." The process begins again. At the end of the second half-hour we switch partners, so that eventually each of the six of us do the practice with the other five.

The collective field of enquiry grows stronger with each passing hour. After lunch we allow ourselves to go for a short walk in silence. Galina tells us what the rules are and all of us agree to abide by them. At one point Don begins writing something in his sketchbook. "No writing anything down," Galina reminds him.

"But I'm just writing in my sketchbook," Don complains. "It's useful to me." "That's against the rules," we all insist. Don is annoyed at the "no writing" rule. I am for following the rules, which have been developed for a reason. Each one of us can see our own ego manifesting in different ways. By the third day, there is not too much talking going on, as it seems we are entering a state of non-verbal communication. We have all grown to know each other quite well in the past seventy-two hours.

Towards the end of the third day, Galina and I sit staring at each other. There is ease between us. Suddenly, what separates us as individuals vanishes and we both recognize what I call "the essence of the Self," which is essentially an experience of awareness that we are one. It is so simple. We both see it and see that the other is seeing it. It leaves us speechless with awe.

The next evening Swami Hridayananda Mataji wants us to demonstrate for her what transpired between us, but of course, with someone watching, we are self-conscious and it doesn't happen. We decide not to talk about it anymore, as the more we speak about it as if it is in the past, the farther away it gets. We are left with a feeling of clarity after the intensive that we hadn't known before.

A couple of mornings later while we are washing our clothes by the showers, I say to Galina, "I feel like my ego will never be able to trick me again." I am so naïve and don't realize that *prakriti*, or the manifest world of names and forms, is full of the tremendous power of *maya*, which can delude us in an instant. The mind falls back into its usual grooves and the clarity of the intellect soon fades. In no time at all, I am right back to where I was before the Intensive, with my ego firmly in charge!

VEDANTA CLASS

Besides attending the daily *ashram* programs of morning meditation, mid-morning *darshan*, evening *satsang* and meals, we begin attending a *Vedanta* class, every afternoon at four o'clock in the Bhajan Hall. Up till now, there has not been any formal *Vedanta* course taught at the Yoga Vedanta Forest Academy, which was inaugurated by Swami Sivananda in 1948 to promote the teachings of *Advaita Vedanta*. Swami Sivananda found that some of his disciples were well versed in the scriptures and he encouraged them to give talks in the Academy. As far as I know, our course, which starts in December 1970 and ends in May 1971, is the first of its kind.[11]

---

[11] It is the prototype for a yearly and later bi-annual Vedanta course taught in the Yoga Vedanta Forest Academy. Hundreds of young Indian men are educated in Vedanta Philosophy through this course. Unfortunately, in later years some foreigners abuse the generosity of the *ashram* and in future are barred from taking the course. Neither are women encouraged to apply.

We count ourselves extremely blessed that we are offered this wonderful opportunity, which has a huge impact on our thinking and our worldview. Our five-month's *Vedanta* course is taught mainly by Swami Tejomayananda, with frequent lectures given by Swami Krishnananda. All the young *brahmacharis* attend, as well as the Western men and women at the *ashram*. We study a scripture called *Viveka Chudamani, (The Crest Jewel of Discrimination)*, and the *Upanishads*. A large chart of the elements, originating in *Brahman* through *prakriti*, to explain how the many came from the One, is printed for the students, in the Sivananda Press.

We students sit cross-legged on the floor, using little wooden benches on which to set our ruled notebooks. The teaching, held in the Bhajan Hall, continues day after day, with us sitting and listening to the lecture and taking detailed notes, either in pencil or fountain pen and ink. Swami Tejomayananda is a methodical teacher and illuminates points by writing them with chalk on a small blackboard, mounted on an easel to one side of him.

I love *Vedanta* philosophy and its practical application to yoga practice. To be told that we are sparks of Divinity, that our true nature is identical with God, is uplifting and inspiring and on a gut level I know it's true. In some religions, equating one's essential nature with God might be considered blasphemy or heresy. I am so deeply grateful to be living in the 20th century, in a place where these ideas are not only being taught as the norm, but where *Vedanta* philosophy is *lived* through our daily spiritual practice. Otherwise, as Swami Sivananda put it, we would just be "dry *Vedantins*," or "lip *Vedantins*," someone with book knowledge, but no experience.

I don't want to be a "dry *Vedantin*," so I study and meditate and do all the spiritual practices with eagerness. I am really interested, so it is not hard for me. One of our classmates is a young *brahmachari* from Orissa, called Ramswarup. Besides studying *Vedanta*, he is eager to learn about the latest gadgets from the West. The tape-recorder is the leading edge of technology and he is interested in how they work and how he can use one to record Swami Chidananda's talks.[12] However, I get the distinct impression that being overly interested in modern technology is frowned upon by some of the senior monks. They don't understand what place it could possibly have in spiritual life, which has been going on for millennia without the use of such devices.

In our free time we don't mix with a lot of people, neither Western nor Indian. Being too social and spending one's time gossiping about this and that, is considered a waste of precious time and definitely discouraged in the *ashram*. It is, however, okay to discuss spiritual topics out in the open, or sitting under a tree in the courtyard. We are fortunate to have each other for company if we need it, and we keep ourselves busy with our sketchbooks, which Don usually assembles himself. He buys the paper and sews the blank pages together with tough thread, covering them with odd bits of cloth we acquire along our journey. It is the only way we can get blank

---

[12] Ramswarup later serves as Swami Chidananda's personal assistant for many years and becomes Swami Ramaswarupananda.

Western devotees

sheets of paper for drawing. The exercise books we use in *Vedanta* class are ruled with thin blue lines.

THE LEPERS

Attending *Vedanta* Class keeps us busy from four to five o'clock every afternoon. Afterwards, we leave our notebooks in our room and head out for a walk. Walking is a common activity for many ashramites, as a lot of time is spent seated on the floor. It feels good to get out and move and stretch our legs. Generally, we walk up the main road to the top of the hill overlooking Lakshman Jhula, where some lepers have built huts on the side of the road. They squat on the roadside, surviving on charity.

Thanks in large part to the attention of Swami Chidananda, who champions their cause they are moved to proper living quarters in their own colonies. One of the colonies we visit with Swamiji is on the outskirts of Rishikesh and the other, further upstream, is being built along the banks of the Ganges, at Siva Puri.

One of Swami Chidananda's missions is to make sure that the lepers are well looked after. As a young *sadhak*, he would pick up lepers from the side of the road and bring them to the *ashram*, where he would tend to their wounds and care for them until they were healed. Not everyone was happy about having lepers in the *ashram*, but Gurudev Sivananda recognized Swamiji's compassionate nature and praised his selfless service. Now, Swami Chidananda encourages people from the West to collect funds and donate sweaters for the lepers to wear in the cold winter months. A young Frenchman, Pierre, has dedicated his life to their care, treating their leprosy with the latest available medicines.

We are told that the disease is only contagious when the carrier has no outward symptoms, like missing fingers, or a hole where the nose should be. A leper might be missing an eyebrow, but other than that, it would be hard to tell if they have the disease. In Biblical times, lepers were shunned and feared by society. Pierre lives with them at the new Siva Puri colony.

He teaches them how to spin thread, to boil it in colored dyes and then to weave it on wooden looms. They learn how to make rugs, mats and bedspreads, which are shipped to European countries for sale. Thus, they are able to earn money and sustain themselves. They also have a permanent place to stay, without having to live in the dust on the side of the road.

The lepers adore Swami Chidananda and regard him as no less than God. Swamiji visits them quite frequently, especially during important Hindu Festivals, like Sivaratri. They are ecstatic to have him in their midst and they dance around in a circle, clapping and beating sticks together. Swamiji joins in with them and dances too, throwing his arms into the air. Later, he sits and talks with them and finds out what their needs are.

One day someone asks Swamiji how he could best be pleased. He thinks for a while and then says, "There is a young man, Pierre, living with the lepers. If he asked anything of me, I would do it for him."

HATHA YOGA

In India, *Hatha*[13] yoga is the discipline that deals with the health of the physical body and mind. *Hatha* is active and translates as "forceful" or "willful" and its practices enhance physical strength and flexibility, which helps to calm the nervous system and bring about mental poise. *Hatha* yoga is about finding balance, ("*ha*" sun and "*tha*" moon), and preparing oneself for the practice of meditation.

From a young age Swami Sivananda was a great proponent of physical fitness and before he took *sannyas*, while he was studying to be a doctor, he learned about the therapeutic effects of *Hatha* yoga and studied with

---

[13] In the early days *Hatha* yoga is a general category, including most styles of physical yoga practice. It is an old system referring to the practice of *asanas*, *bandhas* and *pranayamas*, distinguishing it from the intellectual, devotional and service-oriented aspects of yoga. However, as the practice of yoga becomes popular in the West, a myriad of different styles evolve and develop and "*Hatha*" loses its general inclusiveness and becomes one of these many styles.

one of the most influential teachers in India at the time.[14] Swami Sivananda prescribed for all his disciples a regular daily practice of *Hatha* yoga, which is known in the West simply as "yoga." Without a fit body, how can we be of service to others? Neither will we have the physical stamina nor mental stability to sit still for long periods of meditation.

Swami Sivananda taught his disciples twelve basic poses, or *asanas*, which can be repeated every day with variations, including *Surya Namaskar*, Sun Salutations. He taught his disciples the different forms of *pranayama*, the *Shat Kriyas*—the ancient *yogic* techniques for cleansing the physical body, using the elements of wind, water and fire; the swallowing of a long cloth, then pulling it out through the mouth, to cleanse the stomach; the internal massage of the organs through the practice of *nauli* and the internal locks, called *bandhas*, for regulation of the digestion and promotion of health.

Swami Sivananda's book, *Yoga Asanas*, first published in 1931, is fully illustrated with many *asanas*, *pranayamas* and *bandhas*. Swami Vishnudevananda's *The Complete Illustrated Book of Yoga* was published in the West in 1959, followed by Swami Satchidananda's *Integral Yoga Hatha* in 1970. These are among the first books on the benefits of *Hatha* yoga—flexibility, balance, strength, stress reduction, and increased awareness—to reach the Western world. Through his disciples, Swami Sivananda's influence has a huge impact on yoga in the West.

In our Yoga Teacher Training in Val Morin, we were introduced to the *Yoga Sutras* of sage Patanjali, in the form of 196 aphorisms, written in 400 CE. In Patanjali's system of *Raja Yoga*, the "Royal" or "Kingly" yoga, there are eight steps, called *"angas."* So, sometimes it is called *Ashtanga* yoga— from the eight rungs or limbs. In this system, the third rung, *"asana"* means seat. According to Swami Chidananda this *"asana"* is different from the

---

[14] Swami Kuvalayananda (1883-1966)... blended *asanas* and indigenous Indian physical culture systems with the latest European techniques of gymnastics and naturopathy. With the help of the Indian government, ...*asanas*—reformulated as physical culture and therapy—quickly gained a legitimacy they had not previously enjoyed. (Excerpt from Mark Singleton's book, *Yoga Body: The Origins of Modern Posture*).

system of postures practiced for physical fitness. The definition of "asana" in this context is an aid to the practice of meditation. To meditate we must find a comfortable position on a comfortable seat. If we are comfortable, we are happy (*sukha*) and can sit still for some time. Patanjali describes this as, "*sthira sukham asanam*—seated steadily in a comfortable posture." From this comfortable seat we can practice *pranayama*, regulation of breath and *pratyhara*, withdrawing the mind from the sense objects and turning it within. Once the mind is turned inward and becomes quiet, concentration is possible.

Probably the most well known of Patanjali's *sutras* is his definition of yoga—"*yogas chitta vritti nirodhah*—a complete cessation of thought (*vritti*) arising in the mind-lake is yoga." When we quiet the thoughts and the mind becomes still, meditation is possible. So, a comfortable seat, *asana*, is very important in the process of yoga for a meditative practice.

When Swami Sivananda sent Swami Vishnudevananda and Swami Satchidananda to the West to propagate the science of yoga, they used the physical practice of *asanas* to draw students to them. They realized that the practice of the different postures would engage the students and lead them eventually toward the inner yoga, to meditation. Most of us Westerners are a restless bunch! It is hard for us not to be *doing* something and for many keeping physically fit is a high priority.

At the *ashram* there is a lot of floor sitting, and I find the daily practice of yoga *asanas* a perfect antidote to stiffness, a way to stretch my muscles. I also make time to combine the *asanas* with a few rounds of *nadi shodhana* (alternate nostril breathing) and *ujayi* breath, which always have a calming effect on my mind. Sometimes I alternate with a round of *kapalabati* (shining skull breath) to sweep out the negative thoughts and bring an invigorating sense of clarity to my mind.

During our time here at Gurudev's *ashram* the devotional, intellectual and service aspects of yoga are more emphasized than *Hatha* yoga practice. Perhaps it is because the prominent *Hatha* yogis, like Swami Vishnudevananda and Swami Satchidananda, have gone abroad. There is one swami who practices *asanas* up on the flat roof of Saraswati Kutir and sometimes we join him. But if Don isn't with me, I have a feeling that he is ill at ease. There is also a yoga class held in the Bhajan Hall after prayers, which later moves to the library building, but to my disappointment, it is only for men. So usually, Don and I practice what we have learned from Swami Vishnu, either on the flat roof or on a blanket spread on the cement floor of our room. There is so much offered at Sivananda Ashram and I am learning that everything done with the right attitude of mindfulness and awareness, including *asana* practice, is considered *sadhana* and a possible a path to liberation.

THE TEMPLE PAINTING

Swami Chidananda notices how we are often drawing in our sketchbooks and one day he asks us if we would do some sketches, or little paintings, for a possible backdrop to the black marble statue of Lord Krishna in the Vishvanath Mandir. As you stand at the door of the temple, the statue of Lord Krishna is directly opposite you, in a niche in the back wall. The statue, or *murthi*, is about three feet high and stands in the traditional Krishna pose, with one foot, toes down, crossed in front of the other. His arms are raised, holding a flute to his lips. Krishna charmed the Gopis in Brindavan with the enchanting music of his flute. He also gave the immortal teaching of the *Bhagavad Gita*, the quintessence of the *Upanishads*, to his disciple, Arjuna, on the battlefield.

Swamiji calls us up to the temple at the top of the steps to show us where the painting would go. The swami priest in charge, the old *pujari* of the temple, doesn't know us and tries to suggest someone else. "What about Uma Shankar?" he asks Swamiji. Uma is the German woman artist, who has sculpted the elaborate statues of the Goddess Durga riding on a lion and Saraswati on her swan, which reside at either end of the Bhajan Hall.

"No, no, no," Swamiji dismisses the idea with a wave of his hand. "They will do it."

So, on returning to our rooms we do some drawings and then paint them with our little set of watercolor paints. I paint a pond dotted with pink lotuses and a golden sun with rays radiating out from it. There is a frog sitting on a lily pad and the sun is positioned to go behind the head of Lord Krishna, like a radiating halo. Don draws an upside down map of India with Krishna standing at the tip. I ask him why he is painting India upside down. "There is no 'up' or 'down' in space," he reasons. Over the next couple of days we make a few other options for Swamiji to choose from.

Some days later we bring the paintings to Swamiji's *kutir*, where he is sitting against the wall on a large square cushion, surrounded by Sivananda literature. He spreads the paintings in front of him and begins to comment on each one. "The one with the sun and rays—the mountains represent the spiritual ascent and the river is consciousness, flowing down to merge into the sea of bliss. Beyond both of these is the sun, which represents the Absolute One, from which the rays emanate, such as Krishna, Christ, etcetera. This painting is more in time, as it is has growth, is cyclical, with the rising and setting of the sun."

Swamiji picks up my other painting and comments, "Everything in this painting of the lotuses is in a hushed, quiet condition. The water merging with the air is in a constant state of *samadhi* and the little farthest away lotus is saying, "Hush, hush." Even the frog is silent in awe." He compares both of them. "When Krishna is in this setting, it is as though the Lord has come down to us earthly creatures, while the other painting is motionless, ageless and ethereal. When the Lord is in this setting, it is as though we have to go up to Him, to try to get to where He is. Both are necessary."

Swamiji has such deep insight into things, infusing them with meaning and interpreting every expression that has come from our subconscious minds, making it clear and conscious.

To my surprise, Swamiji chooses the painting I've done of the lotus pond to be transferred to the Masonite board for the larger version. The *ashram* purchases the enamel paints necessary, which are washable and will hold up well. The English girl, Jean, who is a painter of coats-of-arms, offers to do a painting of the Divine Life Society Crest, so she and I paint together on the upstairs verandah of our building.

When the painting is complete, Don and I meet Swamiji in the Vishwanath Mandir to install the backdrop. The seven o'clock evening puja is over and all is quiet. I ask Swamiji, "Will we need to move Krishna?"

"No, no!" He answers. "The *murtis* have been installed by Gurudev himself, when Vishwanath Mandir was inaugurated on 31st December, 1943."

I remember that it was in the same month that the Akhanda Kirtan commenced in the Bhajan Hall. I had read that pundits and astrologers advised Gurudev that the 31st was not an auspicious date for the inauguration, but Gurudev insisted that it should go ahead, because the devotees had their holidays and were visiting the *ashram* at that time. He wanted them to be present at the inauguration.

"Holy *mantras* were chanted for days and days and then only was the *murti* installed," Swamiji explains. We are standing up close to the statue as Swamiji continues. "This is so the *murti* is enlivened by the power of the *Vedic* scriptures. Just before final installation, a written sacred *mantra* is placed under the pedestal. Once the *murti* is permanently installed in the temple, it is never removed."

Fortunately, we are able to bend the Masonite board, so that it goes over Krishna's head and slides into place, perfectly fitting in the niche behind him. We try different lighting effects in the temple and find it looks best with a soft, warmer light.[15]

Now, Swamiji picks up an oil lamp and does *arati* to Lord Krishna, waving the flame all around the *murti* and singing, "*Om Namo Bhagavate Vasudevaya!*"

---

[15] This painting stays behind Krishna for several years, until the temple is remodeled and the walls are covered with marble.

Afterwards, we sit with Swamiji in the dark and follow his lead as he sings a few quiet *kirtans*. Then we fall into blissful silence for some time. Somewhere, deep in my consciousness, I realize that this is an extraordinarily blessed moment, one that I will remember for the rest of my life. When Swamiji stands up, we do too. As we are standing just outside the temple, looking through the opening at Lord Krishna, Swamiji says very slowly and clearly, "And now, He is looking at you—actually." His words send shivers down my spine and I feel something significant is happening. I understand then, even though only intellectually, that while consciousness exists everywhere, that it is especially concentrated in the *murtis* in the temple. After that, I can no longer think of the beautiful statue of Lord Krishna merely as black granite stone. I don't quite understand how, but somehow the statue has the quality of consciousness itself, the living presence of God, looking out through those eyes and knowing everything. I realize that Swamiji has involved us in this project, so that we might come closer to God and thus he has blessed us in a most wonderful way.

DO IT NOW!

One of Swami Sivananda's favorite sayings was, "D.I.N. Do it *now*! Do not postpone." Gurudev taught his disciples to never waste time. Time is precious. Our lives are made of moments and time is really all we have. We are taught that human birth is difficult to get and it is only as a self-reflective human being that we have the ability to realize the Self.

Word goes around the *ashram* that Swamiji is expecting a devotee from Lebanon to arrive soon. A room has been reserved for her in Lakshmi Kutir, the residence block for women. Swamiji asks Mila in the neighboring room on the ground floor to please sweep the empty room and the adjacent verandah and generally prepare for the visitor's arrival. Mila is from Venezuela, a disciple of Swami Krishnananda, and is on an extended stay of six to nine months at the *ashram*. She is a short, dark-haired woman who

SWAMI CHIDANANDA'S RETURN

is always friendly to us. When I see Mila the next day, she is quite upset as she relates to me what transpired between Swamiji and her.

"I thought since the visitor was only coming the following day, I would have plenty of time to do all the cleaning in the morning before she arrived. But, in the morning as I am getting dressed, I hear the sound of the broom sweeping outside. When I look through the window I see Swami Chidananda himself, sweeping the verandah!" Tears fill Mila's eyes and she continues in a shaky voice, "I said, '*Please* let *me* Swamiji!' But he had already finished the job!"

Mila learns the D.I.N. lesson the hard way. I am sure she was willing to do the job, but just thought that she had plenty of time. Perhaps she does not know the aphorism, "Never put off for tomorrow what you can do today." I think Swamiji did what he would have done if Gurudev had asked him to clean the room. The request would take top priority and he would do it as soon as he could. Perhaps Swamiji was also reminding Mila and all of us that Gurudev taught, "Work is worship," Any opportunity to serve should be regarded as a privilege, not as drudgery.

CHAPTER 6

THE POWER OF PRESENCE

VISIT TO UMA SHANKAR

One bright winter morning Galina and I decide to walk up to visit Uma Shankar, the German artist-*yogini* who sculpted the large statues of the Goddesses Saraswati and Durga in the Bhajan Hall. We have heard about this cave-dwelling *yogini* from Krishnapriyananda Mataji, an *ashram* resident, who has remained friends with her since Gurudev's time when they were both young disciples. She still visits Uma on a regular basis. We leave right after breakfast and morning tea. Don and Peter have gone for a two-day hike up the mountain across the Ganga, so we are on our own. The air is cool and crisp as we walk up the empty road at a good pace. We agree on silence as we walk, both to conserve energy and to preserve the quiet of the morning. There are very few cars on the road at this time and the ubiquitous scooter-taxi has not yet reached the small villages of Rishikesh, Muni-ki-Reti and Tapovan.

The turquoise water of the Ganges glistens in the sun to our right. A few shopkeepers at the top of the hill are just opening their stalls, displaying their wares of tea and biscuits, powdered milk, soap, and other simple items. Some have little pyramids of seasonal fruits, tangerines, or guavas. We stop briefly to pay a few *annas* for some fruit, which we hide in a bag from the monkeys. It is traditional in India that when you are going to visit a spiritual person, you bring something, however small, to offer them, usually fruit or flowers.

Ganges looking towards Lakshman Jhula

We walk down the zigzagging short cut towards Lakshman Jhula, the only bridge in the area. We greet the squatting beggars at the entrance to the bridge with "*Namaskar.*" They sit on burlap sacks with battered metal begging bowls in front of them. They do *pranam* back and do not ask anything from us. They sense we are intent on something else today. It is hard to pass by a beggar without giving something, but we have nothing prepared for them this time.

Krishnapriyananda Mataji has given us verbal directions to the cave. "Just after you cross the bridge, go up and to the left. Then look for the scar in the hill from the landslide and walk towards it. The entrance to the cave is farther to your right."

"Will it be alright to arrive with no introduction?" I had asked Krishnapriyananda Mataji. "Can we just show up?"

"Yes, it will be alright. You can just go."

I am eager to meet a woman who has actually left the world behind and lives in a cave. I wonder if her love for God is so strong that she has overcome fear and the need for companionship.

The suspension bridge bounces slightly when we walk across. It is wide enough to allow mules and donkeys and foot traffic, but thankfully, too narrow for larger vehicles. We stop in the middle to look upstream. We are in the foothills of the Himalayas—steep, forested mountains rising on either side of the riverbed, through which the holy Ganga has flowed for centuries. We turn and look at the view downstream. The only significant building in the area is the old temple just above the beach down from the bridge, whose steep dome, once pale blue, is now weathered to grey.

Up the gorge we climb, using the rocky footpath, past a ferny pool of clear water and a banyan tree. Music from a marriage festival in the village recedes farther and farther behind us. The silence of the mountains and the valleys becomes more and more present. We begin walking diagonally across the mountain and eventually we look up and see two young papaya trees full of green fruit and a type of embankment made of natural rocks. A sheep's head pops over the top of the rocks and Galina, who has done some research before our visit, calls, "Sashi!" The big wooly sheep with curly horns has a bell around his neck, which tinkles as he butts his head against a funny looking German Shepherd dog with stubby legs. The dog is tied with a rope and they put their noses together, playing.

"Om! Om! Hari Om!" we call on our approach. Uma does not know us and we had no way of letting her know we were coming. All my preconceptions of what she would be like evaporate when she appears. Galina told me that Uma wanted her skin to become thick and rough like an elephant's, so that she could bear the cold without clothes. But it is smooth and she is quite beautiful. She appears to be in her mid-thirties, fair-skinned with brown hair that has matted evenly into tight ringlets, pulled up and wound around on top of her head, like a Siva statue. She wears an orange piece of cloth wrapped around her waist like a dhoti, and a tiger skin fastened across her chest. Over that, she wears a plain brown sweater with a string of large Rudraksha beads around her neck. We immediately feel welcome and at home with her.

"This is where I live," she says, quite open and friendly, coming out through the gate and patting the sheep. "Sashi—his name means new moon—came with his mother into the forest and suddenly a tiger roared nearby," she tells us. "The mother ran away, leaving the little one to be eaten, so I brought him into the cave with me. The tiger was not happy!" She cackles with laughter. "I made this fence in front here," Uma says pointing to the bars along the mouth of the cave. "Every night the tiger would come and roar outside the cave, because he knew the lamb was with me."

Uma has a stillness about her, a delicate vibration, even when she is talking her eyes look through you, as though she is seeing the beyond. They remind me of Mother Rema, pure and detached, demanding nothing.

The cave is hidden within the side of the mountain and over the entrance she has had workmen construct a tall iron fence with a gate. Leaning against the gate frame is a sculpture of an odd reclining figure. "He is the Lord of the ghosts," Uma explains. Next to him, above the door is an owl sculpture. Just inside there is a statue of Mother Kali, decorated with colored beads and silver things embedded in the cement. Uma's artistic expression has manifested in bas-relief sculptures of gods and goddesses around the walls of the cave, which she has decorated with costume jewelry. "I don't like bare walls," she says, indicating her creations. "So they keep me company."

We take off our shoes and enter the cave, which is about twenty feet deep, and dark at the back with two small oil lamps burning. Gradually, our eyes grow accustomed to the darkness and we sit on a mat, while Uma sits on a small skin on the floor of the cave. Behind us is a three dimensional statue of Lord Siva with his consort, Parvati, next to him, standing on one leg in the tree pose. Near the entrance to the cave is a large rock that couldn't be removed, so Uma has made a statue of Siva's bull, Nandi, on it. There is a black leopard sculpture near the place where she sleeps and Hanuman is coming into shape on one wall. The walls are very irregular, but the floor has been more or less flattened.

"When the sun comes over the mountains, the reflection comes inside and lightens things up," Uma says.

Over on one side is a little fireplace with some cooking pots and a kettle, where a *sadhu* squats, washing either dishes, or clothes. After he finishes his chores, he leaves.

"How do you get your food?" Galina asks.

"Once a week that *sadhu* goes into town to buy supplies for me," Uma says. "Flour for *roti*, some rice, *dahl*, and a few vegetables. I get water from the stream."

We listen as she speaks of many things, telling us about her life. In Germany she had entered a convent in her search for God, but to her great disappointment, found that they would not grant her inner freedom. Reading the Hindu scriptures, the *Vedas*, was forbidden and considered a sin. "Vat is dis? Dis is not Rusland!" she exclaims in her German accent, explaining why she left the convent. "When I came across Swami Sivananda's writings, I came straight to India and was with him for five years." Gurudev encouraged her to express her artistic talent and supplied her with everything she needed to create the statues of Saraswati and Durga in the Bhajan Hall. She also studied the *veena* with Swami Vidyananda and is quite an accomplished musician.

"And what about after Gurudev's *maha samadhi*, when he was no longer here, physically?" I ask.

"After Gurudev passed on, there were those who wanted to get rid of all the women," Uma explains. "But then members on the Board of Trustees said, 'No! These are Gurudev's disciples whom he made himself. They cannot be thrown out! But whether or not more women should be allowed in, will be up to the *ashram*.'"

"So, why didn't you stay in the *ashram*?" I ask.

"It was very unpleasant," she says. "So I came away to the forest."

"So, even though you could have stayed, you decided not to?" I ask further, trying to understand her motive. It seems like such a radical step for a young, single woman to live alone in the forest without any protection.

"I did not want to be a burden on the *ashram*," she explains.

"So most of the time you are alone?" I ask, feeling a longing for quiet and solitude.

"Not completely. Sashi is here. I get wool from his coat and spin and knit it. The dog has come. There is also a cobra that comes in whenever it wants."

"Is it here now?" I ask, turning uncertainly on the mat where I am sitting, looking into the dim recesses of the cave.

"Probably not," Uma says, unconcerned. "It comes and goes. We don't bother each other. Once I found the kill of a tiger and stole two legs of it for my dog," she continues. "But the tiger got angry and came in the night and roared outside the cave. I have lost my culture," she laughs, reaching for a dirty cloth to wipe her nose on.

We sit with her in meditation for some time. Everything is still, outside, inside. My mind becomes concentrated and calm and there is a wonderful quiet that I haven't found even in the *ashram*. The stillness penetrates everywhere and swallows everything, even Sashi's bell and the stream running near the papaya trees. Far away I hear a roar. The thought, *ocean*, comes into my mind. When we finish, Uma says the distant roar is the army firing squad, practicing. "You see all sound is music." We sit and listen in silence. "Someone is chopping wood," she says. We hear it coming through the forest and then the sound of a drum. "When the gross mind quiets down," she says, "the subtle mind comes into play. Like when the blaring music on a fair ground stops, you can hear someone playing the flute."

I am amazed at how simple life can be, if you have the courage to live with very few desires. Uma is one of the old-type of *yoginis*, who has completely withdrawn from the world and all worldly activities. She has seen through *maya* and the world has no allure for her.[16] Where else but in India can one do this and have it understood and approved of? India is the spiritual Mother, sheltering and caring for those who want to know God. I say a prayer that I will never forget the silence within.

We leave the cave, bowing and saying goodbye, but she hardly notices our going. She is absorbed with her spindle and wool.

FOREIGNERS' LUNCH

Swami Chidananda is always on the lookout for ways we may participate and do something useful. He asks us to arrange a "lunch for the foreigners." He wants to honor the foreigners staying in the *ashram* by providing a *sattvic* meal and because he will share the lunch with us, it will be a very special occasion indeed! It is a great honor to share a meal with Swamiji. In India, feeding people is deemed a meritorious act. Food is considered a manifestation of Maha Lakshmi, or Annapurna, never to be wasted. There are so many hungry people on the planet, wasting food is considered unacceptable. Swamiji has a humble way of making it seem like we are the ones doing him a favor, whereas in reality, he creates opportunities for us to be of service.

Besides the food the *ashram* will provide, the vegetables and rice, Swamiji encourages Galina and me to choose other items for the menu. We decide on fruit and yoghurt, what the Indians refer to as 'curd,' for desert. We also decide we will try to make some special bread with walnuts and raisins in it and bake it in the local bakery.

The Rishikesh bakery is a small, dimly lit operation, with metal racks stacked up, loaded with pans of what looks like delicious pastries. But to eat, they are very disappointing. They are heavy and rather tasteless. However, as in many places in India, the people in the bakery are hospitable and friendly and allow us to try baking bread using their pans and ovens.

---

[16] Years later I hear that Uma leaves her cave life and goes to South India to pursue her study of classical music on the veena.

Perhaps it is the flour that is too coarse, or the yeast that is old, but our bread doesn't rise and turns out heavy with a hard crust.

"We can't use this for the lunch!" Galina exclaims. I agree. We deem it a failure as far as the lunch goes, but don't want to waste all the good ingredients.

"Perhaps we can give it to some hungry person in town," I suggest. So we carry the bread wrapped in paper, down a street leading toward the Ganges, where the flower sellers sit with fresh garlands of marigolds, hanging in yellow and orange colors, ready to be offered to some form of the Divine.

We approach a group of barefoot, ragged-looking little children, but when we offer them the bread, they respond by backing away without smiling. They appear to be afraid of us and we are a bit puzzled. "Perhaps their parents have warned them never to take food from strangers," Galina guesses.

We continue down the road, but nobody wants to take the bread from us. "Are we so suspicious looking?" I ask. "Or is it because we are foreigners?"

"Because we are foreigners and I think also because we are women," Galina surmises. In most circumstances Brahmins will not take food from just anyone. Food has to be prepared and served in a pure and sattvic manner. For orthodox Brahmins there are strict rules about where, when and with whom they eat their food.

"Well, let's break it into small pieces and feed it to the fish in the Ganga," I say. It is the custom of visitors and pilgrims to feed the large fish in the Ganges who gobble up little flour balls, thrown from the bridge and from passengers in ferryboats crossing the river. As we make our way to the end of the road leading to the river, we see an old man squatting against a whitewashed wall. He accepts the packet with the bread, mumbling something in Hindi that I can't understand. Relieved the food is not going to waste, we walk the mile or so back to the *ashram*, following a path along the river's edge.

Swamiji has made a special arrangement, allowing us to serve the lunch in Gurudev's Kutir, with windows and doors open to the Ganges. There are about a dozen of us foreign guests seated in two rows on the floor, except for the elderly Herr and Mrs. Franke, who are given small tables. Swami Chidanandaji sits at one end of the long narrow room, opposite a larger-than-life black and white photograph of Gurudev Swami Sivananda holding a book out to the viewer, a beneficent smile on his face. This is where Gurudev lived until he left his physical body on 14th July 1963. Also present at the lunch is Doctor Hridayananda Mataji.

"Where is Galina?" Swamiji asks me.

"She has gone to her room, Swamiji," I say, not mentioning our trip into Rishikesh or the fiasco with the bread.

"Please go and call her," he says. I quickly slip on my sandals and run down the lower road to our building and up the cement stairs to Galina's room.

"Galina!" I knock on the door, breathing hard. "Swamiji sent me to get you! He wants you to be at the lunch!"

"I can't," she says, from behind the closed door. "I just need to stay in my room for a while."

"Are you *sure*?" I ask. "You're going to miss the lunch with Swamiji!"

"I think I just got culture shock," she answers. "I feel overwhelmed."

"Are you all right?" I ask. *What a bad time to get culture shock!*

"I just need to rest," she insists. Her voice sounds tired.

"Okay, then." I realize that she isn't going to budge. "I'll tell Swamiji you aren't feeling well." I hurry back to Gurudev's Kutir, slipping my sandals off outside the door. Swamiji looks up enquiringly.

"She is not feeling well," I report. I know at times India can be overwhelming to Westerners, the sights, smells and clash of cultures. But I never experience culture shock myself. It feels more like home to me.

Swamiji reminds me, "Please put some yoghurt and fruit in a bowl and take it to her afterwards."

"Yes, Swamiji."

It is my job to serve the others. I am wearing an ankle-length Malaysian batik sarong, wrapped around my waist and a plain green T-shirt over the top. My hair is in two plaits on either side of my head. I bend forward, moving slowly down the row of guests, holding the plate of food from which they serve themselves.

"Moo looks like a pukkha Indian squaw," Swamiji says suddenly.

I stop serving and look at Swamiji. "Do you mean a pukkha Indian, Swamiji?"

"Squaw!" he repeats. "An Indian squaw." I smile and continue around with the plate of food. I have always had a strong intuition that I had a past life as a Native American Indian and Swamiji mentioning it confirms it for me.

Finally, I sit with the others and eat. Despite the missing bread, the meal is delicious and all seem to be enjoying themselves. And why shouldn't we be? We are here in Gurudev's Kutir having lunch with Swami Chidananda! We are basking in the grace of two great masters! I wonder what we have done to deserve this good fortune and if the others feel the same as I do.

ABBOT THOLENS

In early February 1971 a tall, thin, very pale-skinned man comes to the *ashram* for a few days. He wears Western clothes and looks like he is gliding when he walks. We find out he is from the Netherlands, but we don't know he is an Abbot until a few days after his arrival, because, while highly educated in theology and philosophy, he never makes a show of his knowledge. His room is next to ours in Gujarat Bhavan and we find that the Abbot has a good sense of humor and likes Don's unusual art, which many people fail to appreciate. He expresses an interest in learning *asanas*.

"It will be hard for you to follow what they are doing in the Bhajan Hall," Don says. "It is not for beginners and there is no instruction, or explanation given."

"We can help you if you want," I say.

"Yes, thank you," he replies. So we meet in his room in the mornings, after the *ashram* prayers and show him the basic *asanas* that we learned at Swami Vishnu's Yoga Camp.

The day before the Abbot is to leave, the three of us go for a walk up to Lakshman Jhula suspension bridge and down the trail on the other side of the Ganga. We come across a *yogi* living on a sandy promontory, in the middle of the river. There is a huge rock jutting up and out at an angle, under which he has taken up residence. A small group of devotees from Haridwar have just come for his *darshan* and are seated on the sand around him. We sit down at the back of the group. He is a rather plump man with a beard, dressed in a *dhoti*, with a fresh flower garland around his neck hanging down to his bare belly. The *yogi's* name is Mastram Baba and we have heard that he is a highly evolved being. Outer appearances are deceiving and if we learn one thing in India, it is that *mahatmas*, great souls, can appear in many different forms. I brush the sand off my hands and close my eyes. Almost immediately, I become aware of the field of consciousness emanating from his being and how his presence creates an aura of peace.

When we return to our rooms, the Abbot asks us the reason for the repetition in *mantra* chanting. We explain how the sounds of the *mantras* have certain vibrations, which have strengthened over the centuries by millions of repetitions by devotees of God.

"If we tune into the vibration of a healing *mantra*, for instance, or send it in another's direction, it definitely has an effect," I explain, even though I am far from expert on the subject. "Some have realized God through the chanting of His name alone, like Swami Ramdas of Ananda Ashram in Kerala. One's mind gets so absorbed into the sound," I continue enthusiastically, "it actually *becomes* the sound. Chanting purifies the mind." I begin to compare *mantra* chanting to Gregorian Chants, a subject I know next to nothing about.

As I am going on about the mind, Abbot Tholens suddenly put his palms together up to his chest and says in a loud voice, "Heart! Heart! Christianity is essentially a religion of the heart!"

I stop talking and stare at him. Yes, of course, he is right! His words strike a chord in me and I realize how ignorant I am next to this wise and humble man.

Most afternoons lately, we have been joining the other Western devotees in the Samadhi Shrine to chant the *Maha Mrityunjaya Mantra*[17] for Swami Chidanandaji's delicate health. When we first start this "health campaign," Swami Krishnananda happens to pass behind us as we are chanting. Our Western pronunciation must sound very jarring to his ears, because later that day he calls us all into his office and teaches us the correct Sanskrit pronunciation of the *mantra*. This *mantra* of Lord Siva is life-restoring and also makes one fearless and calm in the face of death. It holds a high place in the *Vedas* amongst *mantras* used for contemplation and meditation. Besides the promotion of good health, it is also repeated for preventing accidents, including travel of all kinds, and for warding off scorpion and snakebites.

Nagaraj told us how he saw first hand, Swami Chidananda remove the acute pain of a scorpion bite from a boy, using a handkerchief and the repetition of this *mantra*. Swamiji tied a handkerchief around the boy's leg above the bite and while repeating the *mantra*, slowly brought the handkerchief lower and lower all the way to the foot. He asked the boy, "Where is the pain now?" The boy pointed down to where the handkerchief was. Then Swamiji untied the handkerchief and shook it hard. The boy got up and walked away pain free!

While we are chanting on the day after our walk with Abbot Tholens,

---

[17] "*Om Tryambakam Yajamahe, Sugandhim Pushti-vardhanam, Urvarukamiva Bhandhanan, Mrityor Mukshiya Mamritat*," meaning, "I worship Thee, oh Lord of supreme vision, of sweet fragrance and giver of all prosperity. May I be freed from the bonds of death, (as easily) as a ripe fruit from its stem." This is one translation among many.

I can't get his words out of my mind—"Heart! Heart!" Most of my *sadhana* up to this point has been all about the mind, purifying it through the practice of *pratyahara*, withdrawing the mind from the senses, counteracting one negative thought by a positive one, self-analysis, enquiring, "Who am I?" I feel that I am quite familiar this part of my *sadhana*. I think I understand the logic used to purify the mind, but to purify the heart? That's another story! I realize it requires constant self-surrender to God, cultivation of love for one's ideal and living for the good of others. It is beginning to dawn on me how far I have to go!

When Sivananda says, "Give, give, give, give!" he means give of whatever you have—materially, physically, mentally, spiritually. Perhaps this is the reason my spiritual practices don't seem to be progressing. It could be that my meditation and my actions are focused on the mental level and are not coming from the heart. Isn't Christ the Master, whose cosmic mission it is to bring the light down to earth in the form of divine love? Up until now I have never really known *how* to think of Jesus Christ. "Except ye be as a little children, ye shall not enter the kingdom of heaven." I realize that the Abbot has reminded me that I must look into myself and see how to apply this.

The Abbot is a real messenger for me. In his humility, perhaps he doesn't even know that he has shown me where the defects in my *sadhana* are. I am just forming an idea of what Jesus is like and I prefer to think of Him in Vedantic terms, of Christ Consciousness, the all-pervading *Brahman*, like "I and my Father are one." These are very big concepts. Perhaps it is even simpler than that. The next morning, the Abbot leaves very early and I miss my chance to thank him.

MOST HOLY NIGHT

There is a palpable feeling of great anticipation as all ashramites and visitors alike begin gearing up for this most holy day and night of Siva. Siva is the Lord of auspiciousness, also known as the one undivided consciousness, which is the support and source of the manifest universe. Siva is considered the male principle and Shakti the female aspect of God and they are inseparable. The world that we see is nothing but the energy of Shakti in all her multitudinous forms, but her power comes from the silent and unseen consciousness which is called Siva, often pictured in deep meditation, withdrawn from the external world.

According to the lunar calendar this year, Sivaratri falls on 23rd February. The day starts at 4:30 a.m. with meditation in the presence of Swami Chidananda. This is followed by a special ceremony in the Yajna Shala, the room in which the sacred fire ceremony takes place, adjacent to the Vishwanath Mandir. A fire is built in a sunken area, where an especially ordained priest recites ancient Vedic *mantras*. Items like rice and ghee are offered into the fire, representing a burning of old life and the beginning of something new. Today, two young men are taking the vow of *brahmacharya* and receiving their yellow cloth from Swamiji, indicating their first step towards becoming a full *sannyasin*, or the final stage of renunciation.

Don decides this is an auspicious day to shave his head, so I bring the shaving brush and the razor down by the Ganga, where we have access to running water. Peter joins us by the river. I shave carefully so as not to cut Don's scalp.

"Why do you want to shave your head?" Peter asks, fingering his ponytail.

"I want to try something new," Don answers. Shaving the head is undoubtedly letting go of an old image, so a new one can take its place. As the hair falls away his skull looks quite breakable and fragile.

"Besides protecting your head, what else does hair do?" I wonder aloud, collecting the hair into a little tin to dispose of later. "Why do you think it is removed when one takes the vow of *brahmacharya*, or *sannyasa*?"

"It represents renunciation," Don answers. "In my case, it's purely for hygienic reasons."

Like many ashramites, we are fasting on water only in observation of

THE POWER OF PRESENCE

the sacred nature of the day. Don develops a headache and is a bit grouchy, perhaps because of the fasting, or the loss of hair.

"Should we go across the river to visit Sadhana?" I suggest, thinking a walk will do us good. Sadhana is a young woman about our age, from California, who is studying *Kundalini Yoga* with a young *guru* called Bal Yogi. She lived at Sivananda Ashram for six months before we arrived and then chose to live in Bal Yogi's *ashram* across the river and follow his instructions. We heard that Swami Krishnananda did not approve of her living there alone with this young *yogi* and tried to prevent her from leaving the *ashram*, but she went anyway. She told us about some of the practices she is requested to do, one of which is to drink her own urine. It is supposed to be some sort of purification practice, but it seems extreme to us.

"If we go across the river we might miss some of the afternoon lectures," Don says.

"True, but most of them are in Hindi," I answer. So we decide to skip them and take a walk instead.

Bal Yogi's *ashram* consists of a couple of low buildings, set back from the river, hugging the foot of the mountain. In the front is an orchard of shady mango trees, with birds and wild monkeys. We have seen this *yogi* before and are impressed by his expertise in *Hatha Yoga*. He is a man in his forties, but his body looks more like a twenty-year old. On this special day, he is dressed elegantly, in long, flowing yellow robes and shoulder-length, loose black hair. He motions for us to sit before him. We find ourselves in an awkward situation, where he is up on a dais and we are sitting on the ground. It is all a little too theatrical for us. The vibration is strange and unsettling. Don's headache grows worse and he has to go off and lie down.

Almost immediately, I wish we had not come and find myself longing to be back at home, at Sivananda Ashram. I keep thinking of Swami Chidananda and how humble and simple he is. Finally, I can't stand it any more and I say, "It's Sivaratri. We have to go back now!" Sadhana looks disappointed. I know she is lonely for company.

Later in spring, her mother comes from California to see what her daughter has gotten into. She sizes up the situation and does not like the fact that her daughter is living alone with the young *yogi*. She persuades Sadhana to take a break and return with her to California.

Don and I practically run back to the ferryboat to cross the river. We arrive on the Sivananda side with a feeling of great relief and eagerness to participate wholeheartedly in the all-night celebration, starting at 7:30 p.m.

The Vishwanath Mandir is surrounded by an open verandah.[18] All the devotees sit around and on either side of the temple entrance for the next nine hours singing, "*Om Namah Sivaya!*" and other Siva mantras, during the four different *pujas*, which take place throughout the night and early morning hours. I stand and watch the first *puja* through the bars of the temple window, only a few feet from where the senior monks are seated around the Siva *lingam*, mounted on top of a carved white marble slab. I watch Swami Chidananda's face as he presides over the first *puja*, making the offerings with the most reverent attitude and utmost concentration. I imagine he is not merely seeing the shiny black marble *lingam*, but the nameless, formless, absolute consciousness, which it represents.

Only the most *sattvic* of foods are offered to the *lingam*: first milk, then Ganges water, then ghee, mashed bananas with raisins, curds, thick golden honey, milk again and water. The monks have a small clean towel on their laps. As each of these items are poured over the *lingam* from stainless steel vessels, accompanied by rhythmic chanting of *mantras*, the monks use their hands to help scoop the holy food offerings along the shallow channel in the marble base, to the turned down lip and into a stainless steel bucket. In the end they wipe their hands on the small towels. The priest adorns the black *lingam* with three horizontal stripes of holy ash and applies a

---

[18] In the next few years when the temple is remodeled, a roof is built over a wide verandah, which encircles the temple. There is ample sheltered sitting space for many devotees.

silver dollar size glob of sandalwood paste in the center, topped with red *cumcum* powder. Then, as the *mantra* chanting continues, comes the offering of leaves from the Bel tree and marigold flowers, until the *lingam* is completely covered.

I think how strange this *puja* might look to Western eyes. But now I understand that it is not a stone that is worshipped, but the *lingam*, representing Siva, is a consecrated manifestation of absolute consciousness. So, it becomes an expanding and elevating experience. Religious practices only appear strange when we don't understand what is behind them. Because I trust Swamiji and am eager to observe and understand what he is doing and for what purpose, I easily embrace the Hindu pantheon. Don does too. There is no attempt at coercion here. Everyone is free to believe what he or she chooses. I am not as devoted to the gods and goddesses as someone who has grown up in the Hindu faith. But I believe in the reality of their different energies and how they are said to operate in this world. I especially love the ideal of *Vedanta*, which recognizes the essence our nature as one with all life, the consciousness that is at the basis of all existence.

At 4:30 a.m. when the last puja is over, the final *arati* is done, with the big lamp of one hundred and eight flaming wicks, and the loud clanging of the bell comes to an end, all the devotees sit down in rows for a feast. Swami Chidananda carrying a ladle and a bucket of prasad stoops low before each person to serve them himself. It reminds me of Jesus Christ feeding the people, who have gathered together around him.

The day after Sivaratri in the morning *darshan* Swamiji looks over at Don and notices his shaven head. "Ah, very interesting." he remarks. After a moment or two he continues, "I was thinking it would be a good idea for all Western men, staying in the *ashram* for some time, to shave off their hair. I was thinking of making it a rule." He looks again at Don and says, "Very interesting."

As far as we know, Swamiji never makes it a rule. Don deciding on his own to shave his head, seems to change Swamiji's mind and let the decision rest with each individual.

BABA IN DELHI

Soon after the Sivaratri celebration, when Swamiji goes out of the *ashram* on a short tour, Don and I decide to go to Delhi with Peter and Galina, to spend a few days with Swami Muktananda. According to Swami Chidananda, Swami Muktananda is highly evolved and his *guru*, Swami Nityananda, was a very great soul. After informing Nagaraj where we are going, we take a taxi, arriving seven hours later at Mira's apartment, in Karol Bagh, a suburb of Delhi. Mira and Raja, whom we haven't seen since Madras, have invited Don and me to stay in their small apartment with them. Peter and Galina find a hotel in the area and we arrange to meet daily at the venue. When we get there Mira is not in, so we head over to the address we have for Swami Muktananda.

    We enter the gates of a large house, on a quiet, tree-lined street in a residential neighborhood. At this time, India's capital city moves at a slow pace. There are a few cars and three-wheeler taxis on the roads, the air is clear and the sky is blue. The host, a very wealthy member of parliament, has converted his large garden into the venue, with a *pandal*, a colorful, open-sided tent, which fills almost the entire area, except for a separate enclosed section, where special food is being prepared. In Indian culture, it is considered a privilege and a meritorious act to host a holy man or woman, and to feed as guests, all those who gather around them. Food will be served three times a day to several hundred people, for the duration of the ten days of *sadhana*, while Swami Muktananda is in residence. We have a loose plan of staying for a few days, before we return to Sivananda Ashram.

    It is said that being around an enlightened being speeds up one's *karma*. I am not sure if it's true, but I am convinced that coming into contact with great souls, inspires one to go deeper. Whether any fundamental change actually takes place, remains to be seen. When we find a place to sit in the *pandal*, we notice some devotees experiencing various emotional states, with tears of devotion streaming from their eyes. In complete contrast to this, I feel very objective, as though I am some sort of journalist, making a report on a holy man.

As is our habit, Don and I begin to sketch our surroundings. Swami Muktananda sits up on the dais, on an elaborate seat, with curlicues of dark wood protruding beyond an orange cushion. Behind that is a huge circular orange sun, with silver stars radiating from the center. In front of Swami Muktananda is a covered table, where a couple of microphones stretch their necks towards him, waiting for what he has to say. Someone has placed a small tape recorder next to the microphones. It is just beginning to dawn on people that the talks of these *gurus* ought to be recorded. Usually, anyone can put a tape recorder close to the speaker, but to get a seat up front, so you can turn the tape over, is more difficult. A Siva *lingam* adorned with flowers and garlands occupies a central position and a picture of Swami Nityananda, the aforementioned *guru*, is on a small stool to his right.

There is never any thought in this venue, or anywhere else in India, of charging money to the audience for sitting in the company or listening to the utterances of a holy person. Tradition insists that teachings are freely offered.[19] In Hindu *dharma*, it is the duty of the second stage, the *grihasta*, the householder, to support the fourth stage, the *sannyasin*. Without this tradition in the West, we have to resort to using money as the exchange of energy.

By the second day, I can feel Swami Muktananda's tremendous magnetism, as though we have been transported to another realm, with a

---

[19] It is not until a couple of decades later, when Western students return as teachers themselves and institutions are founded around the original Eastern *gurus*, that money enters the picture. The exchange becomes commercial, out of necessity, to support those who have given their lives to bring these teachings to others. Also, in the West, halls and retreat centers have to be rented and so somehow income has to be produced.

higher consciousness operating system. He is called "Baba," father, by his devotees and disciples who constantly surround him, except when he retires to his room, which he does every now and then, without warning. He is reported to be a strict disciplinarian and won't consider anyone a disciple unless they are willing to follow his rules. He awakens within his disciples, the *kundalini* energy lying dormant, coiled at the base of the spine. He transmits the power of shakti, called *shakti-pat*, by touching the devotees either with his hand or a bundle of peacock feathers. Sometimes just his presence is enough. Several devotees get seemingly uncontrollable jerking and shaking and swaying movement of the body, whenever he starts singing or speaking. He allows this to happen around him and every now and then, reaches down and touches someone who has gone into a swoon, bringing them out of it.

I don't doubt that the devotees are experiencing genuine spiritual states in the presence of their *guru*, but for us, this is a surprising contrast to what we are accustomed. There is a lot of spontaneous energetic movement in the devotees, swaying, laughing, crying and dancing. It is different, from the Sivananda lineage, where spiritual experiences are downplayed. Swami Sivananda taught his disciples not to display or use spiritual powers that might come to you as a result of your spiritual practices. In fact, he warned aspirants to shun *siddhis*, as the temptation for the ego to use powers is great, and also distracts one from the goal. The words of Swami Chidananda come to my mind—"A spiritual aspirant must learn to be invisible!" We should not draw attention to ourselves, or indulge our ego.

I wonder to what extent Baba's devotees can control the primal cosmic energy that he awakens in them? They have different responses to his transmission and while they look a little strange, we are learning to accept them all.

A woman in the front says in a complaining voice to Baba, "I am not keeping well."

"Keep well!" he instructs her. Then he gets up and walks out. Those are the only English words I hear him say. His talks are all in Hindi.

THE POWER OF PRESENCE

There is a young Swami with classical features and a shaven head, who seems to be Baba's right hand man. He is always beside Baba, standing slightly behind him. "That is Professor Jain," a devotee tells me. "He translates for Baba."

The *kirtans* are sung with such devotion that they transport me into another awareness, just sound without body. I don't know all the words or their meanings, but am carried in deep by the *bhav*, the intense spiritual feeling. As the kirtan continues we join the devotees as each person walks down the aisle and approaches Baba, to prostrate and to receive his blessings. Some he swats with the bundle of peacock feathers and they fall into an ecstatic state. As I approach closer to him, I can feel my heart beating very fast and I am trembling inside. He notices I am carrying my sketchbook and beckons me to show it to him. I open to the page where I have drawn a sketch of his face and he is quite amused. He takes a red pen and puts a *tilak*, a third eye mark on the forehead, fills in some hair on one side of the face and draws in longer ear lobes. Then, with a flourish, he signs his name underneath the drawing.

Ram Dass is there, sitting on one side of Baba, looking totally blissed out. We know of Ram Dass, the Western psychologist turned *yogi*, from his studies of the mind using psychedelic experiments with his colleague Timothy Leary, at Harvard University and his subsequent trip to India to meet his *guru*. At some point during the day, Ram Dass gives a talk in English, extolling the greatness of Swami Muktananda. He talks about seeing God everywhere, in all people.

Baba Muktananda

"There is only Sita, there is only Ram," he says, referring to the incarnation of Lord Rama, the ideal man, the upholder of *dharma*, and his holy wife Sita, who, according to the Ramayana scripture, is abducted by the demon king, Ravana. "We should see God in all beings," Ram Dass reminds us.

Ram Dass's guru, Neem Karoli Baba, another great saint, is often thought of as an incarnation of Hanuman. Neem Karoli is well known at Sivananda Ashram and is revered by Swami Chidananda and all the ashramites. Once, he stopped by to visit Swami Chidananda unannounced, and spent some time with him, drinking a cup of warm milk. When he was ready to go, he wrapped himself in his customary brown plaid blanket and walked out onto the main road going up towards Lakshman Jhula. Within a minute he had disappeared and no one was able to locate him anywhere in the vicinity. We are told he has the ability to make his physical body disappear at will.

During the mid-morning break, Ram Dass comes over to speak to us. He is mostly bald, with a grey beard, wearing white cotton garb and a garland of orange marigolds around his neck, from Baba, no doubt. Besides the four of us there are very few Westerners in the gathering. "What are you doing in India?" he asks.

"We are studying at Sivananda Ashram, with Swami Chidananda," we tell him.

"Ah, he's a nice man," he says nodding.

"Yes," Don says.

Nice man? I think. *How could he describe Swami Chidananda as a nice man? If only he knew Swamiji better, he would know he is a great yogi and a compassionate saint. It would be an understatement to describe him as a 'nice man.'* Ram Dass smiles and moves off. I am sure he is just being polite. Later, he invites us over to his hotel room, where he is staying on Connaught Circle, in the heart of Delhi. We stand on the balcony and look over the street where a few cars are circling around. The sun is going down and we don't stay long, because

Ram Dass seems preoccupied with someone else who has come to visit him. So, we *pranam* and tell him we'll see him the next day at the venue.

On the fourth day Mira accompanies us to the *satsang*. When Swami Muktananda sees her, he says in Hindi, that he feels as though he has known her for ages. I am impressed that he singles her out of the crowd. Then he turns to Professor Jain and says, "She comes from a divine family." I am even more impressed that Baba is able to look at Mira and know that her mother is a highly evolved soul. Mira simply remarks, "How sweet of him to say."

When we are back at Mira's home that evening we speak to Mother Rema on the phone. It is so good to hear her voice after five months!

The next day, Doctor Mataji Hridayananda comes for Swami Muktananda's blessings. When she bows before him he pats her on the back and garlands her. She shines with what I imagine to be "Sivananda radiance," which makes her an outstanding figure amongst all the other people.

After five days in Delhi, we begin to miss Swami Chidananda and book a taxi to return to the *ashram*. As we pass Haridwar and begin to get closer to Rishikesh, I am overwhelmed by a deep sense of gratitude and am filled with the feeling that we are going home to Shivanandanagar! I feel so happy that we belong to the Sivananda family. Swami Muktananda is really great, but I am more interested in the humility of Swami Chidananda. Now, I feel even surer that Swamiji knows best how to guide me in the way I need to go.

The next day, in Swamiji's morning darshan in the Bhajan Hall, Peter says, almost as though he is throwing a challenge before Swamiji, "Swami Muktananda says that he can give 'instant samadhi.'"

Swamiji smiles. "Well, why didn't you take it then?"

CHAPTER 7

MOVING UP

SARASWATI KUTIR

Galina and Peter leave the *ashram* for a few weeks to travel to a couple of sacred places in India. After they have left, Bhagavan, our building caretaker, complains that a blanket is missing from one of the beds and insinuates that they have taken it. I tell him that I am sure they would not have taken anything, but he can't come to any other conclusion, and so he clings to his opinion that they are thieves.

Don and I are invited by the *ashram* authorities to move up to the main part of the *ashram* at the top of the steps. We gratefully accept. It will be nice to be closer to the Bhajan Hall, the Mandir, to the other inmates and also to Swamiji. Because the inmates are permanent residents, I think of them as having privileged status, one that I secretly aspire to. I assume it means being part of Gurudev Sivananda and Swami Chidananda's "family," and not just a guest. I also assume that the permanent residents are somehow closer to Swamiji, but later I find out this is not necessarily true. Swamiji has devotees and disciples in homes throughout India and many countries abroad, doing their duty according to their *dharma*. Many of them are as close as, or even closer to Swamiji, than any inmate of the *ashram*.

Nevertheless, we are happy to move up to the top of the hill where we feel more included. We move into the upstairs corner room in Saraswati Kutir block, built along the steep driveway leading up to the Samadhi Shrine. On the opposite side of the driveway is a forested hill topped by the little temple of Dattatreya. The first day we are there we meet Swami Krishnananda on the way to the Bhajan Hall.

"I hear you have been promoted," he says, jokingly. "You have come up to a higher level!"

"I hope we don't pull you down to our level!" Don answers, making Swami Krishnananda laugh.

From the corner room we can look across the courtyard to Yoga Sadhana Kutir, Swami Chidananda's residence, where we can see who goes up and down the outside stairs. We can watch in the afternoon when Swamiji's door opens and he comes down the steps, flings his upper cloth over his shoulder and walks away from the building very fast, taking long strides, looking straight ahead, eyes down. When he does this it is clear he wants to stretch his legs and not be followed by anyone. He wants to take some time alone, away from the constant stream of people clamoring to see him from morning to night. Nobody dares to follow Swamiji when he is withdrawn into himself, heading out for a walk. However, sometimes devotees meet him on the road and he slows his pace so they can walk with him on his way back.

We take a walk one balmy evening, with the moon rising from behind the mountain on the opposite side of the Ganges. We have been dealing with some personal problems during the day, which are partly due to being in constant close quarters in our small room. I feel emotionally fatigued and am hoping a change of scenery will shift some of the energy between us. We see Swamiji on the road in the moonlight and when we are about fifteen yards away, he calls out to us, "Work and pray!" As usual, he seems to know and understand everything without our saying anything. We walk up to where he is and he stands with us on the road to gaze down at the dark river, gleaming here and there with reflections of lights from both sides. Sounds of evening *pujas* with chanting and small bells ringing rise into the warm night air. *Arati*, waving of lights accompanied by songs of praise, is being done across the Ganga, on the *ghat* near the clock tower.

Swamiji looks up into the sky where the moon is weaving in and out of the clouds. After a moment he says, "You see, the moon reveals the thickness of the clouds." And as we stand there with him, all the tension of the day evaporates. *Of course!* I think. *That's perfect! When understanding shines forth, problems disappear. Or at least we can see more clearly what they are.* Just spending a few minutes with our beloved *guru* dissolves our problems into insignificance and we walk back to our *kutir* with light hearts. That is the power of a saint. Because his mind is pure and free from illusions or desires, clarity is experienced in his presence and the problems of life fall into proper perspective.

Once again, I see that Swamiji has a way of knowing what is going on with his disciples, even better than we do. How he does this, I don't understand. It is beyond my comprehension. It is not only with the two of us, but with hundreds of devotees, in many different parts of India and other countries around the world. Swamiji's 'knowing' is not limited by time and space and therefore he connects on the deepest spiritual level. His awareness is already there. Ours is always catching up.

One of the bonuses of living in our little room in Saraswati Kutir is that we occupy the same level, with just two rooms in between, as Swami Vidyananda, master musician of the *veena*, a stringed instrument with a gourd on each end. His *sadhana* is worship through music. Every morning at 4 o'clock he can be heard tuning up his *veena*. At 4:30 a.m. he begins playing his morning hymns and prayers. At 5:00 a.m. others are allowed to enter his small room and join in the singing. Visitors sit on the grass mats provided. Swami Vidyananda's room is bare, except for the floor mats and the bed. He plays in a prayerful and divine manner and as his singing ends he quietly and carefully sets his *veena* down on the two large gourds, and puts rock candy prasad into our outstretched palms. Every morning, we hear his stringed instrument tuning up, setting us up for a divine day.

Right next to our room is the room of Krishnapriyananda Mataji, a short lady about as tall as my shoulder. She is a widow, whose husband died unexpectedly when she was still a young woman. She asked her young son permission to renounce the world and come away to the *ashram*, which would mean leaving him to grow into adulthood in the home of a close relative. He agreed, on the one condition that she must never shave her head. He said when he comes to visit his mother he wants her to have hair! Mother Krishnapriyananda is a devout swami who goes to the temple every morning. The *pujari* gives her the flower garlands that have been offered to the deities in the temple the previous evening and she hangs them around her picture of Krishna and other deities in her room. I look in one day and she has orange garlands hanging around every picture.

"Mataji, your room looks like a flower seller!" I say. She laughs and we become friends.

One day she says to me in a confidential tone, "I know you and Mr. Don are just like Sri Ramakrishna and Sarada Devi."

"What? Don't be *silly*, Mataji!" I don't know what she is getting at.

Sri Ramakrishna Paramahamsa was probably the most renowned saint of the late 19th century. He was a mystic from a young age and his behavior was often unorthodox and extraordinary. We purchase and begin reading a large, heavy volume, *The Life of Sri Ramakrishna* by one of his disciples, who just called himself 'M.' It is a daily, first-hand account of Sri Ramakrishna's life and his unorthodox insistence on embracing all religions, not just intellectually, but through his own living experience. As a young *Brahmin* male, he was expected to marry. Rather than declaring himself a monk, he agreed to an arranged marriage with a young girl, fifteen years his junior. At the time, the young girl was only five years old and after ten years had passed, she was sent to live with her husband. Sarada

Devi soon realized that the husband who had been chosen for her was not an ordinary man, and their marriage, by all known accounts, was never consummated. Instead, she became his faithful disciple, cooking and caring for the young men who gathered around him. Later, she found herself the head of an order for the women disciples, who were attracted by the holiness of Sri Ramakrishna and also by her own humble presence.

It finally dawns on me that what Mataji had meant by her remark, was that we are observing celibacy while living in the *ashram*. *Brahmacharya* is one of the tenets of Swami Sivananda's teachings for his monk disciples, along with truthfulness and non-injury. There are different ideas about this subject, but in Swami Sivananda's and therefore Swami Chidananda's teachings, sexual energy is to be sublimated and transformed into *yogic* spiritual energy, activating the higher chakras for meditation and other spiritual practices. *Brahmacharya* is a pattern of conduct or life-style, which ultimately leads to *Brahma-Jnana*, knowledge of God. For monks, *brahmacharya* means total abstinence in thought, word and deed. However, in a broader sense, it takes on a different meaning according to one's role in life. For married people, being faithful to one's partner is considered *brahmacharya*. But since we have chosen to live among the *yogis* and *yoginis* for a certain period, we too observe celibacy. We have taken no vow and no one has actually said anything to us about it. Those on the path of yoga seem to gather knowledge through thoughts and vibrations. The constant contact of living with these highly evolved beings, combined with our own spiritual *sadhana*, lifts our consciousness so that sexual craving falls away into the background, if not totally disappears.

When a great being is there to make God a very real presence, it is obvious that there is something deeper and higher to focus on. We, along with the other devotees, are riveted by Swami Chidananda's holiness. In his presence, doubts and questions that the mind is grappling with and sometimes obsessing about melt away. I understand why Mary, in the Bible story, finds a spot close to Jesus and doesn't budge from there. I must admit I have always felt sorry for her sister, Martha, who is left with all the work.

Shouldn't Jesus have sent Mary back into the kitchen to help with the dishes? But He understands the one-pointed love that Mary has for him. From Mary's perspective, there is nothing more important than to sit in the presence of this great love of the Master. All other obligations disappear.

I understand intuitively, that kind of one-pointed love for God is what is necessary, if one is to make progress on the spiritual path. Especially in the beginning, when one has not yet understood that the spiritual presence is everywhere, in each one of us. In the beginning, the physical presence of the *guru* is really important, until we realize that the *guru* is our own spiritual conscience that guides us from within.

TABLA LESSONS

Our 12' x 12' corner room in Saraswati Kutir has a window on two walls overlooking the courtyard and two more windows on either side of the door, opening onto the upstairs verandah. Most of the doors on these old *kutirs* are double wooden doors with a long iron bolt sliding between them, which can be padlocked from the outside. We hide our key under a rock outside the door, which would be the first place anyone would look, if they were trying to break in. But we have nothing of value that anyone would want, so we don't worry about it.

Most of the *ashram* buildings are painted a pale beige color, but the paint is not waterproof and quickly becomes faded and streaked with black mildew, by the rains and humidity of the monsoon season. Across from us is the one-story music building where Swami Nadabrahmananda teaches individual classes. He can play almost any instrument and we often hear him practicing the harmonium and playing the *tabla*. We love being surrounded by music!

Growing up in Africa, I used to hear drumming coming across the valley at night, a mysterious and soothing sound, like a secret language I did not understand. I decide I would like to learn to play the *tabla*, so I get permission from Swami Nadabrahmananda and soon I begin daily lessons with him. There are two drums in the *tabla* set—the *tabla*, which is played with the right hand and hits the short high notes, and the *dookhee*, which keeps a deeper beat, with the fingers and palm heel of the left hand. Swami Nadabrahmananda is a most patient teacher. Using two fingers, he beats out a gentle rhythm on the inside of my wrist, so I can remember what the right hand has to do. I practice at least half an hour everyday and learn about the double and quadruple speeds of the structured rhythms. It is important to get the sounds of the drums to come out clearly, depending on where they are struck.

Swami Nadabrahmananda decides that if I am serious about learning, I should have my own set of drums. So I accompany him to Dehra Dun one day, where we go to the music shop and he selects a good set for me to purchase. It comes to less than U.S. $20! Once back at the *ashram*, he shows me how to hand sew cloth covers to protect the skins and to make stuffed cloth rings that support the drums while playing. I learn to tune the drums with a little hammer, tapping down the wooden chocks, pulling the skins tighter. I make my *tabla* practice a part of my daily *sadhana*. I'd like to learn to play like Swami Nadabrahmananda who makes the drums sing!

GURU DISCIPLE RELATIONSHIP

When Peter and Galina return they ask to see Swami Chidananda to tell him they did *not* take the blanket. "I wouldn't *dream* that you had," Swamiji assures them. However, they only stay a short while longer. I can tell they are getting restless and want to move on.

"I had an interview with Swami Chidananda and I basically said to him that I was ready to dedicate my life as his disciple," Peter tells us. "I was disappointed that he didn't welcome me with open arms."

We are not able to answer this. We understand that the *guru*-disciple relationship is not like any other relationship. Only the *guru* knows who is really connected to him. An authentic *guru* would not take on a disciple, just for the sake of having a disciple. What I do understand is that it is a very deep commitment. Once a *guru* of Swami Chidananda's caliber takes on a disciple, he cares for the soul of that person and the disciple is connected to their *guru* through their soul and past *karma*.

Swamiji says, "Without *karmic* relationship, it is impossible for individual souls upon this earth plane to be drawn into any type of relationship. And the greatest and most auspicious relationship is between a devotee and God, a seeker and a saint, because this is the one and only relationship that liberates."

Nagarajan, or Nagaraj, as we call him, is Swamiji's primary attendant and is always on the lookout for how he can instruct us in a helpful way. "In life we have many relationships," he tells us. "All of these will pass away. But your relationship with your *guru* is an eternal bond and will go on from lifetime to lifetime." His words make a deep impression on me and bring home the sacredness of the connection.

Nagaraj never tires of telling us stories from the scriptures and relating first hand incidents from his own life and his long association with Swami Chidananda. He came from a humble background in South India and reached Rishikesh by train in the winter of 1953. He was hungry and cold and couldn't speak Hindi, a northern language. He found his way to Muni-ki-reti and lived for six years in an underground cave, where Dattatreya Mandir is located, on the hill opposite Saraswati Kutir.

"Every morning I used to come down to the Ganga to take bath," he says, with his nasal accent. "I only had one cloth and I would wash it and while it was drying in the sun, I would meditate." He relates that he watched a tall, thin monk coming daily to dip in the Ganges and meditate on a rock overlooking the river. "One day, while I was meditating, a shadow fell across me and I opened my eyes to see the monk standing in front of me."

"And was that Swami Chidananda?" I ask, wanting to hear more.

"Yes," he continues. "He asked me why I had come. When he found out I came from the south, Swamiji immediately switched over to my language, Kanarese (or Kannada), so I could understand him." Swami Chidananda introduced Nagaraj to Gurudev Sivananda, who encouraged him to stay in the *ashram* and do some service, as it is "too difficult," he said, "to meditate all day long." From that day onward Nagaraj[20] stayed with Swamiji and became his trusted servant and ardent devotee. It is through him we first get a glimpse of what it means to be a real disciple to a highly evolved soul like Swami Chidananda.

He tells us that Swamiji keeps odd hours and sometimes works late into the night when he will not be disturbed. Nagaraj often stays up with him, taking dictation and sometimes he falls asleep at his typewriter, only to wake up later and discover Swamiji has left him a thermos of hot milk and a jar of Horlicks with a note saying, "You fell asleep while typing."

"You see, such a kind master he is!" Nagaraj says.

"Don't you ever have any questions for Swamiji?" I ask.

"No," he replies. "I don't have any questions." Nagaraj continues, "If it is daytime and Swamiji says, "It is night," I say, "Yes, Swamiji!" If it is night and Swamiji says, "Sky is blue," I say, "Yes, Swamiji!"

To our Western way of thinking, this explanation sounds irrational and a bit daft. But, as Swami Chidananda is fond of saying, "Obedience is better than reverence." And Nagaraj has that down to a 't'. He is able to relinquish his preconceived notions and any "knowledge" he might have in order to accept whatever his *guru* says as the truth by which he lives. I imagine that is why Swamiji has kept him so close to him for so many years. Swamiji knows that Nagaraj can always be relied upon to do what is asked of him. Nagaraj becomes friends with us and many other Western devotees, whom he meets traveling abroad with Swamiji on his many trips to the West. He always fits into whatever we are doing, without expecting to be treated differently. As a devotee of Lord Rama he is often heard repeating under his breath, *Sri Ram Jai Ram Jai Jai Ram!* And he follows Swami Chidananda's example of being a devoted servant of his Master.

---

[20] When Nagaraj becomes a sannyasin in 1972, Swami Chidananda gives him the name of Swami Vimalananda. Later, he becomes General Secretary and then in 2008 he becomes President of the Divine Life Society, following Swami Chidananda's Mahasamadhi in August of that year.

INNER GUIDANCE

In the early days, I am rather intimidated by being so transparent in the radiance of Swami Chidananda's presence. Part of me knows that Swamiji can see deep within my soul, which terrifies my ego. In my ignorance I wonder what he might think if he actually finds out what I really am, with all my imperfections. Sometimes, when I see Swamiji coming from afar, I step behind the corner of a building, so I can watch him without his seeing me. Perhaps we Westerners all carry some sense of shame within ourselves, maybe a cultural "original sin." But Swamiji is so simple and natural that it doesn't take long for his humble presence to dispel this ignorant idea. Soon, I realize that his nature is pure love and he draws the same out of each one of us.

When Swamiji teaches, it is usually with stories from the scriptures, using examples from Gurudev Sivananda's life or the lives of the ancient *rishis* to illustrate his point. In his humility he never uses himself as an example, but when he says, "In the time of the ancient *rishis*…" I think that Swamiji is just like an ancient *rishi*. It sounds like it is himself he is describing! His real transmission happens on an internal level. He relates to the hidden divinity in each one of us and when we respond to that prompting, we begin to awaken.

He says that when he comes to the hall to speak, he does not address individuals. "If anyone thinks I am addressing them personally, it is from their side only. Whatever is spoken is prompted from within. It is the universal speaking to the universal."

My early schooling in South Africa, based on the English school system, was very strict, with the teachers using various kinds of punishment, including in some instances, striking us with a ruler. So, authority figures conjure up fearful memories for me. However, in Swamiji's presence, the image of a teacher as a disciplinarian with a long stick vanishes and is replaced by an atmosphere of loving support. It is such a relief to realize that all of our spiritual practices are done, not because we are told they *have* to be done, but because we are reaching for something truly worthwhile! Swamiji knows how to draw forth that which is highest and best in a person and makes them long to live up to it. He has no hidden agenda. He is one of the pure beings whose selfless actions are only for the welfare of others.

Swami Chidananda is the kind of *guru* who works with you on a very subtle level. If you turn your attention inward and listen, things become clear. Often you will be corrected or encouraged and no one else will know, because it will all happen on such an internal level. Swamiji might not speak to you for days, weeks or months, but all the time changes are taking place internally. I am not able to understand how he does this, being aware of so many details, with so many devotees.

I am very blessed that Don also feels the same love and respect for Swamiji. It makes it much easier for the two of us, that we are both headed, more or less, in the same direction. Because we both have Swamiji's inner guidance we are able to overcome many of the differences of opinion which are bound to crop up between two people, living in close proximity, day in and day out.

RIPE BANANAS

When we move up the hill into Saraswati Kutir, I am given the job of making the rounds and caring for a couple of elderly swamis. Mostly, I just look in on them everyday and see if they need anything. Swami Vedantananda Mataji is the Polish lady *sannyasin* living in a small room on the second floor of Lakshmi Kutir. She never mentions that she is fluent in several languages, both European and Indian, and that she also writes poetry. I never guess that she is a scholar. She writes many compositions describing Swamiji and his divine qualities.[21] She shows me her exquisite paintings of the *pranava*, the *Om* symbol, in beautiful pastel watercolors, which she does as part of her *sadhana*. Visitors purchase these little paintings, giving her a

---

[21] As seen in her book published by the Ashram Press, entitled, *The All-embracing Heart*.

few rupees for her patient art work, so she has some pocket money to spend on the necessities, such as soap, tea, and the watercolor paints and paper, which have to be ordered from Dehradun or Delhi. One day I bring her two ripe bananas, hidden from the monkeys under my shawl, along with the morning ration of dry rusks.

Vedantananda Mataji with Swamiji

"Oh no!" she says, with her eastern European accent. "I don't take ripe bananas!"

"Why not, Mataji? They are nice and sweet," I reply, now hesitant to put them on her small table.

"I know, I know," she says, shaking her shaven head, which is covered by a pale orange, close-fitting skullcap with earflaps. "At one time I took them, but not any more."

"But why not?" I persist.

"Because my mind likes bananas too much!" she confesses. "Especially *speckled* bananas! So I decided some time ago not to take them any more."

"Oh, I see." I move the bananas back under my shawl. "Alright, I won't bring them again." She is practicing control of the mind, by not giving in to what it wants most; not giving way to her craving. I realize that my standing there with the bananas is a temptation to her resolve, so I pranam to her and leave quickly. It seems like such a trivial matter in a way, but it is a good example of how to build will power by self-denial and not always giving in to the mind. Each *sadhak* has to do self-analysis and find out where the work needs to be done. For one, it may be giving up eating speckled bananas, for another, telling the truth. The wonderful thing about Sivananda Ashram is that you are free to chose which particular *sadhana* you need to work on.

ROACHES, RATS AND CAKE

My other charge is Swami Hariharananda, an elderly man, probably in his eighties, who has followed the traditional four life-stages, according to the *Vedic* culture, which form an important aspect of the Hindu concept of *dharma*. The four life-stages, or *ashramas*, are—*brahmacharya*, the student stage, which is meant for studying and apprenticeship; *grihasta*, the house-holder stage, for marriage, children, and work in the world; *vanaprasta*, the retirement stage, where in ancient times the householders would turn their authority over to their children and retire to the forest; and the final stage of *sannyasa*, or renunciation. Swami Hariharananda's wife has given him permission to spend his final years at Sivananda Ashram in the company of the holy. He has a gentle character and seems perfectly suited to this life of utter simplicity.

He shares a room with another man, next to the room where the wood fire is made for heating water for all the morning bucket baths throughout the *ashram*. His bed is pushed against one corner of the room and a straight-backed wooden chair stands beside it. Leaning against the chair is a walking stick and over the bed hangs an orange cloth on a hook. His possessions are very few.

Someone has provided Swami Hariharananda a more modern way of heating his bath water, with a big electric coil, which hangs on a hook by the door. Every morning after breakfast, I go to his room behind the Bhajan Hall to get his bucket of hot water ready for him. The coil has to be put into the water before the electric switch is turned on. While we wait for the water to heat up, I sit on the chair beside his bed and chant the morning hymns to him. When bubbles form on the coil and begin to rise, it is ready to be removed from the bucket. Fearing that I will be electrocuted, Swami Hariharahanda warns me every time, "Don't touch the bucket, Mataji! Don't touch the bucket!"

And every day I say the same thing, "Don't worry, Swamiji. I am switching it off now." Then, as he watches, I safely remove the coil from the bucket and hang it on the hook.

On winter mornings he takes his chair outside and sits in the sun in front of the Sivananda Pillar. Sometimes I drag his mattress out and hang it over the balustrade to air in the sun. This always causes a skittering of cockroaches, which are hiding under the wood frame bed. Out goes the bed, and with a pump-can of Flit, I spray its underside. Cockroaches run helter-skelter looking for a dark place to hide. "I don't like it, Mataji!" he exclaims, afraid that I am going transgress his vow of *ahimsa* and kill something on his behalf.

"I am only spraying the wood, so they will leave you alone," I assure him. "I am not killing anything."

Even scorpions, snakes, and rats are not killed in the *ashram*. Strict *ahimsa* is observed. One day as Don and I are sitting reading in our room, a rat runs through the door and straight up the wall using the electric cord to climb on. To our surprise we find that a mother rat has made a nest on the high shelf in our room where suitcases are generally stored. Before we know it, she has given birth to a whole batch of baby rats! When we report this to the *ashram* authorities, they provide us with a trap that catches, but does not kill. We catch the mother the next day and Don is told to take her down to the Ganges bank and release her there. "Boy, if my Dad could see me now!" he says. "Letting a rat go free would just seem like a crazy idea in the West!" I carry the baby rats outside in a burlap cloth and lay them on the hill across from our building. They don't fare so well, because the hungry dogs find them.

When Swami Hariharananda's birthday comes, I get a small cake from the bakery in Rishikesh, light a candle, and sing, "Happy Birthday to you!" as we sit on the base of the Sivananda Pillar, waiting for the afternoon *chai* to be brought around. He has never had anyone make such a fuss over his birthday and is quite embarrassed, though I suspect, secretly pleased.

Since Swami Hariharananda is too infirm to attend the nightly *satsang*, I am wondering how he might receive Swami Chidanandaji's blessings on his birthday. I know it would mean so much to him to have *darshan* of Swamiji, yet I am unsure and don't know if it's my place to ask for such a meeting. However, I resolve to let Swamiji know after the evening *satsang*. This is a time when devotees often approach Swamiji with questions or information of a personal nature, or if they have just arrived or are leaving the *ashram*, to *pranam* and receive Swamiji's blessings.

As the *satsang* concludes, I am just getting up to approach Swamiji, still sitting in his place against the back wall. He calls out to me, "How is the old man?"

"It's his birthday today, Swamiji," I reply quickly, not surprised that he has guessed the reason for my approach. By now I am used to Swamiji knowing my intention and reading my thoughts.

"What!" He scolds me. "Why didn't you tell me before so we could arrange something?" Now I am kicking myself for not alerting Swamiji beforehand. *Of course I should have told him! Why am I letting my own timidity interfere with Swami Hariharananda's happiness?*

Swami Chidananda turns and motions to the attendant who accompanies him to *satsang*. "There is a new red blanket in my room. Please bring it." The blanket has recently been presented to him, but that will not stop

Swamiji from giving it away. Most things pass through Swamiji's hands and are distributed to others, wherever there is a need. When the attendant runs to fetch the blanket, I know Swamiji will stop by to give Swami Hariharananda darshan, so I run quickly to his room.

"Wake up Swamiji!" I say, switching on the overhead electric light. "Swami Chidananda is coming to see you!" Hardly believing his good fortune, Swami Hariharananda sits up in bed and finding the only thing he can think of to make himself look presentable, ties a red bandana around his baldhead.

Soon, Swami Chidananda enters the room and presents Swami Hariharananda with the red blanket. Then he pulls up the chair and places himself alongside Swami Hariharananda's bed. The attendant and I stand back on the far side of the room, directly behind Swamiji's chair. Giving Swami Hariharananda his full attention, Swami Chidanandaji speaks with him for several minutes, kindly inquiring about his health, his diet and whether he is in need of anything. Quite overwhelmed by Swamiji's loving attention, all of a sudden Swami Hariharananda blurts out, "This is all due to Mataji!" he says, pointing to me. The comment embarrasses me and I wince, covering an ear with my hand.

I am still looking at the back of Swami Chidananda's head and without turning even slightly, he says, "Yes, you can cover your other ear with your other hand also!"

SWAMIJI'S AWARENESS

I have read about certain *yogis* being able to see 360 degrees all around them and now I have seen it for myself. Swamiji knew exactly what I was doing without turning at all. Moreover, I believe that Swamiji can cast his awareness towards us any time, with the eye of intuition, wherever we are on the planet, especially if we tune in to him inwardly. Swamiji would be the first to agree that each of us has to do our own practices, that the *guru* only points the way. But it does seem that in proximity to him and perhaps as a result of his intense *sadhana*, we devotees are being given a leg up. For great souls like Swami Chidananda, at one with omnipresent consciousness, time and space present no obstacle. If he chooses to he can look into our hearts and minds wherever we are and know what we are thinking and feeling. The effect of Swamiji's presence is like a mirror in which our own reflection appears—the defects in our nature staring back at us. As with a mirror there is no judgment. It simply shows what is there. It is up to us to use the information we see to correct ourselves. In Swamiji's presence, we can see how far from *dharma* we have strayed, because his compass always points true north.

Perhaps it isn't that obvious to everyone, but if you are seeking a higher truth, this kind of awareness is a great gift. It is part of the grace that surrounds us as disciples of a God-realized being. If we truly want to know who we are and we really want to clean up our act and live from our divine nature, then there is nothing to hide and moreover, nothing that can possibly be hidden.

My progress towards Self-awareness happens gradually. Those who are ready to give up everything immediately and live only for God are rare. They are like the proverbial dry fuel, which can be set ablaze with one match. I would like to be like that, but I know I am not at that level. Though I have a desire for liberation, I have to live through the momentum of the *karma* I have already set in motion. Nagaraj once told me that as a seeker I am only "half baked." Even though I think my ideal life would be one of renunciation, Swamiji knows better what I need for my evolution. I have a hard time letting go of the idea that it is *my* life. Even though I tell myself that my goal is Self-realization, my ego is still hanging on with a firm grip. However, the light that shines through the cracks is enough to keep me going for many years. Swamiji knows how much we can stand and allows us to develop according to our capacity. His loving heart draws us like a magnet, rather than pushing us beyond our willingness to let go.

Swamiji is infinitely patient with us. He is constantly planting seeds, knowing that something will take root at sometime and we will realize what he is trying to say. The main point is we have to wake up! He is fond of quoting the *Upanishads*, *"Uttishtita jagrata prapya varan nibhodhata!* Arise, awake, having reached the wise become enlightened!" First we have to get up and then we have to wake up! The Sanskrit language has such deep philosophical meaning. The words are not meant to stay on the page. They are to be spoken by *guru* to disciple throughout the ages. I trust that if I keep up my *sadhana*, in time, everything will become clear. As it is, Swamiji, as a living embodiment of the teachings, transmits joy and enthusiasm for this kind of life.

It takes me about four months to get up enough courage to ask to have an interview with Swamiji. Usually, you have to be sure that you have a valid reason to take up Swamiji's precious time. You have to know what question you are going to ask. It has to be important enough that you can't answer it yourself. You have to have thought about it for a long time, day and night, until it is burning a hole in your mind. And then, you have to remember it when you sit in front of Swamiji and he turns his luminous gaze on you.

When it is warm enough to have the evening *satsang* outdoors, we gather around the Sivananda Pillar. One evening, I am sitting in the front and when the *satsang* ends, I blurt out, "I would like to *see* you, Swamiji!"

It is not proper protocol, but instead of correcting me, Swamiji announces out loud so everyone can hear, "You see, I have been trying to see her for four months!" He emphasizes the words *four months*. "And my schedule hasn't allowed it."

The truth is, that if you really have an important issue, Swamiji will make time and see you right away. But it is for our own good that we need to mull these things over in our minds, until our question becomes clear, before approaching Swamiji. Swamiji is always emphasizing the importance of time, and how our lives are made up of moments, minutes, hours, days and months. As seekers, we have to understand the importance of time, that it is a precious commodity, not to be wasted. As seekers, we are encouraged to utilize each moment in some sort of *sadhana*—either in *mantra japa*, study, service, worship, or meditation. Yoga *asanas*, *pranayama* and walking in the fresh air, are also encouraged. All our actions, *everything*, can be turned into spiritual practice. At the end of morning prayers every day we chant, "*Kayena vacha manasendryairva, buddhyatmana va prakrite swabhavat, karomi yadyat sakalam parasmai Narayana yeti samarpayami*—Whatever I do with my body, mind, intellect, self, or nature, I offer all up to the Supreme Divine Reality." Swamiji reminds us, "It is essential that we do not confine our *sadhana* only to the quiet hours inside the *puja* room, but divinize all our actions." He says, "All life is sadhana. Live it as such!"

So, I am given an appointment to see Swamiji in a private interview. It is quite soon and I am happy and nervous at the same time.

MANTRA

When it is the will of God that He must grace an individual soul in this Samsara in a special way, then He out of infinite compassion manifests in the life of that Jivatma as Mantra. —Swami Chidananda

Traditionally, *mantra* initiation, *mantra diksha*, is given to a disciple by a *guru* in order to bring the disciple closer to their chosen ideal, or their *Ishta Devata*. *Mantra* denotes a word made up of certain syllables, which repeated together, describes and invokes a certain form of God. There are many *mantras* praising different deities. If you have the good fortune to receive the *mantra* from a realized being, like Swami Chidananda, it becomes activated for you by his spiritual input and you are linked by it to that Being. Then it is up to you to continue the practice of repeating the *mantra* a certain number of times per day, according to your circumstances. In the *yogic* tradition, name and form are considered one and the same, *namarupa*—name and form. By repeating the name of God as the *mantra*, the mind withdraws from the outside world (*pratyahara*), and becomes quiet and focused, conducive to a state of concentration and meditation. Eventually, the repetition may fall away by itself and only the divine presence remains. After many repetitions of the *mantra* with concentration and devotion, it is possible for that particular form of the Divine to appear. There are Indian saints, like Swami Ramdas of Ananda Ashram in Kerala, who have attained God-realization through repetition of God's name alone.

In *Vedanta*, there is also the concept of pure consciousness, or the Supreme Being in a formless state. These are hard concepts to grasp in the beginning, that formless consciousness also includes all forms. The *pranava*, denoting the sacred syllable *Om*, is a *mantra* without form.

At 7 a.m. I climb the narrow cement steps to Swamiji's kutir and knock on the door. I am told to sit on the bench in the anteroom by the small kitchen, where one of the boys is making tea. The shoes are neatly placed just inside the door. There is a bit of walking back and forth, bringing Swamiji two thermoses, one for hot tea and the other for hot milk. Soon, I am told to go through to Swamiji's room. It is a long narrow room with a lot of open windows facing southeast, which overlooks a courtyard, a large tree and farther down the hill across the road, the Ganges. On the floor, pouring tea from a thermos into a china teacup, Swamiji sits surrounded by stacks of books and papers. Swamiji does all his work, *ashram* business and dictation, correspondence, domestic and foreign, from his seat on the floor.

"Good morning," he says, as I sink to my knees and bow my head in front of him. "Is everything all right?" he asks, to put me at ease.

"Yes, thank you, Swamiji," I readjust my legs into cross-legged posture.

"I got your letter," Swamiji says, carefully adding hot milk into his tea from the smaller thermos.

He is referring to the letter I have recently written him, filling him in with my past history and my questions about the *mantras* I have been using. I explained that first I had practiced Transcendental Meditation (TM) as taught by Maharishi Mahesh Yogi, for two years. Then, I practiced with the *mantra* received from Swami Vishnu at the Yoga Camp in Val Morin for another two years. What I was really saying in the letter is that while I respect and value what I have learned from the others, I recognize on a very deep level that he, Swami Chidananda, is my *guru* and I would like to put the past behind me and start afresh.

Besides that, I wrote that I don't know who my *Ishta Devata* is. I admitted that I don't know if I am Christian, Hindu, Buddhist or what I am. All the paths seem attractive to me in their own way. Perhaps I have said too much in the letter. Suddenly, I feel awkward and exposed.

Swamiji screws the tops back on the thermoses and carefully pours his tea from the cup into the saucer to cool it. He holds the saucer with both hands and sips from it. He takes his time and finishes drinking his tea. He remains silent. Then he closes his eyes and appears to be meditating. I sit still with my eyes down, but every now and then, I glance up to see if he still has his eyes closed. I feel quite small and it seems almost as if he has grown in physical stature, until he is much taller that I am. I can't even tell if I am breathing or not. Finally, he stirs and says, "You will have an experience and it will become clear to you who your *Ishta Devata* is. In the mean time, in the light of what you have explained, I will give you a *mantra* that you can use until later on."

He bends his head and writes on a half-sheet of paper, which he hands to me. "*Om Sri Sivanandaya Namah!*" It is Gurudev's name and I felt immensely relieved! I am happy to say Gurudev Sivananda's name as a way to God, who feels to me like a loving and neutral presence, not pushing me one way or another. Also, because I know how deeply Swamiji reveres and adores his own *guru*, I feel it is a perfect connection for me through Gurudev to Swamiji. I resolve to repeat this *mantra* often throughout the day.

Without thinking, I suddenly confess, "Swamiji, I don't have a religion." Swamiji looks up at me and with great kindness, says, "Why do you need religion if you have God?" With that simple sentence, all the tension disappears and I feel light and happy again.

CHAPTER 8

WALKING THE PILGRIM TRAIL AND OTHER EVENTS

PHUL CHATTY AND NEELA KANTH

Swamiji is called away on a tour of the different branches of the Divine Life Society in India and will be gone for several days. We speak to Nagaraj about walking up the old pilgrim trail to Phul Chatty. "We would like to walk up and around and come back by Neelakanta," Don says. "We might take four or five days."

"There is a Swami Vishuddananda at Phul Chatty," Nagaraj tells us. "I will write a letter to him for you. Don't go to him empty handed," he advises.

I search around for something we can give to the swami when we get there. Amongst our things I find an unopened bottle of vitamin B tablets given to us by the Peace Corps doctor. With that in hand, we set off that afternoon carrying a small bag with some clothes, a flask of boiled water, a book or two and our sketch books. At this point Don still has his old camera and we take that along too.

Some months ago, when we visited a tea plantation in the mountains of Ceylon, we bought a box of the most delicious tea we had ever tasted. Thinking of offering it to Swami Chidananda, we carried it all through

India to the *ashram*, but when we asked Nagaraj if Swamiji still liked tea, he answered, "No, Swamiji doesn't take it any more." Perhaps he misunderstood us, or maybe he thought that we were enquiring because we thought drinking black tea was an unhealthy habit, and he didn't want us to think of Swamiji in a negative way. Whatever his reason, we were disappointed to hear that now the tea could not be given to Swamiji. So we bring it along in the backpack.

We cross by ferryboat to the other side of the Ganga and begin walking along the section of the old pilgrim trail beyond Gita Bhavan Ashram. It is shaded by mango trees and bordered on either side by long cement benches, worn smooth from countless pilgrims resting on them. I love walking along here, where so many prayerful steps have been taken, where seekers walk with the name of God on their lips, where the earth is so soft that the dust feels like talcum powder on the feet. It is very quiet as there are no vehicles of any kind on the other side of the river, which enhances the feeling of leaving the world behind.

We walk upstream beyond Lakshman Jhula until we reach Garud Chatty in the late afternoon, which is no more than just a single *chai* stall, where a man prepares *chai* for the pilgrims. He stirs a pot of hot water with ground ginger, cardamom, and cloves, simmering on the fire, into which he adds milk and then throws in a handful of loose black tea.

On the opposite side of the trail from the *chai* stall is a very old temple in a dilapidated condition. In front of the temple is a square pool of water made of cemented river stones. We sit on the low wall and suddenly a beautiful bird swoops down beside us. "Kingfisher!" Don whispers, recognizing the shape of the head and plumage. We sit completely still, watching the kingfisher as he tilts his head, looking intently into the water. He is hunting for his supper and completely unafraid of us.

"Oji!" the *chai* stall owner calls to us. He has made a couple of *rotis* for our supper, singed over his open fire. They are delicious with our cups of hot *chai*. Since it is getting dark, we decide to spend the night right there

WALKING THE PILGRIM TRAIL AND OTHER EVENTS

on the side of the road near the *chai* stall, where we soon fall asleep on wooden benches.

During the night I have a strange dream. I am sleeping on the bench, but there is an invisible presence nearby that wants to be where I am. I feel that I am being pushed off the bench by this unseen entity. But there isn't any room for another person on the bench. Slowly I realize not only does it want the bench space, but it wants my body also. It is trying to push me out of my body. I become aware of a growing sense of urgency that does not feel benign, that is trying to inhabit my body, pushing and pushing me out, until it has almost succeeded. Suddenly, I scream in the dream, *"Jesus!"*

Immediately I wake up with my heart pounding in my ears. This is one of these dreams that seem as real as the waking state. I sit up on the bench and realize that the name of God has driven away the presence of evil and I am safe. I take a few deep breaths and sit still until the pounding of my heart quiets down. Could this be the experience that Swamiji was referring to, when he said I would find out who my *Ishta* is? It certainly seems so. I do not want to fall asleep again, so I sit on the bench, wondering about being in a human body, as opposed to being a disembodied spirit, caught in limbo somewhere, trying to get back to the earth plane. I think of Gurudev and Swami Chidananda's reminding us in so many ways, that getting a human birth should not be taken for granted, that we should utilize every moment of it to evolve towards God-realization. And indeed, as I sit there in the dark with my feet on the earth, I realize what a privilege this life is. When dawn comes, I wake Don up and tell him my dream.

We thank the kind Garud Chatty host, who is already lighting the fire and grinding spices with a stone pestle in a hollow rock, in preparation for early morning tea. We walk farther up the trail bordering the Ganges to Phul Chatty where Swami Vishuddananda greets us, reads our letter of introduction, and welcomes us to his tiny *ashram*. It seems that medicines and vitamins are scarce in these parts, because he gratefully accepts our offering of the bottle of vitamin B complex. He shows us where we can stay, in a whitewashed room with two cots and nothing else. I love its simplicity, which fills a deep need in me to cast away non-essentials.

There is one simple meal of rice and *dhal* and *roti* served at midday. In the mornings and afternoons tea is available. I find a sandy place in the rocks, away from the river, to go to the bathroom. There are one or two *sadhus* in the vicinity, so I bathe mid-morning with my clothes on in the Bhim Ganga, a small tributary, which runs into the main Ganga, and then I sit on a boulder in the sun to dry.

We are essentially on our own to read, write, draw, and meditate when we like. After three quiet days we thank Swami Vishuddananda, who points us in the direction of a path bordering the Bhim Ganga that leads into the mountains. We walk eastward away from the Ganges, climbing constantly until we are looking down on a footbridge where the trail ends and we find ourselves walking on a narrow path through trees that give way to terraced paddy fields. I wipe the sweat from my forehead on the back of my sleeve and take a sip of boiled water from the U.S. army-issued, water flask we carry with us. We climb up and up, wondering if we are lost, until we reach a cluster of small houses.

We cause quite a sensation in the tiny village where strangers are seldom seen, let alone foreigners. We are immediately invited into one of the thatched huts and told to sit on the wooden bed. The men light their pipes and sit with several young boys on the earth floor, while the girls gather at the doorway, not daring to come in.

We have finally reached a remote village where nobody speaks English, but Indian hospitality is not lacking! We are offered *chai* and there is an excited commotion as one person begins boiling water and another runs somewhere for milk. The young girls around the doorway stare curiously at us. We make the mistake of asking for "*chinni*," sugar for the tea, and immediately regret it, because we are already putting them out. One of the children is sent running to another house in search of sugar. Finally, they get it all together and serve us two cups of tea with milk and sugar.

This is a luxury, which we gratefully accept from the generous hearts or these poor villagers.

I am reminded of a story in the *Mahabharata* in which the rich and generous King Yudisthira prides himself on frequently organizing feasts to feed his subjects. The king cannot help wondering if other rulers also take such good care of their subjects. After one such feast, the king notices a mongoose rolling himself in the leftovers and asks him why he is doing that. The mongoose, whose coat is half golden, then relates a story to the king:

"During a time of great famine in the land, I was searching for food to keep myself alive, when I found a poor family on the verge of starvation. The husband had managed to procure a little flour so that his wife could make *roti*, and I thought I might be able to get some nourishment in case she dropped a few grains of flour. Just as the family was about to eat the *roti*, a starving mendicant came to the hut and begged for food. The husband, believing that the guest is God, gave his part to the mendicant, who ate it and asked for more. Then the wife gave her *roti* to the mendicant, who ate that too. He was not satisfied though, until the son and daughter-in-law had given their portions to him also. Finally satiated, the mendicant left. However, the poor family succumbed and died of starvation."

The mongoose continues, "Witnessing these events, I came close to the hearth where the *rotis* had been prepared and I brushed against some flour lying on the ground. That part of my coat that touched the flour turned golden. Since then, oh great king, I am visiting places where acts of kindness and generosity are performed, so that I can roll in the remnants, hoping to turn the other half of my body golden also. So far, all events have fallen short of the ultimate sacrifice made by that poor family."

King Yudisthira hangs his head, humbled by the mongoose's story.

I wonder if these poor villagers have heard about the story of the golden mongoose? But, even if they haven't, it is ingrained in their culture to offer whatever they have to a guest. We have a little pot of Tiger Balm, which we bought in Singapore several months before, so we give it to them, explaining it is for headaches. I wonder whether they understand what we are saying, but there is a lot of giggling as we demonstrate by rubbing a little on the forehead of one of the children, warning them not to get it near the eyes. It helps keep the flies away from the child's face. We also give them a cloth belt, woven in Ecuador.

"Neela Kanth?" we enquire when we have finished our tea. The village elders point diagonally up the mountain. The children walk with us part of the way and then we continue walking up and around the mountain until, with blisters on our feet, we reach the holy shrine of Neela Kanth.

A huge old tree shelters a small white temple to Lord Siva where countless pilgrims have worshipped for hundreds of years. Swami Chidananda told us that once a year, on Sivaratri, the *sadhus* make a drink out of crushed *ganja* leaves, which they imbibe while chanting the *panchakshari mantra*, "*Om Namah Sivaya!*" all night long, singing themselves into a trance.

There is a little outdoor kitchen where one man squats by the fire making *chai*. He says we can stay the night here and shows us into a completely bare, whitewashed room with a cement floor and wooden shutters. His name is Soham Singh and he begins preparing *roti* and *subji* with mint chutney for our supper. His wife and children spend the afternoon keeping their cows and goats out of the nearby dill patch. While we are waiting for him to prepare the supper, we find a pool at the base of a single stream of water pouring out of the mountain. I stand under it and let the water splash onto my head, washing myself as best I can.

Soham Singh will not accept any payment for the food he is making for our supper, so we give him our last item, the box of tea from Ceylon. There is a saying in India, "Every grain of rice has someone's name on it." If you are meant to eat something, you will travel to the spot where that particular grain, or bowl of rice is being served. I imagine the same rule must apply to tealeaves. We intended the tea to be for Swami Chidananda, but now it will be used here instead.

Neela Kanth temple

There is a legend from the *Puranas* of the *Devas* and *asuras*, the gods and the demons, churning the ocean, using Vasuki, the serpent, as a churning rope. This churning back and forth releases both nectar and a terrible poison, which, if even one drop enters the ocean, will destroy all life. As the legend goes, one of the drops of nectar falls near Rishikesh, which makes it a very holy place. As for the poison, Lord Siva comes to the rescue and catches it in his throat, which turns blue. Hence the name, Neelakanta, blue throat.

We sleep on the floor in a little room off the kitchen, under the giant tree. When everyone is asleep, I sit on my mat to meditate in this sacred place. I think of the blueness of the ocean and the green beauty of the earth. I think of the legend of Siva drinking the poison to save the oceans, which Soham Singh believes happened right here. I am not sure whether it was actually here or not, but it could very well be that we have been given a second chance and I pray that we will look after our planet and make sure the oceans and rivers will not be poisoned by garbage, sludge, and chemical spills of any kind.

Early the next morning we bid our generous host and his family goodbye and set off following the trail diagonally down the mountain. It is quite steep in places and my toes keep ramming against the end of the tennis shoes. Eventually, I take off my shoes and go barefoot the rest of the way, until we reach the ferry, which takes us across the river to Shivanandanagar.

I am happy to be back in our corner room in Saraswati Kutir and I am glad that we took the opportunity to make a short pilgrimage to three holy places, to walk in nature along the river and in the mountains. But we agree that the most impressive thing about our little trip is how welcome we, travelers from a foreign land, have been made to feel, by the simplicity and generosity of these mountain people.

VISITING SAINTS

Don and I make a point of visiting as many of the saints and *yogis* in the area as possible. The other side of the Ganga is still quite wild, with monkeys, elephants, and even a tiger or two. Downriver from Uma Shankar's

WALKING THE PILGRIM TRAIL AND OTHER EVENTS

cave there is another cave halfway up the mountain, occupied by a *yogi* called Tat Walla Baba. When we climb up to the entrance of the cave, he is sitting cross-legged on a mat on the ground, with a cloth wrapped around his waist and a head of thick, black hair. To one side of where he sits is a hand-written sign, which reads, "Cave Hours. 10 a.m. – 11 a.m." We find this sign quite amusing, but it is an attempt to keep unwanted visitors from wasting his time. I suppose that we fall into this category, but we are within the time limits set, so we offer the fruits we have brought him, sitting in silence, as he doesn't speak English. His eyes shine with a deep luster, the mark of a serious meditator and he neither encourages us to stay, nor tries to get rid of us. But he is not someone we feel particularly drawn to, so we take our leave after half an hour.

Perhaps the most evolved soul in India at this time, maybe even the world, is Ananda Mayee Ma, the bliss-filled mother. We are shown an old movie of Ananda Mayee Ma sitting on a dais with Swami Sivananda in an outdoor *satsang*, surrounded by many of their devotees. She refers to Swami Sivananda as "*Pitaji*", or father, and he in turn refers to her as "the most perfect flower the Indian soil has produced." Swami Chidananda also reveres and adores Ma, simply called by her disciples and devotees, speaking of her as "a spiritual phenomenon," one who was already fully awake and enlightened from birth. There was no need for a *guru*. She practiced her own special *sadhana* and initiated herself, when she was a young woman.

On 3rd March, an overcast afternoon for this time of year, Don and I travel by taxi to Haridwar to have Ma's *darshan*. Our neighbor, Swami Krishnapriyananda Mataji, an ardent devotee of Ma, accompanies us and shows us the way to Ma's *ashram* in Kankhal. When we arrive, we find Ma sitting in a small, whitewashed room with a wooden door, much like all the *kutirs* in our *ashram*. The only furniture in the room is a bed with a white

covering and Ma, also dressed in white, is seated on it. Her greying hair is loose to her shoulders.

We have finally come into the physical presence of the blessed and holy bliss-filled Mother. Her consciousness permeates my mind and the unasked questions evaporate. There is nothing that we can give these holy saints, except our love and service wherever possible. I am amazed how divinity has embodied itself in the form of Ma. As a young woman Ma was stunningly beautiful, and even now, in a seventy-four-year-old body, she radiates spiritual energy. Divine light shines through her eyes.

The door to the *kutir* remains open and Don and I sit outside for a while, having full *darshan* of Ma. Then, we are invited inside to prostrate before her and offer the garlands, which we have brought from Rishikesh. My forehead touches the cool marble threshold of her doorway and she bends her neck to accommodate the garland, I am putting over her head. My mind seems to be on hold. My heart is full and peaceful and I feel infinitely blessed by her presence.

Later, back at the *ashram*, I am told by Yvonne, "Oh, you're not supposed to garland Ma! You're supposed to lay the garlands at her feet." I feel regret that I had subjected Ma to the garland, but no one told us the correct protocol. I did not feel any judgment from her and she must have known my intention was good.

One summer morning while we are standing out in the courtyard by the tree where Swami Sivananda used to sit, Swami Chidananda comes outside just in time to greet a bare-chested man coming up the steps. He has shoulder length, curly dark hair and a stocky build. They embrace each other warmly, with a big hug, both of them full of smiles and laughter. "His name is Swami Avadhutendraji. He is a great *bhakta*," someone whispers in my ear. Later that evening, the whole *ashram* is in attendance at *satsang* to listen to Swami Avadhutendra's devotional *bhajans*. We have never heard anything like it! He sings with such fervor, he is so consumed by divine love, that the skin on the center of his chest literally becomes red, the color spreading from the center out across his whole chest. His singing holds the ashramites spellbound.

Another memorable visit is from a *yogi* called Swami Parvatikar, who walks from South India every year up to the Badrinath Temple in the north, to spend the summer months in the cool Himalayas. When the snows begin to fall, he makes his return journey on foot to the south. He has been stopping at Sivananda Ashram since Gurudev's time and continues to do so as long as his health allows. Swami Parvatikar, a lean man with a high forehead and dreadlocks, is a great musician who has fashioned his own instrument—a *Vichitra Veena*—which appears to be a cross between a *veena* and a sitar, having no frets and is played upright with a slide. We are all treated to a concert of his amazing music in the evening *satsang*, accompanied by Swami Nadabrahmananda on *tabla*.

How exceedingly fortunate we are to be present in the *ashram* for these "other-worldly" experiences! Nothing in our Western culture compares to what we are being exposed to here in India among the *yogis*. As far as we are concerned it is all due to the grace of Swami Chidanandaji, because it is by his invitation and encouragement that we are here.

EASTER

We Westerners at Shivanandanagar decide to celebrate Easter by holding a *satsang* on the flat roof of Lakshmi Kutir. Mila, about twenty years our senior, is relatively well off. She always has a supply of cookies on hand, which an errand boy brings for her from the bakery in Dehra Dun. We often visit her in her room and she always offers us a cookie, which is a luxury we can't afford to buy. Even though the cookies are very plain and not up to U.S. standards of crispness and taste, they have that combination of flour, butter, and sugar that reminds us of the food we miss and can no longer get.

Mila takes on the organization of the "Easter overnight *satsang*" and makes arrangements for a big dish of curds and fruit for a midnight *prasad* for all of us. She also gets permission from the authorities for those of us who want to sleep on the roof of Lakshmi Kutir, so that we can wake up in the morning and meditate in the open air.

On Saturday afternoon, between Good Friday and Easter Sunday, Swami Krishnananda gives a beautiful talk about the life of Jesus, the meaning of the Resurrection, and life beyond the physical body. In the evening, Swami Chidananda speaks about the Resurrection as the ascension of man into the Divine. After the *satsang* is over for the evening, we climb the cement stairs to the flat roof. From here we have a good view looking down on the Ganges flowing towards Rishikesh and the outline of the black mountain against the starry sky. There are twenty of us, including Danes, Swedes, South and North Americans, French, English, Indians, and South Africans, all sitting under the Easter moon celebrating Christ. Also present, is one Argentinian man, who met Swami Chidananda on his first trip to the West in 1959-1960.

By the light of candles, we read Easter passages from the Bible in French and English. We sing hymns, *bhajans* and chant in Sanskrit until about 1:30 a.m. All of it seems to work together; everything is impromptu and spontaneous. Just after midnight, Swami Chidananda's young assistant appears on the roof. Swamiji has sent him over especially to deliver some small printed cards, which read, *"God is Here, Now!"* He distributes them to each one of us and I notice that Swamiji has signed and dated each card for "11th April 1971, Holy Easter Sunday". After a closing prayer, Mila distributes the fruit and curds into small bowls and we eat it on the spot.

Those of us who decide to sleep on the roof lie on our blankets, look-

WALKING THE PILGRIM TRAIL AND OTHER EVENTS

ing up at the stars and contemplate grand concepts like space and time. We wonder impossible questions like, when the day of *Brahman* comes to a close, as described in the *Bhagavad Gita*, will all souls in the universe be one with God? How will the night of *Brahman*, the contraction of the universe, begin if even one individual soul is not fully evolved? Will the universe have to wait for that one soul? In fact, it seems, that the universe *is* waiting for us to realize our unity with it and embrace it as our own. The *yogis*, saints, and sages all say that God waits with outstretched arms to welcome His or Her children home. Lying on our backs and looking up at the stars in the vast universe, we realize that *we* are those children and God *is* waiting for us with infinite patience! Why are we not hurrying home?

We sleep on the roof until 4:30 or 5:00 a.m. when the chanting in the Bhajan Hall wakes us. Then we sit for silent meditation facing the holy Ganga. When the sun *comes up over the mountain across the river at about 6:45 a.m. we begin chanting, "Om, Om, Om!"* Everyone joins in. Then the English girl, Jean, and I begin singing the hymn, *"All things bright and beautiful, all creatures great and small,"* through the first verse, but then we realize we don't really know the second verse and burst into laughter.

It is only when we turn around that we see Swami Chidananda sitting on the roof with us and when I see Swamiji's serene countenance, I immediately realize that my ego has taken over. We gather around Swamiji and he asks us to read appropriate passages from the Bible in the Easter morning sun.

Afterwards, Swamiji asks, "Well, did you save me any midnight *prasad*, or did you polish it all off?" We hang our heads in shame, because, while Swamiji had remembered us, we had not thought to save him any *prasad*. Then he reminds us, "Whenever you distribute a quantity of *prasad*, always set a portion aside first and offer it to the Lord."

Swamiji has brought even more *prasad* and distributes biscuits to all of us.

Later that day Don and I are allowed to see Swamiji in his *kutir* to present him with a patchwork picture quilt that I have sewn out of all the scraps of material that we have been given or found on our journey since leaving the West. Each piece of material has a story, a situation, or a person behind it. Right in the middle is a green cross, rising out of the ocean, with a bright red heart in the center. The green cloth with tiny yellow crosses in it, we purchased in Nepal to make cushions. Yellow and green are the Easter colors and it seems fitting that it is presented to Swamiji on Easter day. Swamiji hangs it in his room and apparently, according to the boys that serve him, it stays there for several years.

EYE CAMP

During the summer months Dr. Adhvaryoo and his wife, Bhai, travel from Gujarat to the *ashram* to hold a free eye clinic, commonly known as an "Eye Camp." Bapuji, as everyone calls the doctor, and Bhai, are great devotees of Swami Sivananda and have been coming to the *ashram* for many years. He is tall, early fifties, with grey hair, wide large eyes, and a ready smile. She is short, a little plump and her long black hair is generously streaked with grey. They run a hospital in Gujarat State where he trains a team of surgeons to assist him in eye surgery operations.

Swami Chidananda welcomes them in the evening *satsang*, explaining for those of us who do not know, of Babuji's service to the poor and calling him an "exemplary *Karma Yogi*," for putting Swami Sivananda's teachings of selfless service into practice. Then Swamiji turns towards the women's side of the Bhajan Hall and begins praising Bhai, who like many Hindu wives, serve their husbands in a very self-effacing manner, doing what has to be done without getting much credit for it. Bhai is so embarrassed by the praise Swamiji is showering on her that she pulls her sari over her head, hiding her face.

"There is no need to hide," Swamiji says kindly. I am glad that he wants her to be recognized also.

WALKING THE PILGRIM TRAIL AND OTHER EVENTS

This Eye Camp, specifically for the removal of cataracts, is to take place over the course of several days in the Sivananda Hospital building near the Ganga. Volunteers are needed and I agree to help. Don is not good with sickness or surgery of any kind, so I leave him in our room and walk down the steps to the bottom of the hill. A long line of patients sits in the waiting room on the ground floor of the Hospital building. They come in their everyday working clothes; men in trousers and shirts, women in *kurtas* or saris, mostly poor farmers, down from the hills and mountains of Tehri Garhwal (the Shivanandanagar side) and Pauri Garhwal (opposite side of the Ganges) area surrounding the *ashram*. All shoes are left outside the building.

Operations are already under way and I am shown into the "operating theatre," such as it is. I imagine they want to give me the opportunity to witness an eye operation, or maybe they really are short-staffed. I am immediately handed a flashlight and told to shine it directly into the eyes of the patient lying on the operating table. The room is lit with morning light coming in through a window overlooking the river. There are also overhead electric lights, which are subject to daily power outages.

The next patient, seated on a bench in the hall, does not flinch when he is given an injection right beside the eyeball of the eye to be operated on. While the injection takes effect, Dr. Adhvaryoo's skilled hands are at work on the patient lying in front of him on the operating table. I shine the flashlight in the eye, which somehow remains open, maybe due to the injection, while the scalpel slices right across the cornea of the eyeball in one swift motion and the cataract—a tiny, cloudy oval pillow of tissue—is carefully lifted out of the eye and placed in a stainless steel dish. The cornea flap is laid back on the eyeball and the lid is closed. The team of five young surgeons-in-training then moves the patient very carefully onto a stretcher, which they carry into a recovery room and lower to the floor. They lift the patient carefully and transfer him onto a thin mattress on the floor. Each patient is given a special pair of dark glasses to cut out the light. All the patients must lie still for twenty-four hours and many of the ashramites are helping them to keep them in a steady position.

I go back to the operating room and the man who received the injection in his eye is ready for his operation. Some patients have both eyes done, others just one. Dr. Adhvaryoo's hands are steady and swift. His motions are deft and precise. He does not hesitate and the operations are over in minutes.

"I am not hampered by fear of lawsuits," he tells me later, "and so my team and I are able to do many operations in the time it would take them to prepare for one in the West." He says he can do twenty operations in the time it takes Western surgeons to do one.

The cataract patients have been told in advance what to expect and how they should conduct themselves for a successful outcome of the operation. It is crucially important to keep their heads still for a minimum of twenty-four hours after the operation so the cornea can heal and the fluid not run out. I volunteer to sit with a woman for a two-hour shift, which is what I think I can manage. I am told to sit on the floor behind her and put my hands on either side of her head, with my fingers holding her temples. I sit cross-legged on the floor, gently but firmly holding her head steady and upright until someone comes in two hours to relieve me.

Holding the flashlight was the easy part. It is more challenging holding a head steady for two hours. It is an inner room, so I can't look out of the window and see the Ganges. Isn't now is a good time to do silent *mantra* repetition, to close my own eyes and watch my mind trying to escape from boredom? I tell myself that this could well be a woman from the village on the backside of the mountain who took the trouble to make us a cup of tea. This is the very least I can do to repay the kindness.

After a week when the Eye Camp is over, Dr. Adhvaryoo gives *Raja Yoga* classes, to our small group of foreigners, every afternoon in Gurudev's kutir. He is well versed in the teachings of sage Patanjali and we attend for several days. There is always something to learn from somebody in Sivananda Ashram!

WALKING THE PILGRIM TRAIL AND OTHER EVENTS

*Dr. Adhvaryoo, Swami Chidananda and Swami Dayananda
walking between the Press Building
and the Samadhi Shrine*

BIRTHDAY AND GRADUATION

In April I turn twenty-five and Swami Chidanandaji gives me a stack of Gurudev's books, including, *Thought Power, Ten Upanishads, Fourteen Lessons in Raja Yoga*. He signs and dates each of the nine books and in some writes a little birthday message— "Many Happy Returns. God Bless You!" At this time the quality of the paper of the books printed in the Ashram Press is rather rough. The font letters are set by hand and sometimes mistakenly placed, and the photographs are not always as sharp as they could be. However, because they are Gurudev's books and because Swamiji has taken the trouble to sign and date them, to me they are worth their weight in gold.

When monks take the vow of renunciation and become *sannyasins*, they immerse themselves in the Ganges three times to signify leaving their old life behind. From then on, they do not celebrate birthdays, because the beginning of their new life is considered their *real* birth date. Swami Sivananda, however, started the tradition of celebrating the birthdays of Swami Chidanandaji and Swami Krishnanandaji and it is the wish of the devotees to continue this tradition. Moreover, the *ashram's* annual "Spiritual Calendar" is full of days of celebration of saints and sages and incarnations of God, like Mahavir, Buddha, Krishna, Rama, Chaitanya Mahaprabhu, Jesus Christ, and others. In addition, each day of the week is dedicated to an aspect of God—Thursday to the *guru*, Friday to the Divine Mother, and so on. The calendar has important solar days, like *Maha Shankranti* in January, which, for Hindus, is when the sun begins its summer path and the days get longer.

Consequently, almost every day in the *ashram* there is something important to celebrate. So, the atmosphere is often festive and the celebrations all turn our minds towards God. Though daily life is spare and disciplined and there are no luxuries in the worldly sense, there is a wonderful feeling of joy that permeates the place. There is no sense of dreariness and drudgery in the spiritual life envisioned by Swami Sivananda and his disciples! The teachings are not based on punishment and guilt. They are based on the highest spiritual experience of Gurudev Sivananda, of Swami Chidananda and Swami Krishnananda, and what other great souls have realized through their own *sadhana*. The teachings are based on the truth of *Vedanta*, which says our essential nature is divine. So, whenever we see one of these great beings, we feel our hearts being lifted, as they constantly remind us of who we really are—sparks of Divinity! It is ignorance of our true nature that keeps us in bondage. All the practices are to help us peel away the layers of ignorance and all the celebrations are to remind us, in Swami Sivananda's words, that "The goal of life is God-realization!" How liberating it is to realize that all the mistakes of the past are due to ignorance.

If the monks have relinquished their birthdays, we householders have not. Still, I am surprised when Swami Chidananda mentions in the *satsang* that evening that it is my birthday, saying that I am one of the aspirants who is "rocketing towards the goal." I can't believe my ears! Wow! I didn't know I was *rocketing*! It feels more like I'm just putting one foot in front of the other. I am wary of compliments that boost my ego. However, Swamiji is a great encourager and I figure if he says I am "rocketing," then I better redouble my efforts and live up to his description!

Don has secretly been to the tailor's in Rishikesh to have a *kurta* top and matching pants made, which he presents me for my birthday. It is the first set of north-Indian style clothes that I wear. I gave away my dark blue dress with red hibiscus print, which I wore for months over long pants, to the sweeper woman. After a few days, I saw her young daughter wearing the Hawaiian print. She was smaller than I and her mother had cleverly cut the dress and made a top with long sleeves. It pleases me that nothing is wasted here.

In May, after our final exam, we graduate from our five months course in *Vedanta*. A little ceremony takes place where Swami Tejomayananda reads out our grades from the highest to the lowest and Swami Chidananda hands out diplomas of completion to all of us students. It says we are *Yogacharyas, graduates of the Yoga Vedanta Forest Academy*. Because I love *Vedanta*, I actually study before the exam and receive a good grade. Don doesn't do so well on the final exam. Languages do not come easily to him. On the last question, when asked to describe the *Atman*, he chooses to do a drawing of a burning candle radiating light. I think it is a beautifully artistic way of describing the individual spirit, something that is almost indescribable anyway, but Swami Tejomayananda is not able to think outside the box. He regards Don's drawing as some kind of flippant or disrespectful answer. He doesn't get it and gives Don a poor grade.

CHAPTER 9

PUNJAB TOUR

AN INVITATION

Swamiji is to travel to the northwest of India to visit devotees and give some programs in the Punjab. The secretary of the Divine Life Society, Swami Premananda, a slight man, with small hands and feet, long hair, a beard and a mustache, will be accompanying him. Once a week in the evening satsang, Swami Premananda extolls the glories of Lord Rama from *Ramacharitamanas*, the scripture describing the story of Rama. His lectures are mainly in Hindi, so we don't understand them, but we always enjoy the chant at the end of his talk, "*Jaya Siya Ram, Jaya Jaya Siya Ram!*" Swami Nadabrahmananda is also invited to go and he will provide the musical accompaniment during the public *satsangs*.

Nagaraj appears one morning at the door of our room and asks us if we would like to accompany Swamiji on his tour of the Punjab. "Yes, we would!" we say without hesitation. We will get to travel with Swamiji and see a part of India we haven't seen before. It takes us about ten minutes to pack and be ready. We have few clothes and travel so light, that each of us has just one small carry bag, which we sling over our shoulder. We are to meet Swamiji at the Haridwar train station and travel with the group in the overnight train. At some point, we will disembark and travel the rest of the way by car.

Don and I travel to Dehra Dun by taxi with Swami Nadabrahmananda and one of his music students, Seshikant, a young man dressed in white. Swamis Chidananda, Premananda, and Swamiji's assistant will join the train before it reaches Haridwar. The Swamis are travelling in first class and Seshikant is with us in second. Haridwar is the holy town about thirteen miles downriver from Rishikesh. It is one of the sacred locations where the *Kumbhamela*, a massive gathering of devotees, is held every twelve years. Every evening, a special *arati* is offered to the Ganga by the temple priest, who waves a many-tiered oil lamp of 108 wicks, each with its little flame, making an impressive light. Hundreds of devotees, chanting a hymn praising the holy river, gather beside and on the bridge where the *arati* is performed.

From the train station we cannot see the river, but many pilgrims returning from the Holy Ganga Bathing Day Festival, climb aboard. The carriage is packed with people, on the seats, on the floor, and leaning on each other's shoulders. Despite the crowd, we feel so happy to be traveling with Swami Chidananda's party. Knowing that we are on the same train makes all the discomfort and fatigue of no consequence, as if we are riding a wave of higher consciousness. Don sits across from me and Seshikant has fallen asleep with his head on my shoulder. For a minute I think, *Oh no! Monks are not supposed to touch women. What shall I do? Shall I push him off?* But then I realize he's fast asleep and it would be silly to disturb him. So, we travel on into the night.

At about 2 a.m. the train halts at Ambala Cantonment, an army encampment from eighty years ago when India was still under British rule. The train wheels screech and Seshikant sits up. "Oh, I slept well," he says. "You reminded me of my elder sister, when I was a boy." We disembark and meet the Swamis on the platform.

"Did you have a comfortable journey?" Swamiji asks quietly.

"Yes thank you, Swamiji." We haven't slept a wink but there is no reason to complain.

We follow, as our party moves into the former British first-class waiting room, to rest for a couple of hours. The room, which seems to be reserved for us, is quite stark with walls and floor of grey marble. We watch Swamiji place a small pillow at one end of a wooden bench. His actions are careful and deliberate. He spreads his large orange towel over the bench, lies down, and pulls a shawl over him. Then we all find places to lie down and rest for a few hours. I listen to sounds outside the waiting room, of voices calling in Hindi, steam trains chugging in and out of the station and I finally fall asleep.

At dawn, hundreds of birds that are roosting under the eaves of the station roof wake us with their chirping and beating of wings, as they take off into the sky. Swamiji washes his hands and face in the sink and then sits cross-legged on his bench, facing the wall. He lights one stick of incense and does a silent *puja* with intense concentration. All of us, his traveling companions, stop what we are doing and watch with rapt attention as he moves the incense stick in a slow circle. It makes me think of the nameless, formless Absolute, the essence of God. Then Swamiji closes his eyes and meditates for a short time. None of us moves until he has finished.

After that, Swamiji fills one large thermos flask with hot tea, prepared in the station tearoom and a smaller one with heated milk. He tears a half sheet out of last night's newspaper, making sure it's not the page with all the news headlines and wraps a small quantity of sugar in it. He is set for the journey. We climb into a green jeep waiting outside. Don and I are in front with the driver, and Swamis Chidananda, Premananda, and Nadabrahmananda in the back seat. Behind them is our host, whose name, if I hear right, is Mr. Gilhotra. We travel through the countryside on a narrow, bumpy road with a lot of buffalo cart traffic coming and going.

Swami Premananda leans over the front seat and asks, "Why does a driver never have an accident with a donkey or a buffalo?" We think it's some kind of a joke question, so wait for the punch line. "They have no mind," he says, "and so the driver always has to stop and slow down for them." He cackles at his own answer and elaborates further. "If one person is a fool, then there can never be an accident, because the other can always maneuver around him. It's only when two minds come together that there is conflict." He is on a roll and continues philosophizing. "If the disciple surrenders himself completely, the *guru* will quickly and easily guide him towards the light. But when the disciple is full of ego and mind, progress is slow."

Even if I had anything to say, I am too self-conscious with Swami Chidananda sitting behind us, to make a comment. Don doesn't say anything either. After two hours, we stop on the road for Swamiji to have a cup of tea from his thermoses. We are near a farm out in the country, with a couple of low cement buildings surrounded by fields. The farmer comes over and greets the Swamis, who are all out of the vehicle stretching their legs. I whisper to Don, "I have to go to the bathroom." And I get out of the jeep and begin looking for what might be a bathroom. The farmer sees me looking for something, but he speaks no English. Finally, he understands and leads me behind one of the cement buildings. There is no bathroom. What was I thinking? At this time public toilets in India are few and far between. And in the rural areas, even an outhouse would be a luxury. The farmer and his family probably just use the outdoors. So, after he leaves, I go in the field.

FUNCTIONS, LUNCHEONS AND BLISS

We continue traveling westward toward Jabalpur in the Punjab. The monsoons haven't come yet and the countryside is dry. The roadside, however, is lined with beautiful flowering trees with orange colored blossoms and camels pulling carts. We are about two hours late in arriving at our destination, where a large crowd has been waiting for *darshan* of Swami Chidananda. A cry of joy goes up from the crowd as soon as they catch a glimpse of Swamiji. "Satguru Swami Chidananda Maharaj ki Jai! Swami Sivananda Maharaj ki Jai!"

The procession starts as soon as we get out of the jeep. Swami Chidananda is garlanded first and then the other Swamis. Then, the organizers of the tour come and garland us. This is the Indian custom. Anyone travelling with the honored guest is also shown respect and honor. Boxes of sweets are offered and marigold flowers are tossed towards Swamiji from bystanders in the crowd. We are taken to the Government Rest House where our party occupies all the rooms.

Functions follow in one long, continuous stream of speeches, *kirtan*, talks, walks, lunches and dinners. Everything is *satsang* when Swami Chidananda is present. Most of the talks are in Hindi, and while many of the words and phrases are beginning to sound familiar, we don't know what they mean. But Swamiji's vibration is so strong and his thoughts so powerful that when he speaks, I seem to get the meaning on a non-verbal level, which may be deeper than the words themselves.

We must look quite shabby in our *khadi* cloth pajama outfits, because the hosts decide we need dressing up a bit. They present Don with a long Indian shirt made of fine cotton with a high collar, and me with a yellow striped sari and blouse. I feel like a doll they are trying to dress as they help me wind the sari around my waist. But their intention is generous, so I just succumb to their will and try to be pleasant. I think of what Swamiji goes through in order to please his devotees. The sari material is full of starch and I feel like a yellow cream puff at the next function in a big outdoor tent, where we have to walk to the stage in front of the audience. I keep my eyes down on the ground until we are settled. I seem to be in a constant state of self-analysis, watching my mind and observing my ego. I find I am at ease with Seshikant, who is natural and cheerful, like a younger brother.

At one of the lunches, we are sitting cross-legged on the floor opposite Swamiji, who is giving us a very funny demonstration of how Indians say, "No," when what they really mean is, "Yes." Swamiji looks up at the imaginary server with big eyes and shakes his head, "No," while over his plate he waggles two long fingers, meaning, "Give me two more." Then he says, "No," again, but holds his hands up high enough, so that the server can put some more chapattis on his plate. Swamiji is a natural actor and storyteller. His eyes and expressions are hilarious and we all laugh. I am seated between Don and Seshikant and we are all laughing together. Then I imitate Swamiji, and Don and Seshi laugh again.

The next day when I ask where Seshikant is. I am told that Swamiji had some work for him back at the *ashram* and so he was sent back. The thought crosses my mind that is because of me that he has been sent back. Perhaps I was acting too familiar by Indian standards. We were laughing together. Maybe I was being too open and friendly. We have different standards of behavior in the West, and what would be considered innocent friendliness in one context might be construed as inappropriate in another. No one says anything to me about the incident, so it could be that my imagination is working overtime. Maybe it has nothing to do with me and he really was sent back to do some work.

One afternoon in the Government Rest House, I am so tired of being surrounded by people, I just want to get away and be alone. Don is busy writing in his sketchbook. I walk outside and go around the house until I come to a small covered verandah at the top of three steps. A three-foot wall surrounds it on two sides and a closed door leading into the house on the third side. Hoping no one will open the door, I sit down on the polished cement floor and close my eyes. My head is barely visible above the wall. *Maybe no one will see me. I will just hide here for a while.* I am immediately drawn deeply within and feel an enveloping sense of peace. The peace gives way to blissful awareness. What a relief to be able to retreat within myself! It is the first time in all twenty-six years of my life that I have ever experienced bliss and now I know what the *yogis* mean when they say our true nature is *Sat-chid-ananda*—existence, consciousness, bliss. Suddenly, all the lectures on *Vedanta* make sense. The concept of the three bodies and the five sheaths enters my mind[22] and I realize I have fallen deep into myself. The senses have automatically drawn themselves in, like a tortoise retracting its head and legs. I feel I am getting a glimpse of my essential nature that Swamiji describes in so many ways. It is a revelation to truly know from experience that happiness is not dependent on anything from outside. It is inside us all along! Now I understand what Jesus meant when he said, "The kingdom of heaven is within." This experience releases me on a deep level, undercutting the incessant cravings of the mind with the clear realization that contentment and peace are not connected to acquisition of objects. This bliss is within each and every one of us, like a buried treasure, waiting to be discovered. Yet how many of us live our lives without even knowing it is there? Through the study of *Vedanta* we are told of its existence, but I couldn't begin to imagine how to reach it on my own. I am so grateful for this experience, which I know is a gift of Swamiji's grace that opens a door for me when I least expect it. While I was merely seeking solitude I didn't know I would meet my real Self for the first time!

HINDU REVIVAL

My heart is beginning to open and I realize that the *guru* is actually my own Self. I have caught a glimpse of an internal mystery of communion, of how it is possible for my soul to commune with what is called the Supreme Soul. It's hard to put it into words, because even the word *soul* is hard to define. It seems like an intangible essence of my being, which is not different from the way I experience the *guru*. In meditation this realization is possible, but outwardly our individual roles are resumed. However, just knowing that this exists imparts a deeper meaning to my life.

---

[22] The physical body (*sthula sarira*) of gross matter contains the food sheath (*annamaya kosha*), and the vital sheath (*pranamaya kosha*). Invisible within the gross body is the subtle body (*suksma sarira*), comprised of the mental sheath (*manomaya kosha*), and the intellectual sheath (*vijnanamaya kosha*). Of finer energy than the subtle body and residing within it is the causal body (*karana sarira*), made of the *anandamaya kosha*, the bliss sheath. Beyond these five sheaths is what is known as the atman, the spirit, or pure awareness.

Don and I accompany the Swamis to a morning *satsang*, where a gathering of about two thousand devotees is sitting under a large *pandal*. *What am I doing here at this Hindu Revival meeting?* Don and I are sitting up on the stage to one side, with Swami Nadabrahmananda and the musical instruments, while Swami Chidananda, who is the main speaker, is seated front and center. Swamiji is speaking in Hindi or some other language we don't understand and I can't help thinking how strange this is! It is as if the past has fallen away, all preconceptions dropped and I am looking for a connection in the present. I wonder if Don is having a similar experience.

I look out over the sea of faces and begin to think of the *Virat*, which we have learned in *Vedanta* class is the aspect of God as the sum total of all physical bodies. First, I notice hundreds of pairs of dark eyes. Then, I see many heads with black hair, all seeming to be part of the same body—a moving, living being. Each individual, including myself, is part of this body, as if somehow, those seated in the *pandal* represent the entire human race housed under the billowing, breathing tent. None of us exists outside of our humanity. According to *Vedanta*, we are one vast humanity, "the One which is greater than the Many, yet the Many, no less than the One."

I look at Swamiji's slender figure and see the form of a Hindu monk speaking passionately about God to the people seated before him. My mind objectively wonders about my connection to all this. *What is my connection to Swamiji? How does it work?* The next moment I am flooded with a strong feeling of his spiritual presence, and how powerful is the flow of spirit coming through him. It is quite overwhelming and glorious and all doubts about my relationship with him drop away, because, even though it is strange and unfamiliar, it feels intuitively right.

One day Don and I go with Swami Premananda to an outdoor gathering and I am called upon to give an *asana* demonstration to the ladies. At this time in India, very few women practice yoga *asanas*. It is considered something that is exclusively for men. There is no training that I know of for women; no yoga classes for them, and only a few women take physical fitness seriously. Not expecting to be doing *asanas*, I am dressed in my long

Malaysian batik cloth, wrapped around my waist and coming to my ankles, with a long-sleeved matching top. It must look really odd for a skinny Western woman to be demonstrating the peacock pose in clothes totally inappropriate for the activity! In some ways I feel like we are being shown off to the devotees as an example of how yoga draws people from as far away as the West.

On the last night in the town of Bhatinda, we are once again up on the stage during evening *satsang* and Swami Chidananda begins to sing a *bhajan*. Swami Nadabrahmananda, who is accompanying him on the harmonium, reaches over and taps me on the leg, signaling me to play the pair of *tabla* drums wrapped in a blanket near me. The *tabla* set belongs to another drummer and I can't imagine why Swami Nadabrahmananda wants me to play them. But I follow his lead and obediently begin to play, *Dha-Ghi-Natin-Naka-Dhina*, a basic four-four beat. I try several times to catch Swami Chidananda's rhythm, but he has his own tempo and after the fifth attempt, I give up. The other *tabla* player climbs quickly onto the stage, takes the *tabla*, seats himself, raises his hands to play and just at that moment, Swamiji stops singing. The audience, who has been following this little scenario with interest, breaks into stifled giggles. Swamiji has his eyes closed, but I detect a smile at the end of his song. I am not embarrassed, because it is Swami Nadabrahmananda who is trying to show me off, to show what I have learned, which turns out to be not much. So it is funny, but the joke's on him!

As his music student, Swami Nadabrahmananda always supports and stands up for me, whether it is in music, sketching, or *asana* demonstration. He sometimes calls me "Mooji," "ji" being the suffix added to names to denote affection. While we are in the Punjab, Swami Nadabrahmananda has his seventy-fifth birthday, which seems to me like a ripe old age. He is an amazing example of how yoga can keep one youthful! I've never seen him ruffled in the slightest. He is always calm and easy and doesn't mind being teased, taking everything in good humor. Originally, he is from

South India, but his face looks almost Tibetan. His teeth are perfect and he doesn't use eyeglasses.

"Swamiji, how do you keep so healthy?" I ask him.

Swami Nadabrahmananda
on his 75th Birthday

"No worries." he replies. "You see, every family, every day, a list," he continues in his broken English. "Want rice, want *rotis*, want this, or that. Long list. I—no wants." Each day he wakes at 4 a.m. and plays his music, his offering to God. For half an hour he plays the *tabla* without breathing, without winking, with his eyes fixed on his *Ishta*, a picture of Siva. He has brought along his special pair of *tabla* on tour, which I played during the program, but when I ask if I can practice on them, he says, "I never not give my *tabla*." So, I have to be content with practicing on a table, or the wooden arms of a chair.

ASANAS AND ARRANGED MARRIAGE

After four or five days, Swami Chidananda leaves the Punjab tour to travel elsewhere in India. We are not informed where he is going and we don't feel it is our place to ask. Don and I continue on with Swami Nadabrahmananda and Swami Premananda who has a number of devotees in the Punjab. Once our central focus, Swami Chidananda, is gone our tour is a lot less interesting. But we are learning how our attitude influences our state of mind. We are learning that likes and dislikes push and pull our minds from side to side, but if we surrender to the flow of events, all goes smoothly. As Westerners we hold some interest for the Indians, especially the young ones. So if our hosts seem to be using us to promote the program, then who are we to say that we are not right where we should be at this moment? I wonder if I will ever know what God's will is.

We arrive in the town of Fazilka and are driven to another *asana* demonstration and then on to a devotee's home. In the car of our host, Mr. Gilhotra, we occupy the back seat with Swami Nadabrahmananda, and Swami Premananda is cracking jokes with our host in the front. My eyes settle on the little boy doll hanging from the rear vision mirror, along with a drying flower garland. In *Vedanta*, one of the Sanskrit terms for the mind is *antahkarana*, or the inner instrument, which interfaces with and reflects the world around us. According to *Vedanta*, the world we see is an illusion or a dream, and when the reality is seen behind the appearance, it is like waking up from the dream. The world seems so real to us, but we are told that it is the power of *maya* that keeps us clinging to the illusion that what we see is real. It is not that the outer world doesn't exist. It is that the power of *maya* keeps us from seeing the One Reality that supports and sustains the multiplicity of names and forms. The power of *maya* keeps us in a constant state of separateness, unable to experience the unity of which we are an indivisible part. The doll swinging back and forth with his mind-mirror on his head reflecting the world in it, reminds me that my purpose is to become free from this illusion.

On the 26th April, we travel through this northwestern province of India and arrive at Miss Sharma's primary school in Jallalabad, where we are to give an *asana* demonstration to the children. It impresses me how Indian children are so disciplined and well behaved and learn to sit quietly from a very early age. Even though we are up on a raised platform above the children, we are not there to give a lecture. We choose to demonstrate the animal poses to make it fun for them —the fish, cat, cobra, peacock, crow, etcetera, and then some others that they can relate to, like the bridge, plough, and the tree. I make eye contact and smile at a little girl in the front row. She is embarrassed and sinks slowly out of sight under the platform where I can't see her any more. It would have been much more fun for them if we had asked them to stand up and join in, but we don't think of it until later.

Afterwards, we travel to Faridpur and stay in a devotee's home overnight. Nirmala, the sister of our host, approaches me shyly with broken English. She is twenty years old and in her third year of a co-ed college.

"Do you like your studies?" I ask.

"Yes, I like my studies," she replies, "but the boys are too rough." She has been brought up strictly, in traditional Indian culture, where boys' and girls' high schools are separate. I can relate to this, as it was the same for me growing up in colonial British South Africa. Despite the distraction of the boys in the college, she has developed a thirst for knowledge and she aspires to continue her studies.

"How many years left do you have to finish?" I ask.

"One more year," she says, "but they don't want me to go any more." She tells me that the elders in the family are afraid that if she continues to study, she might grow "too clever" or wise for her position in society, which will be as a wife, daughter-in-law and most likely, a mother.

"What about you?" she asks. "What is your life in America like?"

"We both finished University," I say, "and now we have come to practice yoga and study *Vedanta* with the *yogis*." I can't possibly tell her how much freedom of choice we have in the States. I don't want to add to her unhappiness.

"I don't want to get married," she whispers, "but my parents compel me."

"And if you tell them you don't want to?" I ask, "Wouldn't they listen?"

"They will compel me and I have to obey," she says, with quiet desperation. She uses the word "compel" a lot. "They want me to marry," she adds, "because I am a burden to them."

"Can you choose whom you will marry?" I ask, hoping I am not interfering in their family affairs.

"They have decided already," she says, miserably. "When he comes here, I hide in my room. I don't want to meet him. I am so ashamed."

"But you haven't done anything wrong!" I say, in her defense. I really feel sorry for her. While arranged marriages are traditional in India, the bride or the groom can refuse to accept who is chosen for them if they really don't like the choice. But, that is only if the parents are lenient and honor their children's input regarding the match. It seems Nirmala has no say in the matter at all. She is just expected to obey whatever the elders arrange.

"After marriage, I will first go to the home of my mother and father-in-law for some time and then I will return to live with my husband." Her eyes look so lonely and sad. Her future will be what others have chosen for her.

"Sometimes your kind of marriage works better than ours," I say, trying to cheer her up. I see a flicker of interest in her dark eyes.

"But there is love," she says, not quite a question.

"Marriage for love doesn't always last." I say. "There's lots of divorce in our country. If you are lucky, love might grow between you." It is time for us to go and Nirmala and I give each other a hug. I give her my pen and she gives me a light cotton shawl. "I will remember you always and pray for your happiness," I say, and we part friends.

As we travel by overnight train back to the *ashram*, I realize that while I feel at home in India, the culture has customs that if I applied them to myself, would make me feel constrained. While arranged marriages seem to work surprisingly well for Indians, I am glad that in the West we are allowed, for better or worse, to make our own choice. Don and I have chosen each other. Then again, perhaps our cultures are not so different after all. When I look back over the events of the past four years since I began looking for "a wise person," I wonder *who is it that really chooses?* As I lie in my berth listening to the train wheels clacking over the joints in the tracks, I wonder if it was *my* choices that led me to Swamiji. Or did the universe, in some mysterious way, bring me to him? Perhaps it is both working together.

CHAPTER 10

SUMMER BY THE GANGES

THE GUARD

As the weather warms towards summer, a French doctor, working in India for the World Health Organization, visits the *ashram* and spends some time in the hospital seeing patients. He offers to give Swami Chidananda a B12 injection to boost his immune system. Swamiji accepts and receives the injection.

Don and I become friendly with the doctor who is only staying for a week. He is traveling in India in a Volkswagen Combi van and invites us to go with him to visit the holy cave of Vashishta Guha. We have had no transportation to go there before and we are eager to see this holy spot. The three of us set off early one afternoon, with his driver at the wheel. The road through the *ashram* is the main road leading north up to the border with Tibet, a country that the Chinese are in the process of appropriating by force. India has given asylum to thousands of Tibetan refugees fleeing the violence, including the Dalai Lama, who has taken up residence in Dharmsala, in the mountains northwest of Rishikesh.

Often, the Indian army posts an armed soldier on the bridges over the rivers, guarding against possible suspicious looking vehicles coming down from the mountains. The road to the cave crosses one bridge along the way, as it winds along the north side of the Ganges, climbing and dipping into the folds of the foothills. There are so many curves in the road that by the time we reach the destination, I feel quite carsick and have to sit on a rock until my dizziness and nausea subside.

The driver stays with the van at the top of the hill and we make our way along a well-worn path, past a garden planted with papaya and banana trees, with steps leading down to a sandy beach. A small temple has been built on a raised area and we go there to leave a donation in a secure metal box. A caretaker looks after the cave, keeping the area swept and the oil lamp lit. He makes sure we remove our sandals and leave them outside the cave entrance.

Vashishta was a famous sage of ancient India, the *guru* of Lord Rama. The *Yoga Vashishta* is a scripture dealing with many levels of consciousness, describing in great detail the instructions and teachings that Vashishta gives to young Rama at a critical time, when he is seeking clarification as to his role and purpose in life. Vashishta Guha is the cave where sage Vashishta is said to have lived and meditated and therefore is considered to be a very sacred place. The entrance to the cave is at ground level, leading straight into the side of a steep cliff, covered with scrubby trees and thick vines. Inside, it is narrow and pitch dark, except for the tiniest of lights at the far end. In single file we make our way carefully forward, shuffling our bare feet on the earth floor. As we approach the oil lamp, we see it sits on a rough altar, a natural rock formation at the end of the cave. We are under the hill in a narrow space and we sit down on the floor. It is very cool in the cave and utterly quiet. Not a sound from outside reaches my ears.

Gradually, my eyes adjust to the light of the oil lamp and I am able to see Don and the doctor sitting very close across from me. I close my eyes and enjoy the deep peace that surrounds and envelops me. My mind seems to drop away and I hear the sound of my own breath. Later, when I open my eyes, I am surprised how much light is actually coming in from the cave entrance. Don and the doctor get up and begin making their way out. I bow to the light of the lamp in front of me and follow them.

Leaving our sandals at the cave, we pick our way over and through huge pinkish boulders down to the river's edge. The water is clean and clear and we dip our hands and feet in it. I take a sip from the palm of my hand and sprinkle water over my head, feeling blessed. On the other side of the river I can see the old pilgrim trail where Don and I walked up to Phul Chatty. I take a deep breath of the afternoon air and sit down on a warm boulder with my feet in the water. I spy a rounded stone near me and turn it over in my hands. One half of it is light grey and the other a pale purple, with a zigzag dark line circling the middle. It is a perfect microcosm of the sky and earth, split by the shaded, undulating river in the middle. I keep this stone as a souvenir of this sacred place.

We clamber back over the boulders to our sandals and make our way up to the road, where the driver waits with the van. Feeling happy and refreshed, the doctor opens the sliding roof and we all stand up with our heads and shoulders sticking out of the top of the van, enjoying the fresh air. The driver does a U-turn and motors back down the road. As the van approaches the bridge, we see the guard standing, holding the barrel of his rifle with the butt resting on the ground. He looks up, surprised to see the three of us sticking out of the van's roof. As our vehicle slows to pass him, we all bring our hands together in traditional *pranam* greetings. The guard's automatic response is to *pranam* back to us. He lets go of his rifle while bringing his hands together and then leaps forward to catch it. We burst out laughing and wave to him as our van passes. Is it only in India that this would happen? This is not just a polite response. It is a long-standing cultural belief passed down from ancient times, that the same light of God dwells in each of us. How different would the world be, if soldiers dropped their weapons in order to greet strangers?

SUMMER HEAT

Don purchases a mosquito net for me, which I string up in the room, the net draping down to the red cement floor. As the weather grows warmer in May and June, to keep cool, I sleep directly on the cement floor under the net. I never get bitten, but every morning, I find two or three bed bugs up in the corners of the net where they have climbed during the night. I catch them in my fingers and throw them over the balcony of our shared verandah.

A helpful swami in the next block gives us a little electric stove to use. The electric plug-in, one-burner stove consists of one electric wire coil laying in a spiral groove of a ceramic or asbestos plate, supported by four metal legs. The thin wire coil, heated to red-hot, often melts and breaks. We unplug it, let it cool, and hook the wire back together for another try. It is quite primitive, but enough heat to boil water for tea and sometimes a few vegetables. Nearly everyday Swami Chidanandaji sends a young boy to our door with a handful of vegetables for us.

During these hot, dry months of summer, before the coming of the monsoon rains, we are told that if we hang a damp towel over the bars of the windows, it will help to cool the air in our room on the upper floor. The afternoon sun is especially hot, and the damp towel hardly makes any difference. The heat makes it difficult to study and when I sit for meditation, perspiration trickles down my face and into my eyes.

"Why don't we just stay up all night, when it's cooler?" Don suggests.

"What? And sleep during the day?"

"I think most people are taking an afternoon nap, aren't they?" Don asks. It is true that the *ashram* gets quiet in the heat of the afternoon and it is only around 3 p.m. when the afternoon tea is brought around, that we see the monks coming out of their rooms. As soon as we get the chance, we tell Swamiji of our proposed plan. He is adamantly opposed to it.

"No, no, no! You mustn't sleep during the day!" he says. "You would lay yourself open to *tamasic* forces if you sleep during the day."

According to the practice of yoga, explained in the *Bhagavad Gita*, nature is made up of three major forces or qualities, called *gunas*—*tamas*, the dark force of inertia, lethargy, and dullness; *rajas*, the dynamic force of restlessness and passion, which propels us to action; and *sattva*, the purest and most sublime force, which leads us to higher levels of consciousness. As human beings, we are always subject to all three forces and during the course of the day and night one of them is always predominant. As spiritual seekers, we try to use the energy of *rajas* to overcome the drag of *tamas* and eventually, with practice, we aspire for *sattva* to become predominant in our nature. Ultimately, all the *gunas*, even *sattva*, are to be transcended. In the *Gita* it refers to a liberated being as *gunatita*, one who has transcended the three *gunas* and is no longer ruled by them.

When we hear Swamiji's emphatic reaction to our suggestion, we immediately abandon the idea of staying up at night and sleeping during the day and continue our practices regardless of the heat.

During the summer monsoon season, we often carry umbrellas to the evening *satsang*, which is held outside by the Sivananda Pillar if the weather is fine, or if it rains, under the long roof of the open causeway. Occasionally, one of the free roaming cows wanders up to the gathering where the devotees sit with their backs against the low wall. The cow stretches its neck over the wall and rests its head on someone's shoulder. Animals like to attend *satsang* too and, just like us, wait for the *prasad* at the end.

One night, a dog with a deep, festering, and smelly wound begins making its way into the ladies section. The ladies across from me hold their saris over their faces, gasping and leaning as far away as they can from the dog. Thinking I am doing them a favor, I hold my closed umbrella in front of the dog to stop him moving forward into the group. At that moment, Swamiji looks up and sees me holding my umbrella in front of the dog. He gives me such a fierce, piercing look, which communicates unequivocally, "Don't try to prevent him! He is as welcome here as anyone!" I immediately put the umbrella down, but the poor, smelly creature gives up and walks slowly away. In Swamiji's compassionate heart, all sick animals are to cared for and nursed back to health, not driven away.

During the day, Swamiji is often seen walking around the *ashram*, attending *pujas*, giving darshan, checking on new building projects, or what is being printed in the Sivananda Press. Sometimes he sits under the tree in the courtyard where devotees gather in the open. One sunny morning we are walking with Swamiji down the steps from the Vishwanath Mandir. On the bottom step a puppy is stretched out in the sun like a little sphinx.

"You see, they also have their grandeur," Swamiji remarks, bending down to stroke the puppy's head. Then a few other puppies run over to where the attention is and begin playfully gnawing on their brother. "Enough! Enough!" Swamiji admonishes and they all race over to their mother, who is drinking water out of a bowl by the central water tap. They reach up and start feeding from her teats. Swamiji points out, "Look! They have a built in mess hall and kitchen supply. Isn't nature wonderful!"

STRESS CRACKS

If you've ever shared a small room with anyone for ten months, you will know that no matter how committed you are to the relationship, you will need your own space. Don and I use silence, not as a weapon against each other, but as protective cloak, which we can wrap ourselves in. We read and study, write or draw in our spare time, none of which require talking. It is an easy silence and we often break it to share what we are drawing or reading with each other. When he isn't doing art, Don is working on a field theory which he began developing in college, at Pratt Institute in Brooklyn, about how the universe is structured. He calls it Universal Structure Theory and Swamiji encourages him to continue working on it.

After I start to take *tabla* lessons from Swami Nadabrahmananda, I practice in the room at least half and hour every day. Don seems to like that I am learning a musical instrument. He expresses an interest in learning to play the *sitar*, but I don't really think he is that serious.

In the afternoons at about 3 p.m. we get up and stretch.

"Let's go for a walk after tea," I say and we take our plastic cups and wait downstairs by the courtyard for the *chai walla* to come around with the big teakettle.

However, as time goes on, cracks are beginning to form in our relationship. I know that Don is getting restless living in the *ashram* and every time he brings up the subject of "moving on," a knot of tension forms in my stomach. It seems to me that I have found what I am looking for, am fully immersed in this lifestyle and love every minute of it. Even hunger and ill health are not a deterrent to me. I try to imagine what my life would be like without Don around and know it wouldn't be easy. It is a male-dominated community after all, and as a married woman I am accepted, but as a single woman, perhaps I would not be as welcome.

One day we are walking along the upper path through the forest, Don suddenly says, "I've gotta get out of here!" I feel my body contract with anxiety. I know something is going to change and I will have to make a decision whether to stay, or go with him.

"Your antennae are tuned towards Swami Chidananda," Don says to me. It is true and perhaps I am not paying enough attention to him. But in my view we are both partners in this journey from the "lower self to the higher Self" and that Swamiji is there to guide us through our struggle. The problem arises when one of us finds it easier and makes faster progress than the other. At this point, we are such neophytes we don't understand that realization is not about getting anything for oneself. It is only by getting rid of thoughts and emotions that are dragging us down, that we might succeed in getting a glimpse of a more liberated existence. All our *sadhana* practices are done to purify the mind. They are not ends in themselves.

About this time our student visas, good for six months, need to be reviewed and we ask to see Swamiji about renewing them. We are given a time to bring the visas and we climb the steps to Swamiji's kutir. Entering the long narrow room, we bow before him. After the visa discussion, Swamiji seems open to receive our questions about "personal matters." Don does all the talking.

"We seem to be progressing at different rates and heading in different directions," Don addresses Swamiji, clearly bothered. "Whenever Moo gets ahead, I have to battle that for a while."

I am shocked and just about to deny this, when Swamiji interjects, "Why does it have to be a battle?" His answer takes both of us by surprise. "It is useless to battle such a phenomena. Just accept it as a fact." He goes on to explain that it has nothing to do with this lifetime and how we conceive of ourselves now. "It is just the evolution of the soul," he says. Swamiji makes it seem so natural, as though it is just something that has happened over the process of many lifetimes and is nothing to be attached to or afraid of.

"Instead of battling, why not rejoice that your *karma* has thrown you together?" Swamiji asks. "If your marriage was done as a sacred act in the eyes of God, then there's no need to think that this sacred tie has to be renounced. On the contrary," he assures us, "the spiritual gains made by either of you should be shared as common property and should serve to take you higher, towards the goal of God-union. You must think of yourselves as a unit, not as separate."

I am so relieved by Swamiji's explanation and I glance at Don who is nodding his head also. All the tension is dissolved, for now.

Soon after this, Don has a couple of private interviews with Swamiji, in which Swamiji offers to send him, should he wish, for higher education to a university in India, to pursue his scientific studies. Swamiji offers to pay for this education and also to pay for a trip back to the States every couple of years, for Don to visit his family. Don tells me that during one of these interviews, he asks, "Swamiji, who *are* you?" Swamiji, seated on the floor at the end of his long verandah room, pointed immediately to the large photo of Gurudev Sivananda on the wall near him. "There was no hesitation in his action," Don says. "There was no doubt he meant that he and Sivananda are one and the same!"

Swamiji suggests that we go up to Barlowgunj, a village near Mussoorie, up in the mountains, where the *ashram* owns a small cottage. It is much cooler up there, away from the steamy heat of the monsoon. The view looking over the Mussoorie valley is beautiful and we stay in this rarefied atmosphere for two weeks, living in one side of the cottage. During the day we spend some time working on the *Adventure of Yoga*, an illustrated yoga book for children. In the other side of the cottage, Pundaji, the cook, lives with his family. He cooks one simple meal a day for us while we are there. It is very plain food, but my stomach is not functioning properly and I can hardly digest anything.

One Sunday afternoon, Pundaji and his family invite us to go for a walk with them down the mountain to another village. We accept their kind invitation, but after about fifteen minutes walking downhill, I realize that I am already fatigued and that if I keep going down, I will not have the energy to climb back up to the cottage. "I have to go back," I announce. They look surprised, but after a brief discussion, Don goes on with them and I make my way slowly back up the hill to rest. My energy is so low it is all I can do to get back to the cottage.

The change of scenery does us good, and thanks to Swamiji's generosity, it's refreshing for us to be on our own for a couple of weeks. I am crazy enough to think that we could actually be happy living up here indefinitely, above the clouds. But Don thinks I am unrealistic and he's probably right. After two weeks we return to the *ashram* and the heat of the foothills.

PAULA AND THE TONIC

Downstairs from Nagaraj lives an old lady of German origins, named Paula. She had immigrated to America and met Swami Chidananda in California, when he first visited the United States in 1959. Deeply attracted by Swamiji's kindness and humility, she left everything and came to live in India to be near Swamiji, whom she adores. She now appears old and dumpy, with short straight hair that looks like it needs washing. She wears

Western dresses with hem length below the knee and moves about slowly, tending to numerous mangy dogs, which share her room in Om Kutir. Perhaps that is why she looks unkempt and unhealthy. The ashramites understand and respect devotion to a *guru* and they accept her for who she is, without criticism. Sometimes I see her outside of the *kutir*, moving about slowly with a dog bowl in her hand.

My own health has begun to deteriorate even more and Swamiji sends me for a blood test to the doctor in Dehra Dun. Don does not think it important to accompany me and I don't really see the point either, especially since he is not helpful with anything having to do with blood. But, when I leave the doctor's office and come out onto the busy street, I feel light-headed and quickly sit down on the front steps so that I won't faint and fall into the road. I put my head down on my knees and sit there for a while, until I felt steady enough to walk to the bus station. Swamiji expects me to report to him on my return and when he finds out I have gone to the doctor's on my own, he is not pleased. Swamiji is a great proponent of *dharma* on all levels, in all stages of life. He considers it a husband's duty to accompany his wife to the doctor, if she is feeling sick.

When the blood test comes back it shows that I have hookworm, whipworm, and amoebas.

"Have you been walking barefoot?" Swamiji asks. His voice sounds stern. Many of the monks go barefoot, so I don't think he could possibly mind. One of the worms that showed up on the blood test often enters through the skin of the feet.

"Well, when we lived in South America, we did walk through the muddy fields with bare feet sometimes," I said, remembering a time when we had taken our shoes off and run through a farmer's field.

"There is some special medicine for that," Swamiji says. "It is very bitter. You will have to take a dose. This," he says, handing me a brown bottle of some sort of tonic for my liver, "you can take at any time."

"Thank you, Swamiji," I say. Once back in the room I read all the fine print on the bottle Swamiji has given me. I am surprised to find that one of the ingredients is liver extract.

"This isn't vegetarian!" I inform Don. "I wonder if Swamiji read the ingredients?"

"He must think it will be good for your health," Don answers without looking up.

"But I'm vegetarian!" I say. I am committed to a vegetarian diet and so I'm in a quandary about whether to take the medicine or not. The diet at the *ashram* is vegetarian, all the swamis are vegetarian, all the Hindu *yogis* and *yoginis* are vegetarian and Swamiji himself is vegetarian. And so am I! *So, why has he given me this non-vegetarian tonic? Maybe it's a test. He wants to see if I will break my vegetarian diet. Or, maybe he thinks when we are ill we should overlook such things and take what is good for us.* My mind spins with all kinds of possible scenarios, but it is hopeless to try to guess what Swamiji's intention is.

I put the bottle of extract on the shelf in our room and stare at it. I am happy that Swamiji has given me something that is good for my health. I am happy that he even thought of me. But, I just don't know what the right course of action is. I wish I had just accepted Swamiji's gift for my health and not scrutinized the label so carefully. I finally decide to think about it for a few days. I just can't bring myself to take the medicine containing liver extract and the bottle remains unopened on our shelf.

A few days later Swamiji is coming down his steps into the late afternoon shade of the courtyard. As usual, several devotees are gathered there to see him. When he spots me he says with a smile, "Have you taken the medicine I gave you?"

"No, Swamiji, I haven't taken it," I reply, my confusion returning.

"Can you send it back to me?" Swamiji asks casually, "There is someone else in need of it." *Of course! Medicines are hard to come by in these days of scarcity and are not to be wasted!*

I go back to the room immediately and fetch the bottle and hand it over to Nagaraj. "I made a terrible mistake," I confess. "I should have taken what Swamiji gave me as *prasad*! I shouldn't have bothered about the ingredients."

"No, it's alright," Nagaraj assures me, taking the bottle, "It's alright." But I suspect he's just trying to make me feel better.

A few days after the medicine incident, I am called to Swamiji's room for some reason. Paula is seated on a chair with her feet soaking in a basin of warm water. Swamiji is sitting cross-legged in front of her with a pair of nail scissors and a towel to dry her feet. Paula cannot reach her feet to cut her toenails and no one has volunteered to help her. So Swamiji, himself, is doing the service in a respectful and careful manner.

"Someone has sent me some packets of powdered soup from America," Paula is saying, happy to have her nails cut and even happier to have Swamiji's full attention. "Would you like to try some, Swamiji?" she asks.

"Oh, thank you," he answers courteously and distinctly, "But I have to be careful. I can't be sure they are vegetarian." As he says these words, he turns his head and gives me the sweetest smile. Then I know that whether I have done right or wrong regarding the bottle of tonic, all is forgiven. Swamiji has let me know, in his own way, that there is no blame.

BITTER MEDICINE

After the incident with the liver tonic, I vow that whatever Swamiji sends for me to consume, I will regard as *prasad* and I will take it without hesitation. I won't even read the label.

On Swamiji's instructions, one of the young *brahmacharis* who serves him gives me a stainless steel tumbler of Alcofiar medicine for the worms. I take a deep breath and glug down the entire amount without stopping. I feel like Siva drinking the poison! But I know it is for the ultimate health of my body. Later Swami Krishnananda questions me about the cure.

"So, you drank the medicine?"

"Yes, Swamiji. It was the most bitter thing I have *ever* tasted!" I shudder, just remembering it.

"That's the one!" he replies, pleased that I have taken the medicine. We are here at the *ashram* at the invitation of Swami Chidananda, but Swami Krishnananda is also concerned with our welfare in a detached and friendly way.

We are not the only ones the senior swamis take care of. Their concern is for everyone, visitors from abroad and inmates alike. They want us all to make use of the facilities that Gurudev created for seekers, so that we can all take full advantage and spend our time at the *ashram* fruitfully. The simple necessities of life, food and shelter are provided, so that we can dedicate our time to doing spiritual practices without worrying about where our next meal is coming from.

The senior swamis are quite familiar with the difficulty of doing *sadhana* when one's ill health is a constant distraction. Each of them has learned to live with their physical limitations as part of their practice and surrender. Swami Krishnananda suffers from chronic asthma and the climate of Uttarpradesh[23] is not at all conducive to his illness. Even though the winters do not usually dip below freezing, there is no heat in the cement buildings and no glass in the windows, so there is no way of getting warm except for bolting down the wooden shutters and wrapping ourselves in blankets and shawls. Summers are very hot and dry, with dust blowing in from the plains until July or August, when the monsoon rains come and turn the area between the green mountains into a steam bath. This makes a daily dip in the cool waters of the Ganges a special blessing. But by the time you have walked back up the hill, you're dripping with perspiration again. There is a month of pleasant spring weather in March and a mild fall in October and November, but the rest of the year is quite extreme.

Swami Chidananda has a delicate constitution and has to be very careful with his diet. He eats very lightly and fasts on water only every Ekadasi without exception. Ekadasi occurs on the eleventh day of every fortnight in the Hindu Lunar Calendar, which means it falls twice a month, on the

---

[23] Uttarpradesh is split off from Uttaranchal which is eventually renamed Uttarakhand.

waxing and waning phases of the moon. On Ekadasi, the rest of the *ashram* is free to fast as they please, but generally fruits and milk are allowed, or some vegetables, but rice and *chapatti* are not cooked or served.

The diet and the climate are hard on everyone and my health is already compromised with amoebic hepatitis from living in Ecuador. Besides the worms, the blood work report shows my red blood cells are approximately 33% low and the Hemoglobin is 20% low. Don calls the Peace Corps doctor in Delhi and iron injections are recommended for anemia, ten separate injections, or one big infusion of the drip method over five or six hours. He also recommends injections of glucose and something called neomethedine and vitamin C, one-a-day for six days, for pepping up the liver. It would mean a trip to Delhi and staying there for a week. Even though the Peace Corps would pay for the treatment, the trip sounds too exhausting to me and I don't want to be away from the *ashram* that long, especially now that Swamiji has returned. This is no doubt foolhardy on my part, but I am living in the present and not thinking of the long-term benefits to my health.

Swamiji has been away touring to the various branches of the DLS in India and he returns in ill health. We are all concerned to see him in such a weakened state. I wonder why these great souls have to suffer so much? God realization doesn't mean that one's life will be easy. It often seems to be just the opposite. Gurudev teaches, "You are not this body, not this mind, immortal Self you are!" Our Swamis are living examples of this teaching. Swamiji's spirit is anything but weak. Perhaps it is very subjective, but it does appear to me that as soon as Swamiji returns, everything in the *ashram* is imbued with a radiant consciousness that was lying dormant before. Everything and everyone seems enlivened.

In evening *satsang* Swamiji makes the statement, "Only when there is rebirth into higher values, can there be any real evolution."

At the finish of every evening *satsang* Gurudev's *Universal Prayer* is recited. Swami Shivashankarananda always leads the Universal Prayer with his distinctive intonation that rises and falls in the same way every evening. It is not a strong voice, and I find out later that he is not a very healthy man. As an Indian living in Malaysia during the WWII, he was imprisoned in a Japanese concentration camp, where he learned to speak fluent Japanese. Apparently, in order to keep the prisoners subdued, the prison guards put arsenic in their food, which kept them in a weakened state, but was not enough to kill them. Swami Shivashankarananda still suffers from stomach problems due to the poisoning.

His main service is to greet devotees from Japan[24] and show them around the *ashram* and make them feel at home. Because Swami Shivashankarananda knows their language, he considers it his privilege and duty to serve them. Despite his ill health he is able to live in the spirit of forgiveness and transcend all sense of personal suffering.

TOUGH LOVE

In June, when the hot weather is in full force, a family of devotees arrives at the *ashram* with a problem, which they put before Swami Chidananda. Their twenty-year-old son, according to his parents, is beginning to act in such a way that is out of their control. "We can't do anything with him, Swamiji," the parents complain in morning *darshan*. The wife is close to tears. "He won't listen to us! We feel that he is going in a direction that he will later regret!"

Indian culture is very family-oriented and the children, even when grown, obey and respect their elders. In this culture, the institution of arranged marriages has existed and flourished for centuries, because the children, for the most part, obey their parents. In this case though, it has nothing to do with marriage, as far as we can tell. "We leave him with you,

---

[24] After Swam Chidananda makes several trips to Japan, in the '80's and '90's where his ardent devotees, Mr. Kawabata and his American wife, Linda, run a yoga center, many Japanese devotees visit Sivananda Ashram HQ. Swami Shivashankarananda greets them and helps them in whatever way he can.

Swamiji," the distraught parents say. "If anyone can bring him back to his senses, it is you."

Before departing, the husband and wife prostrate at Swamiji's feet, believing with all faith in their *guru*, that he is the only one who can remedy the situation. At this time, psychologists and psychiatrists are almost unheard of in India. If there is a personal or social problem, people seek the advice and wisdom of a holy person. Even heads of State prostrate before saints and sages. Many families are attached in some way to the lineage of a holy saint from the past, or a living *guru* in the present. Thus, wisdom is imparted from generation to generation and the moral code of *dharma* is upheld.

We are more than a little surprised to hear Swamiji say in a loud voice, "Lock him up with no food for a week!" The young man has a slightly crazed look and a goofy smile on his face, but he does not resist the two *brahmacharis*, one on either side of him, firmly holding his arms, as they guide him to a small building opposite the Music College.

"No one is to speak to him," Swamiji announces as the *darshan* ends. Swamiji is not afraid of taking what seems like drastic steps in order to bring the young man around.

"Wow!" I say, "Locked up for a week! With no one to speak to."

"Swamiji isn't messing around," Don observes.

All of the windows in the *ashram* have bars on them, to keep the monkeys out, but these add to the "jail effect" of the one-story building, located between Saraswati Kutir and the block where Swamiji resides. After evening *satsang* we walk back to our room, finding our way in the dark with our flashlights. As we walk past the "jail" building we hear the young man calling out to us in a loud whisper from the open window. "Foreigners! Foreigners!" He sounds desperate for someone to acknowledge him. I feel sorry and I want to stop and console him, but Swamiji has said no one is to talk to him, so we can't answer and walk by without speaking.

From the side window of our upstairs corner room in Saraswati Kutir, we look down on the building where the young man is kept. Very late at night, when all others in the *ashram* are asleep, Swami Chidananda carries a chair down the steps of his *kutir* and places it outside the building. He sits in the chair and quietly talks to the young man through the open window. He does this night after night, sometimes sitting in the chair, sometimes standing near the door. Although their voices are low and we can't hear what is being said, we can make out that Swamiji is asking him questions and the young man is answering.

By the end of the week, with Swamiji's middle-of-the-night attention, the young man seems to have talked though all his problems and promises to follow Swamiji's instructions. He is released from his lockup and stays on a little while in the *ashram*, before Swamiji returns him to his parents in a normal state of mind.

CHAPTER 11

SWAMI SIVANANDA'S DISCIPLES

TOUCHING HOME BASE

We are very blessed during the summer that several of Swami Sivananda's senior disciples choose to come and visit their spiritual home, Sivananda Ashram Head Quarters. It is a wonderful opportunity for us to meet them for the first time, or reconnect with those we have already met. Even while Gurudev Sivananda was still in the body, several of his disciples went out to different countries across the world where they started their own *ashrams* and yoga centers in his name, to share their understanding of his teachings in their own particular way. Swami Chidananda travels extensively worldwide, but always comes back to Shivanandanagar as his home base, while Swami Krishnananda, as General Secretary, stays put and runs the *ashram*.

Firstly, we are informed that one of Gurudev's top disciples, Swami Satchidananda, will pay a brief visit to the *ashram*, as he is traveling with some of his students to holy places in India. Swami Satchidananda started his own brand of Sivananda's teachings, which he calls "Integral Yoga." He founded the Integral Yoga Institute with many centers in the U.S. and

Europe, emphasizing the four main paths in yoga—*Karma, Bhakti, Raja* and *Jnana*. Swami Satchidananda was the first swami I ever met. I was traveling through Boston on my way to South Africa in 1967 and I attended a small yoga class with him. He founded Yogaville in Connecticut, and later moved the center to rural Virginia on the James River. There, he built the Lotus Temple to honor all known and unknown religions. Swami Sivananda made it clear that we need an integral approach, so that all aspects of the personality can be used to forward our evolution.

At the appointed time, many of us gather at the bottom of the steps awaiting Swami Satchidananda's arrival by road. For six decades the Ambassador, with its rounded form and spacious interior, is the only make of car on the road in India. Nearly all of them are plain black in color. So we are quite surprised when a shiny new beige vehicle comes sweeping up the road and stops in front of us. Swami Satchidananda alights from the car, his long wavy hair topped off with a stylish turban.

Swami Satchidananda

He appears rather lavish to us with clothes pressed and immaculate and he greets all in a friendly *pranam*. Peter has a conversation with him and later comments, "He is like the city cat visiting his poor country cousins." We can't help smiling in agreement. We have forgotten what new clothes and fancy cars look like. After greeting everyone, Swami Satchidananda walks down to Gurudev's Kutir for *darshan* of the holy Ganga before returning to his car. We don't see him after that and soon he is on his way again.

Both Swami Satchidananda and Swami Vishnudevananda are well known in the West. Swami Vishnu settled in Montreal, Canada in the 1950's and later started the Yoga Camp in Val Morin, where we did our teacher training. He also opened a center in the Bahamas, as well as many yoga centers in the United States, Europe and later South India. Swami Vishnu specializes mainly in *Hatha Yoga* and *pranayama* practices and Patanjali's teachings of the eightfold path.

Both Swami Vishnu and Swami Satchidananda became pilots and fly their own small planes. Swami Vishnu has just flown in on a "peace mission" from the U.S. to India. There is tension in the Middle East, and while crossing Israeli airspace, fighter jets escorted him to the border. His plane is decorated with brightly colored paintings of Peter Max, a popular New York graphic artist. While in India, Swami Vishnu pays a short visit to the Sivananda Ashram H.Q. for a couple of days and Swami Chidananda praises him in the evening *satsang* for his "heroic spirit."

During his visit, I bring a plate of fruits and flowers to Swami Vishnu's room.

"How are you getting along?" he asks, graciously accepting the small offering.

"Very well, thank you," I reply. I tell Swami Vishnu that I am grateful to him for giving us the training that we had at the Yoga Camp in Val Morin.

"Do you like it here?" he asks.

"Yes, I do, Swamiji." He must see that I am completely hooked and doesn't ask me when I will be coming back the States.

Then, sometime in May, after our course in V*edanta* is completed, Swami Venkatesananda visits the *ashram* and stays for a couple of weeks. Swami Venkates, as he is called, is a brilliant man, who worked as an undersecretary in the Indian government before he took to the life of *sannyas* and became Gurudev's private secretary. After Gurudev's *maha samadhi*[25] Swami Venkatesananda left India and started yoga centers in Australia, Mauritius, South Africa and the UK.

He was also a guest speaker at Swami Vishnu's Yoga Camp in 1969 and Swami Chidananda makes it a point of inviting us to a private lunch held for him, so that we can renew our acquaintance. Not that we know him very well, but he is certainly fun to be around! He is a handsome man who looks a bit like Yul Brynner with his shaven head. He sits on the ground in the half lotus pose, laughing and cracking jokes one minute and the next minute becomes serious and dignified. Swami Venkatesananda loves to make puns and play with the meanings of words.

"Not all teachers are *gurus*," he announces. "*'Gu-ru'* means 'remover of darkness,' and some who call themselves teachers are actually *cheaters*." And then he says, "You know the difference between a disciple and a pupil?" When no one answers, he continues, "A disciple has *dis-ci-pline*!" he looks around, "And what happens to a pupil?" He grins. "When you shine a light into their eyes, they close and contract!" He laughs and slaps his knee and says, "If you don't know who your *Ishta Devata* is, wait until a scorpion drops onto your lap! It will be the first name that springs to your lips!"

Swami Chidananda and Swami Venkatesananda are very fond of each

---

[25] The final samadhi, the absorption of the atman or spirit into the Ultimate Reality; when a fully realized saint, sage, or yogi consciously departs from the body; the death of the physical body.

other. Both served Swami Sivananda closely as young men and stayed with him until he attained *maha samadhi* in July 1963. Swami Venkatesananda used to take notes on Gurudev's daily sayings and activities and type them up at night when others were asleep. Thus he produced the *Biography of Swami Sivananda*. Among other writings, Swami Venkatesananda wrote commentaries on Patanjali's *Yoga Sutras*, the *Bhagavad Gita* (Song of God), the *Bhagavatam*, and two volumes translating the *Yoga Vashishta*, the scripture dealing with different dimensions, worlds within worlds and different levels of consciousness.

At the same time that Swami Venkatesananda is staying at the *ashram*, another of Gurudev's prominent disciples, Swami Chinmayananda visits. As a young man Swami Chinmayananda had been a resistance fighter against the British, who ruled India until its independence in 1947. He is well educated and became a journalist for one of India's main newspapers, *The National Herald*. He set out with the purpose of writing a piece which would expose the *yogis* and swamis as good-for-nothing, lazy people, living off the charity of others. "I went not to gain knowledge, but to find out how the swamis were keeping up the bluff among the masses." After several months at Sivananda Ashram, he was won over by Gurudev's magnanimous personality and decided to leave the newspaper and join the *ashram* instead. After a few years, Swami Sivananda recognized his propensity for *Jnana Yoga*, the path of wisdom, and sent him higher into the Himalayas to study with a different guru, Swami Tapovanam. Swami Chinmayananda made it his life's work to revitalize Indian culture, both in India and abroad, by reminding and teaching Indians about their great heritage.

Swami Chidananda greets Swami Chinmayananda with a loving embrace and they sit on the raised seat under the shade of the tree in the lower courtyard, chatting to each other. Some of us gather around them, sitting on the ground enjoying their company and their conversation. A feeling of great joy and lightheartedness prevails.

Swami Venkatesananda, Swami Chinmayananda, and Swami Chidananda

As we are sitting at their feet, Swami Venkatesananda comes up the steps from his morning dip in the Ganga, wearing wooden sandals and bare-chested with a cotton cloth wrapped around his waist and another thrown over his shoulder. He greets Swami Chinmayananda with hugs and laughter. The three of them sit together talking about old times. It is such a privilege for us, the next generation, to witness this meeting between the three of them. Each of them has become a *guru* in his own right, but when they are together, they are disciples again, sharing memories and their mutual love of Swami Sivananda.

A BIRD IN THE HAND

Swami Chinmayananda doesn't stay long at Sivananda Ashram, because he is on his way to the higher regions of the Himalayas. One of his former disciples, Swami Dayananda, takes up residence in a small *kutir* on the riverbank where the Ganges curves to the west around the outer edges of Rishikesh. There, he begins giving mid-afternoon classes on Vedanta.

We are familiar with Ramakrishna Paramahamsa's story, which the swamis are fond of re-telling. It's about a man who begins digging a well in order to find water. When he doesn't find it right away, he digs in another place and then gives up on that one and starts digging a third well elsewhere. In the end, he has dug many shallow wells, but none of them deep enough to find water. The point being that once you have found your *guru* and your path, you should stick to him or her and follow their instructions in order to make any real progress. Changing from one teacher to another and another could ultimately lead to confusion and no real depth in spiritual progress. But that doesn't mean to say we shouldn't learn from others too! Even Sri Ramakrishna, a realized saint, studied with different teachers. Some of our Swamis came to Gurudev Sivananda through the Ramakrishna lineage.

As long as it doesn't interfere with our attending the ongoing programs offered at the *ashram*, Swami Chidananda encourages us to visit other teachers once in a while in the larger Rishikesh-Tapovan area. Swamiji seems to be of the opinion that whatever we learn will enrich our India experience and therefore will be valuable for us. Within our *ashram* there are so many different teachers, but all are bound together by the love of their *guru*, Swami Sivananda. When you know in your heart who your *guru* is, all other teachers become manifestations of his or her grace. In a broader sense all the teachers of *Advaita Vedanta* are following the common thread of the Adi Sankaracharya lineage.

So, we are interested when Ann, a young American woman, also staying at Sivananda Ashram, comes to tell us about Swami Dayananda's afternoon class. The three of us decide to go and see for ourselves. I sometimes see Ann conversing with one of the young Indian men dressed in white and I am worried that she does not know the etiquette and that her familiar behavior will be frowned upon by the *ashram* authorities. "Be careful," I warn her. "Single women are encouraged to keep to themselves." I like her and I hope she doesn't get into trouble.

I cannot help wondering why Swami Dayananda has broken away from Swami Chinmayananda and gone out on his own. We are so used to Swami Chidananda's *guru bhakti*, his devotion and reverence for Gurudev Sivananda. He never starts a talk or a satsang without first paying homage to his *guru*. It seems to me that his whole life is dedicated to the service of his master. Swamiji says, "Just looking at you, the world should understand the divinity of your *guru!*" This is certainly the case where Swami Chidananda is concerned. We know how great Swami Sivananda must have been, by observing and spending time with Swami Chidananda and some of the other senior disciples. While some of them live abroad in their own *ashrams*, they have not broken the connection with their *guru*.

However, for any number of reasons, some disciples do leave their *guru* and go off on their own. We are beginning to understand that the *guru*-disciple relationship is a delicate balance of giving and receiving, of service and surrender that can be misinterpreted and even misused. We come to realize that Swami Chidananda's utter dedication to Gurudev and his mission, is the ideal rather than the norm.

The *kutir* where the afternoon talks are being held is a typical one-story building, a couple of inner rooms, with an open verandah facing the river. In this Tehri-Garhwal area of Uttarpradesh, most buildings are made of cement, using broken river boulders as the foundation. A few devotees sit quietly on the verandah waiting for Swami Dayananda to come outside.

At three o'clock he appears and takes a seat on a grass mat on the floor. He wears an orange bandana cloth around his head, holding his long black hair in place. He has a beard, following the style of Swami Chinmayananda and he speaks like him too, in a dynamic way with shining eyes, a confident voice, and gesturing hands. This is quite a contrast to the quiet and methodical way in which our *Vedanta* course teacher, Swami Tejomayananda, instructed us. Don and I are both riveted to what Swami Dayananda is saying and we return to listen again the next afternoon, and the next.

Swami Sivananda used to make up little songs to convey his teachings, which could be easily remembered by his devotees. One of them is, "Eat a little, drink a little, do *asana* a little, meditate a little…etcetera." It is the middle path, the path of moderation that Swami Sivananda put into verse, to encourage seekers to practice everyday and not become unbalanced. Another is, "Be good, do good. Be kind, be compassionate." Gurudev's songs sound so simple, even a child could understand them. But to really put them into practice requires a deep surrender and renunciation of the ego.

One afternoon I hear Swami Dayananda say in a mimicking voice, "Do *pranayama* a little, meditate a little…" Then he stops mid-sentence and says, " A *little* won't be enough! It's going to require a *lot* of meditation!" Maybe he's right, but I don't like the fact that he is mocking one of Swami Sivananda's songs to make his point. Sivananda also preached putting full effort into one's practices. He did not approve of half-hearted measures when it came to spiritual life. Gurudev himself meditated for hours and hours everyday for a period of twelve years. "Thought creates actions, actions create habits, habits create character, and character creates one's destiny. Be up and doing!" Sivananda sang. Swami Dayananda is an excellent teacher of *Vedanta*, but after I hear his criticism, I stop going to his afternoon classes.

Don, however, is so inspired by the discourses that he decides he is going to follow Swami Dayananda to the next venue, another town in India, where he will be teaching. "Do you want to go?" Don asks me.

"No thanks, I'll stay at the *ashram*. But if you want to go, I'll walk with you to the station to see you off." Swami Chidananda is away from the *ashram*, so we inform Swami Krishnananda that Don is leaving for a while to attend Swami Dayananda's lectures. Swami Krishnananda doesn't make much comment. I am not sure how long Don will be gone. He packs a small bag and we walk to Rishikesh, where he buys a ticket at the train station.

As we stand on the platform by the side of the train that is to depart shortly, Don looks down at the ticket in his hand. "I've changed my mind," he says. "I don't think I'll go after all."

"Good!" I say feeling a bit relieved. "Let's go back to the *ashram*."

When we see Swami Krishnananda that evening, Don tells him he changed his mind and decided not to follow Swami Dayananda. Swami Krishnananda is highly amused. He chuckles and quotes, "A bird in the hand is worth two in the bush!" And that is the end of the matter.

GURUBHAIS

One of the most important advantages in a life where spiritual aspiration takes priority is the fellowship of like-minded people, the community. Perhaps this is especially true in spiritual life, which often moves contrary to where the mainstream of society is heading.

One morning in late February, when the weather is mild, I walk down to take a dip in the Ganga and I come across a woman in her early-forties, down on the sandy beach drying her hair in the sun. For bathing, we women go further up the beach, away from Sivananda Ghat, to swim in the privacy of the large grey boulders. In February, the water is almost turquoise, without the sand stirred up by the swollen turbulence of the July monsoon rains, when the river turns brown and folds back on itself, swirling into waves. In February and early March it is clear and clean, but still icy cold from the snowmelt in the high Himalayan peaks around Gomukh, the source of the Ganges.

A familiar-looking bottle of shampoo is propped up on the sand near her towel.

"Oh," I exclaim, "it's all in Afrikaans!" I am reading the backside of the label on the bottle. Sunlight Shampoo, I recognize a South African brand. The woman lifts her blue eyes to look at me. Her wavy brown hair is almost dry. "Oh?" she says, "How do you know Afrikaans?" She speaks with an accent that I am trying to place.

"That's where I grew up," I say. "You too?"

"*Ag*, no. I'm from Holland, but I live in Johannesburg now," she says. This is how Jyotsnamata and I first meet. Despite the difference in our ages, she being about seventeen years my senior, we become fast friends. She has three daughters, one of whom is still a teenager. She has come to India with the secret longing to become a *sannyasin*, but Swamiji says the time is not right yet and that her youngest daughter still needs her. She and her husband, Bharat, are founding members of the Sivananda School of Yoga in Johannesburg.

Chidananda Jyotsnamata (she is the only one that I know of that has Swamiji's name as a prefix) is like an elder sister to me, and I draw on her wisdom and life experience with all sorts of questions about the spiritual path. "Don't ever wish yourself into the next stage of life," she advises. "It is important we live fully the stage that we're in."[26]

I meet Sita Frenkel, who is visiting the *ashram* for a few weeks. She came to the *ashram* as a teenager on her own in 1957 and stayed for several months under the guidance of Swami Sivananda. She and her husband, Hans, are taking turns coming to India, because they have three children at home.[27]

---

26 Jyotsnamata keeps very much to herself at the *ashram* and I don't get to know her well until later when we visit each other's homes in South Africa and the United States. When she becomes Swami Ramanarayananda she remains unpretentious and practical, with an almost childlike sense of fun. We share many good times together.

27 The following year, I study with both Sita and Hans at their *ashram* in Harriman, New York. When their marriage breaks up, we move close to Sita in Maryland, so we can participate in the monthly satsangs and summer retreats of the DLS of MD. We become good friends and her two daughters, along with her right hand companion, Marcia, are like part of our family. She lives to serve and share with others what she learned first from Gurudev Sivananda and later from Swami Chidananda. Their teachings come before

Sita stays for a few weeks and does a lot of *sadhana* in her room, so I don't see much of her. When she returns to the States, her husband comes and stays for some time in the *ashram*.

One afternoon, Nagarajan, standing in the courtyard with a young woman, calls up to me on the verandah, "Moo, this is Carol Dyall from America. She is just here for a day." We greet each other and I learn she is taking a year off her flight attendant job with Eastern Airlines, to volunteer with the Dooly Foundation, serving the poor in Cambodia or Thailand. Carol[28] becomes one of the spiritual sisters with whom we share a common bond in our love for Swami Chidananda.

My most faithful correspondent during this year at the *ashram* is Diane Dufault from California and Oregon. Our friendship started at the teachers' training at Swami Vishnu's Yoga Camp in Val Morin and we exchange letters frequently. I notice that she often sends me cards with Native American Indian motifs on them. In one exchange, discussing past lives, I write, "Were you ever an American Indian? I was once." A couple of weeks later I receive the answer: "I *am* an American Indian." I learn that Diane's grandfather was a Lakota Sioux and she is on the official tribal role of the Klamath River Indians. We are drawn together in friendship by our love and reverence for Swami Chidananda.

Bill and Melissa Schnirring, who are traveling the world as journalists, visit the *ashram* during 1971. There are not many married people on the

---

everything else in her life. She is initiated into the holy order of Sannyasa by Swami Chidananda and becomes Swami Gurudevananda in 1993.

[28] Carol takes Sannyas and becomes Swami Karunapremananda.

path of yoga and we find we have a strong connection. They come to our room one day to compare notes and exchange stories. In the course of our conversation, we show them some artwork and Bill buys three of Don's watercolor paintings, which depict the evolution of the soul in the form of a peanut, for U.S. $10 each. This keeps us going for another couple of months. Melissa stays at the *ashram* doing sadhana and Bill travels as far as Greece, pursuing a story. Later he returns and they continue their travels together.[29]

There are many others, drawn as we are, into Swami Chidananda's orbit, with whom we become life-long friends, but it is the above-mentioned whom we meet during our early days at Shivanandanagar.

---

[29] The following year Don and I live with Bill and Melissa in Connecticut for nine months, and become godparents to their son, Luke. Like us, they are trying to figure out how to reorganize a relationship around a commitment to these yogic teachings, how to live a married life on yogic terms. Yoga demands that one faces and then tries to live the truth, which often puts a strain on a relationship, shining a light in all the dark corners and exposing our faults. Yoga is not for the faint of heart and sometimes relationships, at least in the West, do not survive.

CHAPTER 12

A SIREN CALLS

DON PREPARES TO LEAVE

Don mentions again that he would like to learn to play the *sitar*. He goes with Swami Nadabrahmananda to Dehra Dun to the same music shop where I bought my *tabla* several months ago. While he is waiting in the front room where the selection of the *sitar* will be made, someone in the back room puts a record on the turntable. The moment Don hears the voice of Carol King on the record player he knows he will have to return to the West. He tells me later, "The voice was like a siren beckoning to me, calling me home. The only way I could possibly stay here is if I become an Indian and that's never going to happen! I am a product of the Western world and for all its drawbacks it is where I belong. I need to get back to my own culture. It's the only way I can make my way in this world."

When he returns that afternoon from Dehra Dun, I know a line has been crossed. He is carrying the *sitar* he purchased, ostensibly to learn to play it, but I intuitively know a decision has been made. Now, it is only a matter of time before the decision will become *my* decision—Should I go with him and abandon this *ashram* life? Or should I stay on and continue a life of spiritual practices and self-enquiry, of delving deeper into the wisdom of the East? From an outside point of view, *ashram* life looks like hardship—illness, lack of food, living in Spartan conditions, with lizards, scorpions and rats, with no running water. But I have found a joy here that I didn't know existed. I have found that the *yogis* understand that the luxuries of life can become a distraction, especially to a neophyte like myself. They have encouraged us to ask the questions, "Why we are here? Why are we born? What is the purpose of a human birth?"

"Realize the Self and be free!" Swami Sivananda taught. "You are the children of immortality!" Minimizing one's desires frees the mind to focus on what is truly relevant— experiencing one's essential nature. This life of simplicity and renunciation fosters its own internal rewards of clarity and bliss. Don and I have both recognized this truth, but his destiny is pulling him away.

We have tried to share our experiences with some of our friends and members of our family, by letters written back and forth—ten days for a letter to reach the States, another ten, if we were lucky, to receive a reply. Some of our friends think we have gone too far; changed religions, or worse still, joined a cult. My parents in South Africa don't appear to understand what we are doing here. Don's parents in the States, don't say much, but when they do write, it is to urge us to come back home and start our "real" lives.

Only fellow seekers and those who have met Swami Chidananda know that what we are doing in India makes perfect sense. It is the best choice we can make for all time to come. To spend time in the presence of a great being, especially one of Swamiji's caliber, puts the world and all its incessant activities into the proper perspective. Spiritual seekers don't question the choice we have made, to spend the energy of our youth seeking company of the wise. Swami Chidananda makes us aware of the *mahavakyas*, the 'great sayings' from the *Upanishads*—"*Tat Twam Asi*, That Thou Art; *Aham Brahmasmi*, I am Brahman (God), or I am the Divine; *Ayam Atma Brahman*, this Self is Brahman." We have found those rare beings on this planet that actually embody these utterances, through direct experience in the living of their lives. We count ourselves extremely fortunate to have stumbled into their camp.

We have spent the past several months through daily reading and study of religious texts, through attending lectures on *Vedanta* philosophy and the practice of meditation, becoming acquainted with the concept of non-duality, *Advaita Vedanta*—that all is indeed One and we are not separate from *That*. "God alone is, without a second." All of creation, including our selves, is of the nature of divinity. It will take us the rest of our lives to actually absorb this truth and digest it, so that it becomes the underlying basis of our daily living. No amount of study, however, of the various Yogas, of the different paths to God, can take the place of sitting at the feet of a liberated master.

It is our love for Swami Chidanandaji that brought us to India. He is our spiritual friend and guide on the path of life. One does not leave such a love lightly. I know Don has struggled for weeks with his decision to leave the *ashram*.

Despite Swamiji's exceedingly generous offers Don makes it clear that he wants to go back into the world to work and to create. He wants me to go with him, but he understands how invested I am in the life here and how unthinkable it is for me to leave at this point. I feel that I have just barely scratched the surface and believe it is important for me to stay longer in the holy presence of my *guru*. Swamiji understands my deep longing to stay and gives me permission to continue on at the *ashram*.

Now that Don has taken a definite decision to go, Swamiji is fully behind him, encouraging him in everything he does. On 8th September, we celebrate Gurudev Sivananda's 84th birth anniversary, 1008 moons. We celebrate this auspicious event in the new library building and Don is invited to participate in the *puja*. It is one of the ways that Swamiji has of honoring Don before he leaves.

Swami Sivananda's padukas

With a devotee's grandchild sitting on his lap, Swami Chidananda explains how *puja* engages all the senses of the worshipper—seeing the form worshipped, chanting the name of God, hearing the music, tossing the flowers, smelling the incense—all elevating and expanding the mind. *Chakras* are opened during such a *puja*, as the expanded consciousness rises through the psychic subtle body of the worshipper. Swami Sivananda's *padukas*, the silver-plated wooden sandals that Gurudev used while in the body, are worshipped with milk, water, sandalwood paste, *cum-cum* and thousands of rose petals.

Later, down on Sivananda Ghat the Divine Mother is worshipped in the form of the holy Ganga. As I am standing on the bottom step, the petals tossed from behind fall all around me, on my hair and feet, until the river close by is covered with pink petals floating downstream. I look down toward the clock tower and see Don sitting on one of the cement platforms jutting into the river, silhouetted by the sunset. He looks sad, and I imagine he is thinking of his immanent departure and all he is about to leave behind. I imagine he is trying to take it all in. I get an empty feeling in the pit of my stomach.

The following day, Swamiji invites us to lunch with him in his kutir and later arranges a special afternoon gathering in the Bhajan Hall, during the 4 o'clock *Vedanta* class hour. He asks Don to come up and sit beside him and describe in a nutshell, the work he is doing on the structure of the universe. Then Swamiji explains, "Don is bringing Western science into the realm of Eastern metaphysics, to make it known that the two must work together for the harmony and unity of the world." Swamiji concludes the satsang, chanting the holy names of Jesus and Krishna and presents Don with fruit and boxes of sweets, cookies and nuts, as well as a big cake, with "Bon Voyage Don, Happy Landing," written on it. Swamiji never does things in half measures! Don is in tears and does a full prostration to Swamiji. Yvonne also garlands Don. Then we cut up the cake and share it with all.

After the satsang Swamiji again invites us to his *kutir* for coffee. He gives Don some parting advice, "Even if you don't understand what these teachings are now, cling to them and practice them and one day they will flower and bear fruit. When you are with people be like them, but never forget your true Self. Be always rooted in your God nature." We sit in silent meditation for five minutes.

Then Don prostrates again to Swamiji. I feel sincere love and deep gratitude passing from Don to Swamiji, who is radiating light. Then Don, still kneeling before him, lifts his hands to either side, palms open in a gesture of surrender.

"We'll see you again some day," Swamiji says.

"I hope I'll be better material to work with next time," Don answers.

"Everything is inside," Swamiji replies, touching the center of his chest.

DEPARTURE

Neither of us has any long-term plan. We are just taking each day as it presents itself. Before Don leaves India he wants to first visit the Taj Mahal, so after reaching Delhi, we take the train to Agra. We spend a whole day in the garden, sitting, sketching, and walking barefoot in the mausoleum, under the big marble dome.[30] A few gardeners are at work trimming bushes with hand shears and tending the flowerbeds. We only see one or two other tourists in the afternoon, which means we practically have the whole place to ourselves.

We leave our sandals at the bottom of the steps and stand by the tombs of Mumtaz and her devoted husband, marveling at the intricate designs of white marble carved into lattice, inlaid with semi-precious stones. We walk around the Taj and through the huge arches of red stone that flank the marble dome and we gaze over the River Yumuna, which runs along one side. The king mourned his wife's death so deeply that after building the Taj Mahal as her tomb, he intended to build an identical Taj in black marble across the river, so they could face each other throughout eternity. But it never came to pass. His son rebelled against him and usurped the throne, imprisoning his own father until his death.

The following day we take the train back to Delhi and make our way to the airport from which Don's flight is scheduled to depart that afternoon. Some months ago, my parents sent us tickets from Delhi to Durban, South Africa, with a stop off in Mauritius, thus insuring that we would visit them on the homeward journey back to the States. It feels like the right decision and since we have all but run out of money, we don't have much choice. Don plans to visit Swami Venkatesananda's *ashram* on Mauritius for a week

---

[30] This is long before the explosion of Western tourism to India, and the Indian middle class has not yet blossomed, so there is very little tourism at the Taj Mahal.

and then on to Durban, where he will stay with my parents and look for a job in his field of industrial design.

"I love you," Don says, turning at the gate in the fence through which passengers cannot pass. I uncurl my palm and give him the little bronze statue of the Tibetan monk with a begging bowl, which we had bought together in Katmandu a year earlier. We both like this little figure, which somehow symbolizes the austerity and the simplicity of the path, and it seems right that he should accompany Don on his onward journey.

We hug each other. "I love you too."

Then he turns and I watch him walk across the tarmac to the Indian Airlines plane, waiting to take off for Bombay. We have no idea when, or even *if* we will see each other again. We have entrusted our shared destiny to the Cosmos, hoping that somehow, love will prevail. We don't know what will happen to us. At the top of the steps Don turns and waves. I wave back and then he disappears into the body of the plane. I watch the plane taxi down the runway, propellers whirling. I don't know what will happen to our relationship, but I know each of us is following what we feel we must do, so I try not to think too far ahead into the future.

When I can no longer see the plane, I sling my cloth bag over my shoulder and make my way to the Delhi train station, where I take the overnight train back to Haridwar. I share a taxi from Haridwar to Rishikesh and a *tonga* brings me to the *ashram* steps.

It is 11:30 a.m. and if I hurry I can make Swamiji's morning *darshan*. I walk quickly to the Bhajan Hall and sink to my knees at the back of the group of people gathered in front of Swamiji.

"Did Don get off alright?" Swamiji asks kindly, when he sees me. "Everything alright?"

"Yes, thank you Swamiji," I answer.

Thus begins a new phase for me, living singly in the *ashram*.

CHAPTER 13

GOING SOLO

SWAMI CHIDANANDA'S BIRTHDAY

Swamiji's birthday, which sometimes coincides with Navaratri, is celebrated on the 24th September. As the birthday nears, I decide I would like to make Swamiji a cake. It has to be eggless, so I use peanut butter as the glue to hold it together. After I mix up all the ingredients, Ann and I go off to the Rishikesh bakery to use the only oven in town. After baking it in one of their pans, Ann helps me to carry the cake back to my room in Saraswati Kutir so I can decorate it with icing. Placing the cake on the low table and painting the legs with kerosene from the lamp, solves the problem of keeping the ants away. Thus, the cake is made "ant-proof" until the next morning, 24th September.

At about 6 a.m. one of Swamiji's attendants calls me to come quickly to Swamiji's *kutir* for darshan. There are just a few of us Westerners here who celebrate birthdays. Technically speaking, once *sannyas* is taken there are no more birthdays. One has already figuratively burnt one's body in the fire of renunciation. Swamiji is graciously allowing himself to be celebrated, not for his sake, but for ours. We light the candles on the cake and sing, "Happy Birthday to you!" He enjoys our happiness. Then, keeping everything in perspective, referring to his eternal essential nature, he reminds us, "You are celebrating the birthday of someone who has never been born."

Later that morning, after the *puja* to Swami Sivananda's padukas, Swami Chidananda takes a seat just outside the Samadhi Shrine against the low wall in the long, open-air verandah. Here, there is more room for everyone to have Swamiji's *darshan*. Soon, the senior swamis and many *ashram* inmates gather around him to pay their respects. Everyone, it seems, wants to garland Swamiji to honor him on his birthday. Swamiji sits patiently, as devotee after devotee prostrates before him and puts their garland over his head. Each time, Swamiji brings his hands together in *pranam* and inclines his head, bowing his thanks, gracefully acknowledging each person in turn.

I watch as the garlands pile up, growing heavier and heavier around Swamiji's neck and shoulders. Marigolds are used because they are easy to grow, last well once they have been cut and strung into garlands, and because their bright yellow and orange colors are the colors of renunciation. Finally, a couple of Swamiji's assistants begin removing the garlands from his neck and arrange them in a pile on a huge brass platter. Once they have gotten the bulk of the garlands off, they remove each garland after it is put on. When an important event like this takes place, it is not necessarily quiet. The assistants talk if needed, passing things back and forth, making sure that devotees don't crowd Swamiji; and yet an atmosphere of reverence pervades.

There is a great outpouring of devotion to Swamiji, as the pile of flowers on the platter grows into a small mountain. Perhaps it is hard for the Western mind to imagine how much these great spiritual beings are revered in India. When the culture of the country agrees with its ancient sages that the goal of life is God-realization, and one of its sons or daughters attains that goal, they are revered and adored for having done so. These great beings are more valuable than diamonds, because they have given up everything for the sake of God and they have reached the goal of Self-realization. India is a unique country in that it recognizes the worth of those who have attained the pinnacle of spiritual experience, and looks to them for wisdom and solace.

With all the attention and hubbub going on around him, there is never any sign or feeling from Swamiji that he considers himself better than anyone else. He bears it all with patience and humility, allowing the devotees to express their love for him, because he knows it is what they want and need to do. I watch closely as Swamiji is sitting in a cross-legged position with his feet protruding from his orange cloth. I see a young man, a devotee from Orissa,[31] come from behind, kneel down, and kiss the bottom of one of his feet. Swamiji notices this, but he makes no motion to move his foot, or to reprimand the devotee. It is as though Swamiji has seen someone kiss the foot of a statue. What is appropriate for one person may not be the right thing for another. I know my love for Swamiji is much more restrained, but that is all right also. He receives and works with each one of us as we are, as long as we were being true to ourselves.

NAVARATRI

Navaratri, or the nine nights of *Devi Puja*, follows soon after Swamiji's birthday. The worship of the three aspects of the Divine Mother as Durga, Lakshmi, and Saraswati is one of the most important celebrations in the Hindu year.

I decide to ask Swamiji if he thinks it would be a good idea for me to eat only fruits during this nine-day period as a means of purification. I climb the steps and knock on the door of his kutir. The outer room has other people waiting to see Swamiji and I am about to sit down, but just then Swamiji comes through the door. Before I can ask anything, he says, "Yes, you can fast on water for nine days." I am a bit shocked. I wasn't planning on eating *nothing*! But Swamiji has raised the bar!

Swami Devananda, a short, rotund disciple of Gurudev whose job it

---

[31] In 2011 reverts to original name of Odisha

is to take care of Gurudev's Kutir, takes it upon himself to decorate the altar for the celebration. For the first three nights, a large picture of Mother Durga dressed in a scarlet sari sitting astride her tiger, adorns the altar. The altar is set up in the brand new hexagonal library building, built over a meditation room, a dark room for developing photographs and a small private kitchen, used by Nagaraj and Nagarkar. Strings of marigolds are hung from the library ceiling in loops around the altar, which is draped with an ornate silk cloth.

Mother Durga is the purifying aspect of the divine power of Shakti. It is She who helps spiritual seekers to destroy all the negative aspects of our personalities, ultimately extinguishing the ego, which separates us from our divine nature. While Mother Durga has a terrifying and fierce aspect, we cannot make any inner transformation without Her grace.

On the fourth through sixth night Mother Lakshmi is worshipped. She is the Goddess of abundance of all material and spiritual wealth. She is pictured with four arms holding a lamp for light, a conch shell to blow in praise of God, a lotus blossom representing purity and often, gold coins are streaming down from one of her outstretched palms. She blesses us with abundance of all kinds. The full moon and an abundant harvest are also reminders of the fullness of Lakshmi.[32]

Mother Saraswati, the Goddess of wisdom, arts, and learning, is celebrated on the seventh, eighth, and ninth nights. She blesses us with artistic ability and skill of all types—music, dance, acting, writing, painting, as well as scientific knowledge and wisdom. I, along with many ashramites bring our books, wrapped in cloth bundles or tied together with string, and place them at the foot of the altar, along with many musical instruments. The belief is that Saraswati helps us with our learning, our understanding, and our artistic talent.

---

[32] Some years later when Swamiji is a passenger in our car traveling through the Maryland countryside, he notices the tall farm silos filled with grain and remarks, "Lakshmi has been very gracious to these farmers."

FASTING AND INITIATION

After the first two days of drinking only water, my stomach stops growling for food as the hunger pangs subside. Whenever I feel hungry, I drink water. I continue my *sadhana* as before, although I conserve my energy by refraining from talking. I become aware of how much energy is spent in talking. Every thought requires *prana*. When I stop thinking about food and what I am going to eat for dinner, it frees up lots of time and my thought process seems to slow down. I notice clarity in my thinking that was not there before. Thoughts don't have the energy to run in circles or jump around as they usually do. In Sanskrit it is called *vikshepa*, or tossing of the mind, when thoughts hop non-stop from one thing to another. Now, they slow down to the point where I can observe them clearly.

On special days, a recording of Swami Sivananda's voice is broadcast by loudspeaker throughout the *ashram* for all to hear. "You are not this body, not this mind, immortal Self you are!" The words of Gurudev's song ring in my ears. I hear his clear alto voice singing the words and for the first time, I experience their real meaning. If I can observe my thoughts, it means that they are different from me. The *yogis* say, "The mind is a bundle of thoughts." That is its nature. But now the senses are not drawing the mind outward as they usually do. I assume it is because of the fasting that the thoughts have turned inward. Realizing this brings me one step closer to understanding myself. Swamiji says, "The more you know yourself, the more you know." Once we stop looking outside of ourselves for the answers to our questions, often the answers come to us from within.

During Navaratri the evening *satsangs* are especially glorious, as the whole *ashram* comes together in the library for the worship of the Divine Mother. No matter which aspect one might relate to personally, everyone is uplifted by the *bhav*, the intense spiritual feeling that we are all in this together. The *Devi Mahatmyam* is chanted during the day and at night the new library is filled with devotional singing of *kirtans* and *bhajans*.

As the fast progresses into the sixth and seventh day, I begin to feel physically weaker, so I start squeezing a fresh lime into the water that I am drinking. Then, the last few days I add a spoonful of honey. I feel I need the sugar in the honey to keep me going. While I can feel my body shutting down, I felt very clear and uplifted mentally and spiritually.

I decide to write a note and ask Swamiji if he would consider giving me *mantra diksha*, at the conclusion of Navaratri. I have been daily repeating the *mantra* of Gurudev's name that Swamiji gave me in the spring, five or six months ago. But I am still longing for a formal initiation, which would make me, in my mind and heart, a proper disciple. In the India of the *yogis*, *mantra diksha* or initiation, is the sacred link that connects the disciple not only to a realized master (if you are so fortunate!) living in the present, but through him or her to the whole lineage of *gurus* before them. Swami Sivananda's disciples are all representatives of this lineage dating back to the 8th century when Adi Shankaracharya, the brilliant scholar-monk, founded the philosophy of *Advaita Vedanta*, non-dualism. The monks of the present time are accountable to their lineage, which in turn serves to keep them humbly proceeding on the path to God realization. In the *ashram*, located between the Vishwanath Mandir and the Samadhi Shrine, there is white marble statue of the seated figure of Sri Adi Shankaracharya. I have often seen Swami Chidananda bowing before this statue honoring the founder of the lineage. For my part, my main concern is about my relationship with Swamiji himself, who bridges the divide between the East and the West.

I write a letter in pen and ink, address it to Swami Chidananda and seal it. I bring it into the evening satsang and sit down on the marble floor. Swami Nadabrahmananda is in his element, playing the *tabla*, accompanying a devotee who is singing a *bhajan*. I close my eyes and I can soon feel the beat of the drum moving up and down my spine. Just like any other musical instrument, the *tabla* drums are tuned before playing, so they have a resonance to them. It is just as though every note is being played inside my body.

When the *satsang* is over and devotees are prostrating before Swamiji, I approach him, kneeling down and place the letter at his feet.

"I had already thought to do it," he says. *Is he speaking to me?* I look up at him, just to see if I have heard him right. He doesn't need to read the letter. He already knows what is in my heart. I get up quickly and leave the hall. I go back to my room and am thrilled that I will finally be accepted as a disciple! I sit still in the dark for a long time, until I fall asleep in the early hours of the morning.

I keep the idea of initiation to myself, but as the day draws nearer, I wonder what the proper thing to do is when one receives initiation from the *guru*. Shouldn't I offer him something? I decide to seek the advice of my next-door neighbor, Krishnapriyananda Mataji. She advises me that one should offer fruits and flowers to the *guru* and immediately takes it upon herself to send a boy to purchase some fruits and a flower garland from Rishikesh, as well as some Indian sweets made with boiled milk and sugar.

The next day, on the morning of Vijaya Dasami, the tenth day—the day of victory—I am ready with my little tray of fruits, sweets, and the flower garland, which I keep covered with a damp cloth on the low table in my room. Krishnapriya Mataji suggests that it would be auspicious for me to attend the morning *paduka puja* in the Samadhi Shrine. I am beginning to feel uncomfortable with her involvement, but I obediently go with her and sit down behind a small group of swamis and other devotees who are performing the *puja*. They are sitting cross-legged in a tight half circle, chanting and tossing marigolds onto Gurudev's silver sandals. The entrance to the Shrine is quite narrow and it is already crammed with devotees, so there is no room for anyone else to squeeze in. But there is no dissuading Krishnapriya Mataji, who has taken me under her wing and is determined to do what she thinks best for me! I am already getting a sinking feeling, as something in me knows this is not the right thing to do, but Mataji is already announcing, in a voice trembling with emotion, "She *must* be allowed to participate in the *puja*, because she is going to receive *mantra diksha* this very day!" I am mortified when she announces it out loud. I intuitively know it is a mistake and I wish I had never asked her advice! The last thing I want is to draw attention to myself and I cringe inside, as the swamis, with no break in their chanting or flower offerings, shift reluctantly over so that I can squeeze my skinny body in.

When ten o'clock comes, I attend the special morning *puja* held outside near the Sivananda Pillar, where nine little barefoot girls from the village are to be worshipped as representatives of the Divine Mother. They sit in a row on a bench, their black hair combed, oiled, and drawn back into two plaits on either side of their heads. They wear their best clothes, brightly colored blouses with long skirts. They are too young to know what is really going on, but to the adults, worship of the Divine Mother in the form of these little girls is a serious matter.

With great reverence, Swami Chidananda applies sandalwood paste and bright red *cum-cum* powder to the center of each young forehead. He does this with the fourth finger next to the little finger, pressing first a small amount of moist sandalwood paste against the forehead and then dipping his finger into a little vessel of red *cum-cum* powder and dabbing it lightly onto the sandal paste. Then he garlands and prostrates before each girl in turn. Finally, he gives them some sweets for *prasad* and a set of new clothes. All of them go home giggling and happy.

I return to my room and wait. No messenger appears at the door to call me and I spend the afternoon meditating and reading. I feel deeply disappointed, but accept without hesitation that something I have done has made Swamiji change his mind about the initiation. My ego feels the sting of rejection and humiliation, but I know that what Swamiji does is always for the best. The tray of offerings remains covered on the table.

Towards dusk, Krishnapriya Mataji comes out of her room when she hears me moving about on our shared verandah. "Did you receive *mantra diksha?*" she whispers, not that anyone is listening.

"No, Mataji."

After a moment, she says, "Swamiji must have come to know that I told you to purchase those things." Her voice trails off, subdued and remorseful.

I do not try to second-guess Swamiji any longer. I remember how

Mataji had insisted that I be given a place during the *puja* at the Samadhi Shrine, but I don't say any more about it. Somehow, word must have filtered back to Swamiji, or, in his mysterious way of knowing what is going on in other locations he has come to know about Krishnapriyanandaji's attempt to intervene on my behalf.

The lesson that I digest from these events is that the *guru*-disciple relationship is extremely sacred, ever so subtle, and not to be revealed to anyone else, because that brings in another element. Even the goodwill of someone else is an interference of vibrations that don't belong in the relationship.

Later, I come downstairs and give the fruits and sweets to a passing *sadhu* on the main road. I retrace my steps up the hill and pause to listen to Swami Nadabrahmanandaji giving someone a harmonium lesson. It dawns on me that whatever disappointment I have experienced is also a manifestation of *guru's* grace. I trust Swami Chidananda completely to make the decision that is right. In every situation I have ever seen him, he always does what is correct and in line with *dharma*. That is one of the marks of a realized saint. As I am standing outside of the Music College building in the twilight, Nagaraj appears at the foot of Swamiji's steps and calls out to me, "Moo, dry your face and come with us! We are going to Dehra Dun to see Ananda Mayee Ma!"

"I'll just get my shawl," I respond without hesitation and run upstairs to the room, relieved to have something to take my mind off mulling over my recent mistakes. I wonder what Nagaraj meant by "dry your face?" Does he think I have been crying, or is that an Indian expression? I feel a bit light-headed from lack of food, but a chance to have *darshan* of Ananda Mayee Ma cannot be passed up!

I get into the backseat of the taxi that Nagaraj has reserved to take us the forty-five minutes to Dehra Dun. I am to accompany him and Narasimulu, his friend and fellow devotee of Gurudev. When Narasimulu sees me sitting in the back seat, he hesitates. I suppose it is because Swami Sivananda has told his monks to avoid close contact with women. "It's alright," Nagaraj assures him, and Narasimulu gets in next to me.

Ananda Mayee Ma's Ashram is close to the outskirts of town, on a tree-lined, residential road leading from downtown Dehra Dun towards the mountains. There's a large outdoor *satsang* in progress. Most of the devotees are dressed in white, as is Ma herself. Ma is sitting on a dais and below her a devotee plays the harmonium, singing *bhajans* and leading the gathering in *kirtan*. The words are the various names of God and as I sing along with all the devotees, I feel the disappointment of the day washing out of my mind and joy filling my heart.

When the *satsang* comes to an end, the three of us prostrate to Ma and get back into the taxi. We take turns singing *bhajans* all the way home to the *ashram*. I even dare to sing the song that Mother Rema taught me in praise of Meenakshi. It is late when I climb up to my room physically exhausted, but blissfully happy and ready to redouble the efforts of my spiritual practices, trusting all is as it should be.

MOONFLOWER

I am getting used to being on my own. I continue to study and write and draw in my room, as Don and I used to do together. We could spend hours without speaking. But now that there's no one else to speak to, I find myself examining my own mind, its thoughts, motivations, fears, and doubts. *Vichara*, introspection and self-enquiry, as well as *viveka*, discrimination between the real and the unreal, are a necessary practices in yoga. How else are we to know our own mind, unless we analyze our thoughts and choose what is right over what appears to be more appealing? Choosing the good over the pleasant is also an important practice on the path of self-analysis—*sreyo marga*, the path of righteousness leading to higher consciousness, over *preyo marga*, the path leading merely to the pleasant. The *Vedantins* have studied the mind so well that there are terms for every nuance of thought. When I observe my mind I find that it has turned inward.

One day a Western visitor to the *ashram* gives me some seeds. "What are they?" I ask, always fascinated by how small seeds contain the complete unique program for what they will become. As seeds go, these aren't very tiny, but more like dried peas that roll in the palm of his hand.

"They are moonflowers," he says, tipping his palm so that the seeds roll into mine. "Somewhat related to morning glories."

"Thanks," I say, "I can't wait to see how they turn out." Growing things has always fascinated me and I haven't had the opportunity to do that for a while. Don and I had spent one morning down at the *ashram's* cow farm south of Rishikesh, planting sunflower seeds, but it was too far for us to go to water them and nothing came of it.

Back in my room, I find a plastic bowl that can serve as a makeshift flowerpot and then set about finding some soil. I climb the hill opposite our building, and begin digging with a stick under the tree with yellow flowers. The ground is hard, but I loosen up enough soil to fill the plastic bowl and look around for some cow dung to serve as fertilizer. Within the *ashram* premises cow dung isn't hard to find.[33] I mix the cow dung with the soil as best I can, plant the seeds, and water them.

After a week or so the first green sprouts start coming up in the pot. I am excited and tend them carefully, watching their progress and hoping the fresh cow dung won't be too strong for them. The idea that it would be nice to give Swamiji a flowering plant to brighten up his room comes to my mind. I wait until the third set of leaves and what I think is the beginning of buds appear, before taking the pot up the steps to Swamiji's *kutir*. As I am standing in the anteroom, Swamiji comes out with his walking stick, ready for his afternoon walk. I have the chance to explain to him that I have been given some seeds of the moonflower plant and that he

---

[33] Before there is an ordinance to contain the cows in their own special place, they wander around freely and poop wherever they feel like it, often a messy affair, especially when it rains. Later on, when the Divine Life Society Board of Trustees decides to clean up the *ashram*, the stray cows are the first to go. Some of the monkeys are also caught and released into the jungle.

might like to see the flower. In his usual attentive manner, he receives the little plant as though I am presenting him with a pot of gold. He places it carefully against the wall under a window where it will receive light. On the way out, he calls his attendants, pointing to the plant with his walking stick, "You must make sure it receives enough water."

About a week later I am called up to Swamiji's room. I gasp when I see the plant all dried out and limp under the window. Swamiji calls the attendants, who shuffle in with sheepish smiles on their faces.

"Did you water the plant yesterday?" Swamiji asks in a stern voice.

"She watered it," one of them says, pointing to me. As I hardly ever come up here without being called by Swamiji, it is obvious he is just making it up. I haven't been anywhere near the place.

"No, I wasn't here," I say, realizing that it was a mistake to bring the plant here. My desire that Swamiji should have a flowering plant has created trouble. Not everyone has the same feeling for plants that I have.

"You see," says Swamiji. "If you think this plant can go without water, this Swami," touching his chest with his hand, "will also fast. Tomorrow I will not take food." He is already so thin, I feel bad that Swamiji won't eat tomorrow. But it is out of my hands and that is the end of it as far as I know.[34]

I am given a task to do another painting, this time for behind the little statue of Devi inside the Vishwanath Mandir. I think it is the pujari's idea and I am not provided with a proper board, but only a large sheet of stiff paper. Don has taken most of his paints and brushes, so I have to use what the *pujari* can scrounge up. There is no fine-tipped brush and I cannot get

---

[34] Later, one of the young men attending Swamiji at the time tells me that the incident made such an impression on him that it completely changed his relationship to the natural world. When Swamiji fasted because the plant had not been watered, he became intensely interested in plants and learned how to cultivate beautiful flower gardens wherever he took up residence.

any proper detail. I use poster paints and do what I can with the materials provided, but the finished product is not to my satisfaction.

For a while I keep attending *Vedanta* class at 4 p.m. and then one day I don't feel like listening to any more lectures on *Vedanta*. I mention to Swami Chidananda that I have stopped going to class and I can tell he does not approve.

"You can take a few days off and then resume the classes," Swamiji says. He knows I need some structure to my days. "There was once a lady who came to live in the *ashram* and after a long time, she had not made any progress at all. She remained exactly the same." This is a warning that I am to make best use of my time here, not to find a comfort level and sink into it.

Moo beside the Ganges

LOOKING OUT FROM WITHIN

In the afternoons I often go down and sit on a rock by the Ganga. Watching the flow of water is soothing and peaceful. Sometimes, I climb up to the little Dattatreya Mandir on the hill hugging the north side of the *ashram*. It is very quiet up there and deserted. I am alone, yet not too far from the *ashram*. There is a cave-like room[35] underneath the temple, but it is dark and I imagine may be the home for scorpions, so I don't go in it. I prefer to sit on the cement foundation surrounding the small, steep dome and meditate.

I hear that Swami Chidananda is about to leave on tour of the many branches of the Divine Life Society throughout India. He will be gone for about six weeks and return just before Christmas. For the first time I feel lonely. I realize I am still dependent on Swamiji's physical presence. Everything seems all right when he is in the vicinity. I know I share this feeling with many other devotees who long for Swamiji's *darshan*. Even a glimpse is enough to re-inspire us.

Swamiji is very sympathetic to a true devotee's love for the *guru*, but at the same time will discourage others from coming near him and making a show of their devotion. Swamiji can always tell what motivates people from within and two devotees may appear to do the same thing, but because of the inner feeling, are given different instructions and treated differently.

One day he remarks drily, "Too much *darshan* gives spiritual indigestion!"

Swamiji encourages us to grow less dependent on his physical presence and begin to find the true *guru* residing in our heart—as our own Self. But it will be a long time before I reach that stage.

One morning after early morning prayers, there is a knock on my door and the young boy says, "Come. Swamiji is calling you."

I wrap my shawl around my bony shoulders. The chilly wind off the

---

[35] Nagaraj actually lived in this cave-room for six years, when he first came to the *ashram* in 1953.

mountains blows Swami Vidyananda's *veena* music along the verandah. Bells are ringing down by the Ganga and all around me the sounds of people getting ready for a new day. The thought that another winter is approaching invigorates me.

Swamiji invites me to a cup of morning tea, which I gladly accept. "After speaking to someone for a very long time," he begins, without explaining whom the "someone" is, "I have drawn up a daily *sadhana* schedule for you to follow." He passes me a single sheet of paper with hand-written instructions. "You will follow this for forty days, until I return before Christmas," he says. "Then you will have your *mantra diksha*."

"Thank you Swamiji," my voice comes out in a whisper.

"This should be kept to yourself," Swamiji continues, "not shared with anybody or anyone."

"No," I say. I knew it was a mistake to mention it to Krishnapriyananda Mataji! I knew it! I am so grateful Swamiji is giving me another chance. "Yes Swamiji. Thank you." I am so happy to hear that he will initiate me that I never think to ask him who the "someone" was he was talking to "for a very long time." But my guess is it was a communication with someone not in this physical world.

CHAPTER 14

REALITY GETS REAL

SPECIAL SADHANA

I begin the new sadhana routine that Swamiji has given me in earnest. Mine was not a family that went to church on a regular basis. Growing up, I spent most Sunday mornings roaming free on our farm in South Africa. The great outdoors was my church, with the result that whenever I was connected to the natural world around me—the grass, rocks, wild creatures, deep valleys and flat-topped hills of Natal—I felt at peace. I spent most of my free time outdoors, with siblings, friends, and quite often alone. I knew I had to be careful of ticks, poisonous snakes, lightning, and fires, which sometimes swept up the valley, burning the dry grass, the wildflowers, and the wattle trees oozing with sap. I felt completely at home in the natural world, which gave me the first inkling that there was something in me connected to everything else.

The school I attended, Durban Girls' College, also had an influence on my religious outlook. Natal province, mostly settled by the British, followed the Church of England with morning prayers in the high-ceilinged school hall. Every day, we lined up in classes, from Standard One through Matric, to sing a hymn from the Oxford Hymn Book and recite the Lord's Prayer. Then a short passage was read from the Bible.

Later, as teenagers, my sister and I attended Sunday evening services at the Presbyterian Church, a few blocks down the hill from our house in Durban. We were confirmed in that church, but as I remember, we were more interested in the young men attending the service than the substance of what the minister was preaching.

So, it is almost surprising to me that I have come all the way to India, only to discover in a predominantly Hindu *ashram*, that I feel drawn to the teachings of Jesus Christ. I say predominantly Hindu, because Swami Sivananda's enlightened, generous spirit embraced all religions, all prophets, saints, holy men and women of all religious persuasions. He taught, "There is only one religion, the religion of love."

In the Hindu tradition there are many forms of God. Each seeker is encouraged to discover his or her *Ishta Devata*, which is usually the deity worshipped by the family in which one is raised. It is important in the *yogic* tradition, as in Christianity, to have a personal relationship with some form, or with some idea of God. In *Vedanta*, the idea of God could be formless. Swamiji often says, "In whatever way you can connect yourself to God, do it." In order to make God *real*, you have to know that He, She or It is *very* near you, "nearer than your hands and feet, nearer than your very breath."

During the first few months spent at the *ashram*, Swamiji encouraged me in various ways, to discover and identify my *Ishta*. When he involved us in the painting project I became very attached to Lord Krishna. We learned about Lord Rama, the ideal human being, who incarnated to establish *dharma* and rescue his wife Sita, abducted by the wicked demon king, Ravana. I love to hear the chanting of *"Sri Ram, Jai Ram, Jai, Jai Ram!"* Hanuman is the perfect devotee of Rama, the perfect servant. From Mother Rema in South India, we learned first hand about the power of Shakti, in all the forms of the Divine Mother. I am drawn to Shakti, because I see nature shimmering with Her power. She is both soothing and terrifying. The multitudinous forms of God found in India do not in the least make me think of ignorant primitive idol worship. Rather, it is the overwhelming generosity of God who has appeared in so many forms so that *everyone* can find a connection to Him, Her or It. All are included! All are welcome!

The spiritual practices that Swamiji has written out for me to follow are designed to involve me in constant remembrance of God. Besides the regular programs and classes, I am to do twenty-five *malas* of *japa* morning and evening; read one of the four Gospels from the New Testament each day, so that by the end of forty days, I will have read each one ten times; one chapter of *Bhagavad Gita* per day; *mantra* writing 108 times per day or night; 6 rounds simple *pranayama* daily, a.m. or p.m. and half an hour of meditation at the Samadhi Shrine. I am to observe silence from noon until 4 p.m. every day and am not to leave the *ashram* premises to go shopping in Rishikesh, or even over the river. A walk up the road is okay.

Shortly after I begin the *sadhana*, Swamiji leaves on his tour of the DLS branches in India. The practices take me from four o'clock in the morning until the evening. I begin to feel fatigued and sometimes skip the evening satsang in favor of a longer night's sleep. One morning Swami Krishnananda meets me at the top of the steps. "I haven't seen you in evening *satsang*. Are you ill?"

"I have been doing *sadhana* which Swami Chidananda gave me to do," I explain.

"Does it take you all day?" he asks.

"Sometimes it does, Swamiji."

"Well, try to come at 9 o'clock at least, just for the end of the *satsang*." Swami Krishnananda is so kind to me. I know he cares that I get the benefit of coming together with others for the evening meeting; so from then on I make the effort to go to *satsang*.

My already precarious health begins to deteriorate even more with the long hours, coupled by the fact that when Swami Chidananda leaves the *ashram*, the young boy who normally brings a handful of vegetables for me to cook stops coming. I try to eat what I can from the *ashram* kitchen, but I become thinner and am often hungry. I make it a habit to visit the Vishwanath Mandir as the bells begin to ring for the 7 a.m. worship when they sometimes give *kicheri*, *dhal* and rice cooked together, as *prasad*. It is usually served warm in a little cone-shaped cup made of newspaper printed in Russian. I wonder how this Russian newspaper comes to be at the *ashram*. Who would be reading it? But I am more interested in the warm contents of the cone, not because I am holy and devoted, but just because I really need something to eat.

WAR

In the days when Swami Sivananda was alive, he discouraged his disciples from reading newspapers, so that they could focus solely on their spiritual practices without distractions from outside. More or less the same applies today. However, when Don was here he used to go down to the little tea stall at the bottom of the hill by the Ganga and get a cup of *chai* and read the newspaper from Delhi. He would relate to me bits and pieces of stories he had read. He felt it was important to keep up with what was happening in the States and in the world at large. The hideous war in far away Vietnam is still raging. I believe Nagaraj has a radio in his room, where he listens to the world news from the BBC.

Towards the end of November, the news filters through the *ashram* that India and Pakistan will soon be at war. Not knowing much about Indian politics, I assume it is over the territory of Kashmir. I know that both of them claim the territory and tension has been bristling along the border between the two countries for some time. The worst part of the news is that the United States is backing Pakistan! The Nixon administration has promised to send arms to Pakistan, so they can fight India! What is *wrong* with our country? The Indians love America. Why would we Americans not side with another friendly democratic country? I can't understand it.

"They'll round up the Americans and put them in camps," I overhear someone saying. The news dismays me. Many members of my family were interned in concentration camps in China and the Philippines during WWII and the possibility that I will end up in a camp scares me. However, as long as I am living in the *ashram* I feel safe and protected. A young Indian woman whom I have come to know a little smiles at me and says, "It's just like Lord Krishna tells Arjuna in the Mahabharata. 'All those who are going to die, are already dead.' So don't worry. There's nothing we can do about it!" If she is trying to cheer me up, it doesn't have the right effect. I find that as long as I concentrate on the *sadhana* Swamiji has given me, I am fully occupied and the idea of the war is out of my mind. That is my saving grace.

I often visit Gurudev's Kutir in the evening, where Swami Devananda holds *kirtan*, as twilight falls over the Ganges. Both Swami Devananda and Swami Hamsananda are caretakers of Gurudev's Kutir, sleeping on the floor at night. After the evening *kirtan*, we shuffle our bare feet into Swami Sivananda's small inner rooms where he wrote his books, slept, and meditated. In the small *puja* room a beautiful, classic picture of Lord Krishna playing the flute stands on an altar in front of which nightly *arati* is performed. An oil lamp is waved and we receive the blessing from the light. Then the *kutir* door is opened and we walk down the cement steps to the river. *Arati* is then done to Mother Ganga, while the devotees chant a hymn singing her praises. Dotted along the Ganges banks I see the flames of other *aratis* and sometimes, tiny boats made of leaves carrying little flaming wicks down the river. It's a beautiful sight!

One evening, after *arati* I find myself in the *ashram* office where Swami Premananda, the *ashram* treasurer is working after dark.

"How long do you intend to stay at the *ashram*?" he suddenly asks me, in his slightly squeaky, high-pitched voice.

"I don't know." I answer, taken by surprise. "Forever." I don't even know why I say "forever." There is no such thing. But I have no plan for departing, so I just say what comes to mind.

"That will not be possible," he informs me, enunciating each word.

Then he resumes working at his desk, absent-mindedly stroking his long greying beard. His words hit me like a blow to my heart. I don't ask him why he says I won't be able to stay. I am too stunned to speak. I leave the office and walk slowly up the hill, taking the long way to avoid the steps. I realize that without Swami Chidananda here and now that Don is gone, my position in the *ashram* is tenuous. Everyone knows me as a married woman, I reason, but now I am a *single* married woman and I have heard they don't like single women staying too long in the *ashram*. Apparently, it's too distracting for the young monks. I remember a Zen story about a young woman seeker who asks permission to enter the Zendo. The head Roshi refuses her, because she is too beautiful. So she leaves and to show her determination, burns her face with a hot iron and returns the next day to ask permission again.

Thinking about this story, I stop walking and realize that my desire for liberation does not include burning my face with an iron. Maybe I am half-hearted after all? Sri Ramakrishna said that the desire for liberation should feel so intense, like a drowning man wanting air. Anyway, I don't have to worry about beauty being my downfall. My face is all broken out and I am as skinny as a rake. It has never dawned on me that the reason could be monetary. It is true that I have very little money left from our original batch of traveler's checks and no prospects of receiving any more. It just hasn't crossed my mind until now that I may be a burden on the *ashram*. Swami Chidananda never, *ever*, gave us any inkling that we, and now I, would not be welcome because we could not afford to pay our way. But then, no one is like Swamiji. How naïve and stupid I am! After all, I remind myself, the running of the *ashram* depends mainly on donations from the devotees, as well as income from the sale of publications.

I don't mention this to anybody. I will wait until Swamiji returns and then discuss it with him. Meanwhile, the best thing to do is to keep doing my *sadhana* as he instructed me.

AMOEBAS AND A SHEEPSKIN COAT

I cannot ignore the gnawing feeling in my left side any longer. Four years ago I was hospitalized for ten days with amoebic hepatitis, so I am familiar with liver disease, which I first contracted in Ecuador. Now, it seems to be back. I was told that once amoebas have established themselves in your body, it is almost impossible to get rid of them. After a course of antibiotics, the only thing you can do is to fortify your immune system with good nutrition and vitamins, plenty of rest, and moderate exercise. My immune system is full of holes through lack of all of the above, except for the exercise. I still do a few yoga *asanas* on a daily basis and take walks along the road and down to the Ganga every day. With a curious objectivity, I find that despite the ill health, I love being here.

One morning I walk down the hill and sit on a large rock on the Ganges bank, upriver from the bathing *ghat*. As a young *sannyasin*, Swami Chidananda used to meditate on one of these rocks. I have come here to do *japa* and some *pranayama* in the fresh air, but the morning sun feels so good, I lie back on the rock to absorb the warmth. I am so fatigued, that the thought of walking back up the hill is almost overwhelming. I know I should go to the doctor in Dehra Dun, but how can I? Swamiji's instructions are for me not to leave the *ashram*.

Dr. Kutty, the OBGYN who comes to the *ashram* to serve the poor women of the area, is not in residence at present, so I cannot seek her advice. Finally, I decide I will ask Nagaraj, who is most helpful when Swamiji is away. Next morning, as I am crossing the courtyard, I see him at the top of the steps leading to the door of his room. I tell him about the pain in my side and that I am sure it is an indication that the amoebas are back.

"You go to the doctor," he says, matter-of-factly.

"But what about the instruction not to leave the *ashram*?"

"Then you bear the pain," he replies. Nagaraj has a pure mind and keeps everything as simple as possible. It is either this or that. He doesn't overanalyze or split hairs.

The pain is not so bad. I could easily bear it, but I really don't want the amoebas to get a foothold in the liver again. So I opt for going to Dehra Dun by shared taxi the next day and take the Bible with me, so I can read a gospel while I am waiting at the doctor's.

"During partition," the lady doctor tells me, while taking my blood pressure, "my family left everything in Pakistan and came to India to settle." I listen as she writes out a prescription for antibiotics. "Partition was not a good thing. Look at all the trouble they are having now!"

"Yes, I've heard about it," I say. She hands me the slip of paper.

"Take twelve tablets a day for five days," she says. "With food."

"Thank you," I say, turning to go.

"Have you paid me?" she asks, a sharper edge to her voice.

"Oh. I'm sorry," I turn back, reach in my bag and take out my zip purse. Living at the *ashram* where food and shelter are provided, I have gotten quite out of touch with the way the world works. People *do* actually have to earn a living and money *is* exchanged!

"Twenty rupees," she says. It's not even two dollars. Very cheap by our standards, but I have become accustomed to Indian prices now. I thank her again and cross the street to a little pharmacy and fill my prescription. The Flagyl tablets are only a few rupees.[36]

The following week a young Western man called John, turns up in the *ashram*. He seeks me out, as I am one of the few Western faces here. He is having a hard time with his digestion and the spicy food does not agree with him. I can sympathize with that!

"If I buy the vegetables," he proposes, "would you cook them? Then we can have lunch together."

"Alright," I agree, taken by surprise. "But you will have to go to Rishikesh to find vegetables."

---

[36] Later, I find that these exact same pills cost ten times as much outside of India.

REALITY GETS REAL

He turns up before noon, and I boil the vegetables in a little water, in my enamel pot. They taste very good with salt and pepper and we sit on the floor and eat. It's strange having someone else in my room. He's from one of the western states, like Wyoming or Montana. He's about my age and height, with reddish blond hair. After we have finished he says, "What if I buy the vegetables every day and you cook for us, while I am in the *ashram*?"

"Oh, no, I'm sorry I can't." It's a simple request and he's a nice person and I would like to help him, but I know it would be too much socializing for me. He looks disappointed, so I explain. "I am here for a specific purpose, to do *sadhana*, not to be a cook. I'm afraid it would be too distracting."

"I understand," he says, getting up. "I'll make other arrangements."

I don't see much of John after that and I hope he is managing with his food. A week later, I hear a knock on the door and John is standing on the verandah with a sheepskin coat slung over his arm.

"I came to say goodbye," he says. "I'm leaving today. I wonder if you would make sure this coat goes to some needy and deserving person." He hands me the coat, which feels heavy in my arms.

"Won't you be needing it?"

"No. I'm heading to South India and it's warm down there. It would just be in the way."

"Then yes, of course I will," I say. "I hope you have a safe journey."

"Thanks. Goodbye!" he turns and walks to the narrow stairs leading outside. I lean over the railing, until he appears on the driveway. "Drink only boiled water if you can!"

"Yes, okay. Thanks!" he raises his hand.

"Safe travels!" I wave back.

I carry the coat inside and spread it over my thin mattress on the floor. I kneel down and run my hands over it. The seams are on the outside and the sheep's wool is on the inside. What a well-made coat! And warm too!

Winter is approaching and the nights and early mornings are chilly with wind blowing down from the Himalayan peaks. We cannot see the peaks from the *ashram*, but we can feel in the air that they are covered with snow. The temple at Kedarnath, in the high Himalayan range, is closed in November. A single wick lamp in a big vessel of oil is left to burn inside the temple all the winter months, until the snow melts and the doors are open again in spring. Here in the *ashram*, everyone wraps themselves in thick shawls or blankets with warm scarves wrapped around head and neck. Indian men, visitors from towns and cities, also wear short wool jackets with high collars, the "Nehru jacket," over their cotton *kurtas*. In my room, I spread the coat over the top of my cotton blanket and Tibetan shawl, which I bought in Nepal a year ago. It is nice to be really warm for a change!

Next day, I try the coat on for size and it fits me perfectly, but I take it off quickly and throw it on the bed. It could never be worn in the *ashram!* For one thing, it is made out of skin, which means an animal has been killed. The swamis don't wear leather. It would violate the principle of *ahimsa*. Their sandals are either rubber flip-flops, or faux leather. Some of them still use the traditional wooden sandals, with a wooden spindle sticking up between the big toe and the second toe. Neither do they use belts or leather bags. Mostly everything is made from cotton.

I notice that the thought of the sheepskin coat will not leave my mind. John's words were, "a needy and deserving person." Who could that be? I will have to make some enquiries. In the meantime, no harm in enjoying the coat myself for a little while! Having spent the last year studying *Vedanta*, I have some idea of how the mind works. If there is an object that one desires, the mind immediately goes to the idea of that object and attaches itself to it. It obsesses over it, until it can possess or acquire it and then it is satisfied. But only for a little while, until the next desire comes along. The same process is repeated again and again. Thus we are caught in the never-ending cycle of desires. With the experience of temporary satisfaction, the thought-waves in the mind subside and happiness arises. The mind mistakenly associates the internal happiness with the object of desire and becomes more attached to it. The feeling of attachment, thinking "this is mine" and the subsequent fear of loss, is what brings about our suffering. I remember Swami Krishnananda saying that attachment to even a worthless bag can prevent you from God-realization!

The coat has been in my room for three days and I am already attached to it. One part of my mind thinks of it as *my* coat and another part observes, *Interesting! You already think this is your coat. You have fallen into the trap of the mind!* The *yogis* say, "Mind is the cause of both bondage and liberation; the feeling of 'I-ness and mine-ness' comes from ego. Attachment is bondage. Detachment is liberation."

It appears now that the war is coming for sure. For all I know, it might have already started. My health is broken. And the fact that I was not able to stick strictly to my *sadhana* by going outside of the *ashram* to the doctor in Dehra Dun is beginning to nudge me in the direction of leaving. My thoughts run on and on. *How nice that coat would be in the cold Pennsylvania winter! I could really use it.* It is a struggle for me to let go of the idea of keeping the coat. *Could I be the deserving person? After all, no one knows about the coat except me. I could easily keep it.* Then I berate myself for such a selfish thought. I would deprive some poor Indian from enjoying the warmth of the coat, which might even save his or her life. Finally, it dawns on me that the coat has ruined my peace of mind. As long as it is in my room, I cannot think of anything else for very long. I resolve to take the coat to Nagaraj tomorrow. Then I lie down and am soon asleep.

I have a strange dream. I am at some sort of a party in a room crowded with people. They are all talking and chatting with each other. I feel left out. I miss Don. Suddenly, on the other side of the room jammed with people, I see Don standing in the doorway. He sees me too and begins to wave. He is trying to communicate with me. Then I hear the distinct sound of wings, like the fast flutter-beat of humming-bird wings, coming from afar and getting closer. Thrrrrrr! Something lands very lightly on the back of the neck and I wake up with a start. I am lying face down on the mattress on the floor. For a minute I don't move at all, until the sensation of the kiss on the back of my neck fades slowly into waking consciousness.

It feels like an angel, or someone just brought me a message. Or, perhaps it is Swamiji sending his blessings.

After breakfast that morning, I carry the heavy coat up the steps to Nagaraj's room and knock on his door. He opens it right away. "Someone left this coat with me," I explain, "and he wants it to go to a needy and deserving person. Do you know anyone?"

"What about *you*?" Nagaraj asks. "Aren't you a needy and deserving person?" I wonder if he is joking with me.

"Oh no! It's not for me!" I say decidedly, not wanting to give any leniency to my mind, which has tormented me long enough.

"All right, then. I will give it to one man who lives down on the plains. The place gets very cold in winter."

"That sounds perfect," I say, handing over the coat. I thank Nagaraj and return to my room. I am flooded with a great feeling of relief. The decision has been made and the coat is no longer mine, nor my responsibility. My mind feels the sense of loss, of what could have been, but that is quickly replaced by an awareness that peace is returning to my heart.

TELEGRAMS

The war between India and Pakistan officially starts on 3rd December 1971 when Pakistan launches air strikes on eleven Indian air bases. East Pakistan is fighting for its independence from West Pakistan. India takes sides with the Bengalis in their liberation struggle, and attacks Pakistan on both the eastern and western fronts.[37]

I receive a telegram from Don in South Africa, telling me to get out of India. He has obviously heard the news and he is afraid I am going to get trapped here. He doesn't say all that in the telegram but I get the message.

---

[37] Eventually, Pakistan will surrender and they will sign an agreement in Dakka, creating the new nation of Bangladesh.

REALITY GETS REAL

Now I'm now torn between trying to continue my *sadhana* and following Don's request to leave. I'm not sure what to do. Yvonne, the French lady living in Lakshmi Kutir, advises me to have a bag packed and ready to go at a moment's notice. I don't know where I would possibly go, but I pack a bag anyway and put it by the door. I listen to Yvonne who was active in the French underground, during the German occupation of France in WWII and has been in all sorts of dangerous situations. Still, I know I must wait for Swamiji to return. I can't imagine leaving without his permission, or officially saying goodbye to him. So, I continue my *sadhana* as best I can and take each day as it comes.

That evening, while sitting on the floor in front of my little altar, which is no more than a cloth over a board, with two black and white photographs, one of Gurudev Sivananda and one of Swami Chidanandaji, something unexpected happens. Perhaps it is because I am under so much stress wondering about my situation, but as I am staring at the photos, the eyes suddenly became conscious. Instead of photographs of people in frames, the people in the photographs, namely the two great beings mentioned above, are alive! The photographs have a conscious presence to them. They are not just being looked at—they are looking back at me, with eyes full of love! I feel so blessed to have both Swami Sivananda and Swami Chidananda in the room with me, helping me get through this crisis.

The following morning the Indian Posts and Telegraphs Department delivers a telegram to me from Swami Chidananda. It is from Bombay through Tehri-Garhwal, the official government office of this area. Written on flimsy pink paper, it is addressed to: Mrs. Moo Briddell, care Sec'ry Divine Life.

It reads, *Dear Moo, in view of present situation, if you desire to leave India urgently as Don wish you to do, then you have my permission, blessing to depart. Stop. Myself shall be able return only 22nd hence, this telegram. Swami Chidananda.*

It is wonderful to get a telegram from Swamiji! As always, he is aware of the entire situation. Distance is no obstacle to him. The telegram has a round ink stamp with the date, 10th December 1971.

I run with the telegram to show it to Yvonne. She agrees that now, with Swamiji's permission, I am free to leave. It is a bittersweet release. My heart feels heavy that I will not get to see Swamiji before I leave, nor will I receive initiation from him. I will have to wait and trust that on some unknown future date, I may meet him again. I go back to my room and write a long letter to Swamiji, telling him that as of tomorrow, it will be exactly one year since we arrived in the *ashram* on a full moon evening. I tell him that everyday has been like a jewel on a necklace. I have loved every minute of each day. Thinking of Swamiji's delicate constitution, I make a final request. I know it sounds irrational, but I write it anyway. I ask Swamiji please not to leave his body until I have a chance to meet him again. Then I give the letter to Yvonne to hand over to Swamiji when he returns on 22nd December.

Now that I know I'm leaving, I walk around looking at everything with a fresh perception, trying to absorb and record in my memory the sights that I may never see again. My possessions are few and it doesn't take me long to pack my backpack.

When dear old Swami Hariharananda hears that I am getting ready to leave, he sends five rupees up to the *pujari* of Vishwanath Mandir, requesting a *puja* for my safe travel abroad and reunion with "Mr. Don." He is such a sweet man and teaches me two verses from the *Bhagavad Gita* (Chapter 18, verses 65 and 66),[38] which he insists I learn in Sanskrit by heart. "These are the most important verses," he says, as I sit with him on the last day.

I take the mud statue of Ganesha and lower it into the Ganga, as requested by Mother Rema's daughter, Mira, who gave it to me. It is easy to give things away now that I have no more need for them. I give away my little blue enamel pot and the electric burner to Ann.

---

[38] 65) Fix thy mind on Me, be devoted to Me, sacrifice to Me, bow down to Me. Thou shalt come even to Me; truly do I promise thee, for thou art dear to Me.

66) Abandoning all duties, take refuge in Me alone: I will liberate thee from all sins; grieve not.

"Where's the Ganesha?" she asks, looking around my empty room.

"Oh, I followed the wishes of the person who gave it to me and put it in the Ganga."

"Oh," she says, disappointed. "That was the one nice thing you had."

"Sorry! Yes, it was a nice Ganesha," I say. "I just thought I should honor her request."

We tell each other that we will stay in touch.

On the last evening, I take leave of Swami Krishnananda. I have made a candle for him, by pouring wax into a hollow bowl of sand. I put it on a plate with some walnuts, which I have heard he likes. He is staying on the other side of the gully in a double-story red cement building, overlooking the Ganga. "All this is not necessary," he says, when I put the plate with the candle and walnuts in front of him. We talk for a while and I thank him for all his guidance and support. In the absence of Swami Chidananda, Swami Krishnananda has always shown me such kindness. I am sad to say goodbye to him.

"Come back again to Gurudev's *ashram*," are his parting words to me.

The next morning, I go down to the river one last time and fill a little plastic bottle with Ganges water to take with me. My heart is brimming like the river. I am so sad and so grateful at the same time that I cannot speak. Nagaraj takes me by car to the Rishikesh train station, where he helps me to book my spot, by spreading my Tibetan shawl on an empty wooden seat. Then I bow to him and get on the train to Delhi.

Mira meets me at the train station and I stay overnight with her and Raja. We talk about Mother Rema and I leave them with the Tibetan shawl. Next afternoon, when I settle into my seat on the plane for Bombay, the gentleman in the seat next to me calls the flight attendant.

"Look," he says to her, pointing through the window at several jets lined up on the tarmac. "It will be so easy for the Pakistanis to bomb them all! Please alert the captain to have them moved." The young lady nods and disappears down the aisle. I am not the only one with anxiety about the war.

THE WAR ENDS

In my bag is a letter of introduction from Nagaraj to Mr. Siva Narayan Kapoor, who is a trustee of the Divine Life Society. I have two or three days to wait in Bombay for a flight to Mauritius and then South Africa. Nagaraj has asked Mr. Kapoor to put me up for a few days. The Divine Life Society members take care of each other, treating strangers like family and devotees from abroad are no exception. Apart from the first couple of nights in Madras when we arrived in India, we have rarely stayed in a hotel. We've nearly always been put up in a home with a family or in an *ashram*. Indians are probably the most hospitable of all people in the world—from the richest to the poorest they will share what they have with you. They imbibe from their culture the belief that God can appear in any form or disguise. The unexpected guest might be the Almighty dropping in to see whether they are acting in accordance with *dharma*.

Mr. Kapoor happens to be a wealthy man and his family occupies some spacious apartments in a block of flats in a good residential area of Bombay. I am given my own room and offered tea and then supper. I feel quite shabby wearing my worn-out cotton clothes in this place of opulence. However, my hosts are very gracious to me and give me plenty of time alone. I decline the offer to go shopping. I know a trip into a crowded shopping area would simply short-circuit my brain at this point. I prefer to stay in my room, continuing with my practices as much as possible, or sitting in a chair in the living room, reading.

I take down one of three copies of a large, thick book called *Sadhana*, which is a compilation of a series of transcribed talks given by Swami Chidananda about fifteen years prior. I saw this book in the *ashram* library, but I was told it was out of print. I settle into a chair to read. At some point, Mr. Kapoor sees me engrossed in the book and offers it to me.

"Would you like to take a copy with you? I have extra."

For reasons even I can't understand, I feel that I can't possibly accept such a gift from him, even though I would really like to have the book. "Oh, no thank you," I answer. "It would be too heavy for me to carry." Why do I say "no" to accepting this book, especially when I can see that he has three copies on his bookshelf? I am so used to having nothing, that the thought of receiving something valuable, triggers my mind into automatic recoil. Perhaps it is the experience of my struggle with attachment to the sheepskin coat that lingers in my memory. Or, maybe I am thinking of myself as one who wants nothing, still holding renunciation as the highest ideal. As if refusing to accept a gift is more honorable than accepting it! Mr. Kapoor just smiles. He must think me very strange.

The Kapoor children, a son and a daughter, are about my age, maybe a little younger. They are going out with friends and they invite me to go to dinner with them. I am grateful that they have included me in their outing and accept their invitation. I have been inside for three days now. Perhaps their parents are worried about me and would like to see me get out for a while. The restaurant is in the apartment building, so we just have to go downstairs in the lift.

The young women are very stylish, with short haircuts and modern clothes. The irony is not lost on me that while I am dressed in traditional India garb, with my long hair braided behind my neck, they are having none of it. The young, upper class Indian is adopting Western ways as fast as they can. The men are handsome and the women are beautiful, with glossy black hair and large lustrous eyes. They are full of *joie de vivre*, bursting with exuberance, happy to be together and having a good time. I feel like a fish out of water and sit quietly, wondering if I will be able to digest the Indian food we are about to order.

They try to include me in their conversation. The handsome guy at the end of the table is a young actor, who has played a part in a recently made film called *Siddhartha*.

"I played Siddhartha's friend," he tells me. "We were up where you were, in Rishikesh and Lakshman Jhula."

"Oh really?" I look up, interested.

"The film opens with an early morning scene by the old temple in Lakshman Jhula," he continues.

"I know that old temple," I say, encouraging him to tell me more.

"It is a special place, with a special atmosphere," he hesitates. "But we were just playing roles. You are the real thing!"

"I? The real thing?" I shrug self-consciously. "I wouldn't say that." I don't attempt to explain how completely *unreal* everything has seemed for the past few weeks. I can only think of how much I have left behind, of how my spiritual life seems torn in two. Yet my body and mind are relieved to be away from the war zone.

After dinner, they have plans to go off to a club somewhere and I thank them politely and return upstairs to the apartment, happy to be on my own again. I suddenly feel extremely tired and as soon as I undress, I crawl into bed and fall asleep.

The next morning, I pack all my belongings into my backpack and lean it by the door. "My plane leaves this afternoon," I remind my hosts at breakfast. The daily newspaper is on the table. "The war is *over*?" I read out loud, picking up the paper and reading the headlines on the front page.

"Yes, the war is over," Mrs. Kapoor says, serving me an *idli*. "Thank goodness! Now we can relax again!"

"How did it end?" I ask. "Who won?"

"Oh, India! India won," Mr. Kapoor replies. "And they have made East Pakistan into Bangladesh."

I feel slightly stunned. I am glad the war is over and no more lives will be lost, but it seems so ironic that I am departing India on the 16th December, the day the war ends. If I didn't know better, I would think the cosmos has pulled a fast one on me to get me to leave this country that I have come to love.

"I expect your husband will be glad to see you," says Mrs. Kapoor.

"Yes," I smile, "I expect he will."

EPILOGUE

When I left India in December 1971 I knew it was the end of an important aspect of my life and that nothing would ever be quite the same again. While it was true that the experience changed me on a fundamental level and I had gained a deeper understanding, it was not the end of my spiritual life. It was the beginning.

The year I spent in holy company at the *ashram* changed my worldview and rearranged my priorities. After living amongst the *yogis* and studying *Vedanta*, I had a different understanding of life and its purpose. I learned that human birth, according to the teachings, does not come easily and is not to be taken for granted. That it is only as a self-reflective human being, that we are able to be liberated from ego and realize the Self, our oneness with all existence. I learned that we are here to evolve and express our divine nature through every thought and action. This message, that our precious human birth is not to be wasted, made a lasting impression on me.

When I left India I feared that I would most likely never see Swami Chidananda again. In those days, traveling overseas meant you were going somewhere far away and leaving something or someone behind. In 1971 long distance trunk calls were very expensive and only made in emergencies. Telegrams had the limitation of length and the telephone was used sparingly. It was not something we carried around in our pockets. Our earth seemed like a bigger place and communications, especially in what was then the third world, were few and far between. It is hard now to imagine how much our world has changed, how digital technology, computers, email and cell phones have shrunk the planet.

Leaving spiritual India and all that it stood for was such a wrench that both Don and I had a very difficult time. Encountering the material values of the West, we found ourselves survivors in a land where we had all but forgotten how to speak the language. We suffered from acute culture shock. Living simply and having few possessions is not the goal of our Western civilization.

We stayed with my family in Durban for six months. None of them asked what we had been doing in India over the past fifteen months. No one asked what our life had been like, what we had seen, whom we had met, or how our experiences had changed us, or why I stayed on in India after Don had left. I have no doubt that they cared for us deeply, but they couldn't relate to our spiritual search and had no interest in what had become the most important subject of our lives. We had been so thoroughly immersed in the spiritual values of the *ashram* culture, that at first we could barely function in the world. Gradually, we learned to become more accepting of the ways of people around us.

We returned to the States and in 1974 Don and I settled in Pennsylvania where we started a family and a business. After the partial meltdown of nearby Three Mile Island Nuclear Plant in 1979, we sold everything and moved to the Maryland countryside.

Fortunately for us, Swami Chidananda came to the West many times over the next thirty-five years. A core group of Swamiji's devotees settled around the Maryland area. Swamis Gurudevananda (Sita Frenkel) and Samarpanananda (Marcia Davies) started a small branch of the Divine Life Society of Maryland, in Urbana and later Keedysville, where we gathered for thirty years for a monthly *satsang*. After Gurudevananda's passing in May 2006, we members decided to share the responsibility of hosting the *satsangs* in our homes.

As circumstances allowed, we would travel to wherever Swami Chidananda was to attend his programs. Whenever possible, we would include

EPILOGUE

our children so they could experience in their own way, his higher state of consciousness. We were fortunate to host Swamiji in our home more than once, several days at a time. I also returned more than a dozen times to India from 1975 to 2014 to replenish my spirit. We regarded the many occasions that we were able to spend time with Swamiji as evidence of divine grace in our lives.

Swamiji's message was always about love for the Divine— how to live in a divine way, how and why we should do spiritual practice, how to come closer to God. He insisted on the importance of meditation in one's practice. "A day without meditation is a day wasted," he used to say, because it is in meditation that we find our essential nature, beyond the mind and beyond time.

Swami Chidananda's presence always affirmed that truth triumphs over ignorance, light over darkness. He also made it clear that we have to work for it! We must never give up our *sadhana*. God's grace works together with self-effort. A *guru* paves the way, but we have to do the walking. We must have faith and be ready to step into the unknown.

Swamiji taught us to be of service to others in whatever way we can and to look within our own selves to find the truth. He showed us that even the smallest of actions must be done with one's full attention. In Swamiji's final years he said to us, "I have told you everything. Now the ball is in your court. It is up to you."

Don and I have kept up our *sadhana* throughout our marriage of forty-nine years. Putting the teachings into practice has kept us together through all the ups and downs of life, anchoring us in something greater than our individual selves.

I have found the importance of listening serves me well. Often, I recognize the *guru* using people or situations to transmit teachings to me. Young children teach me to stay curious about the world. Nature is also full of lessons on how to live. Animals, plants, the earth, sun and moon, family and friends—everything and everyone shine with the consciousness of God. I came to realize that the *guru* is essentially my own Self. I am reminded of the saying, "We are the ones we have been looking for." The voice of intuition can be drowned out by the distractions and noise of the world, but if I stop long enough to listen to my inner voice, I usually find my way.

There have always been scoundrels and charlatans in every field of endeavor, and they become more apparent in the spiritual field, where integrity and righteousness are assumed to be the bedrock and foundation of all the practices. Submitting one's ego to a spiritual teacher can be tricky if that teacher is not trustworthy. So, it is important if you are looking for a mentor, either in the East or in the West, to find an impeccable teacher, one who is beyond reproach, who embodies the qualities of love, compassion and humility as the foundation of his or her character. Some teachers begin with good intentions, but due to lack of humility and moral integrity, abuse their position of power over their students and disciples. They give spirituality a bad name and seekers become rightfully suspicious and wary. Students are taken advantage of, sometimes physically. In the worst cases these "so-called *gurus*" have confused and psychologically damaged their students by betraying their trust.

Swamiji Chidananda was one of those pure beings whose only thought was to help others and bring them to God. Even though hundreds of seekers regarded him as their *guru*, he gave all credit to Swami Sivananda, not accepting any of it himself. This constant self-effacement kept him humble and obliterated his ego.

In 2016 the Indian government issued a stamp to honor and commemorate the Centenary of Swami Chidananda's birth.

How generous the universe is to have connected us to such a great being!

It is important to keep studying and learning on a daily basis, never to think we know all the answers. According to the *Yoga Vashista*, the ancient spiritual text, there are four gatekeepers to liberation—self-control, spirit of enquiry, contentment and good company.

EPILOGUE

The *yogis* and sages have told us, "The goal of life is God-Realization." For many years I was under the impression that this was some sort of linear journey. However, the longer I am on this path, the more I realize the goal is intangible and unfathomable. It isn't really a path at all. There is nowhere to go. It has been said that, "The path and the goal are one." The mind can only grasp at the truth, but because it objectifies everything, it will always remain separate. How fitting that this mystery can be consciously experienced, but as soon as the mind tries to define it, it slips silently away.

Since the 1970's yoga has flourished in the United States and around the world into a booming business. While there are many excellent yoga teachers teaching different styles from different lineages and many more coming along behind, I wonder how many of them will have the opportunity to actually immerse themselves in this ancient science of yoga. Will their definition of yoga include the spiritual component? Will they realize that *awakening* is the essence of the teachings, and that *asana* practice is one path leading towards it? Sometimes I wonder whether the coming generations will be able to find a true and humble teacher. Were we just the lucky ones who happened to be in the right place at the right time? Will the awareness of spirit be overwhelmed by the sheer speed and abundance of information in the digital age?

Then I remember the saying, "When the disciple is ready the *guru* appears." If it were true for me, for us, then why shouldn't it be true for others also? I remember the Sanskrit verse from the *Vedas*:

> *Om Poona Madah Poornam-idam*
> *Poornat Poorna Mudachyate*
> *Poornasya Poorna Madaya*
> *Poorna eva Vashishyate*

> Om, That unseen Absolute is infinite, complete and full.
> This, the manifest universe is infinite, complete and full.
> This manifest universe emanates from That unmanifest Absolute.
> After the coming of the manifest universe from the Infinite,
> the Infinite remains.

So I conclude, knowing that there is nothing lacking in this universe, now or ever. Times change, civilizations rise and fall, but consciousness is never absent, never depleted. It is and will always be as full now as when I first began this journey. It is always here for each of us to awaken to its loving and intelligent presence, in our own time, as our own awareness.

> Om Shanti, Shanti, Shantih!

EPILOGUE

The Universal Prayer of Swami Sivananda

O Adorable Lord of Mercy and Love,
Salutations and prostrations unto Thee!
Thou art Omnipresent, Omnipotent and Omniscient.
Thou art Satchidananda – (Existence, Consciousness, Bliss Absolute).
Thou art the Indweller of all beings.
Grant us an understanding heart,
Equal vision, balanced mind,
Faith, devotion and wisdom.
Grant us inner spiritual strength
To resist temptations and to control the mind.
Free us from egoism, lust, greed, hatred, anger and jealousy.
Fill our hearts with divine virtues.
Let us behold Thee in all these names and forms.
Let us serve Thee in all these names and forms.
Let us ever remember Thee.
Let us ever sing Thy glories.
Let Thy Name be ever on our lips.
Let us abide in Thee forever and ever.

GLOSSARY/DICTIONARY

ajna chakra – sixth energy center between the eyebrows
ahimsa – non-injury
akhanda kirtan – continuous singing of a mantra
amma – mother
ananda – bliss
anna – currency unit, one sixteenth of a rupee
antahkarana – the inner instrument, the mind
arati – worship by waving of lights around the deity
ashram – place where a saint resides
Atma(n) – the Self, spirit
avadhoot – yogi who goes without clothes
Ayurveda – Ayurvedic, adjective; a 3,000 year-old holistic healing system based on the belief that health and wellness depend on a delicate balance between the mind, body and spirit.
baba – father
bal – baby
Bhagavan – Lord
bhajan – devotional song praising God
bhakta – devotee of God
bhakti – the path of devotion to God
Bharatavarsha – original name for India
bhav – intense spiritual feeling or attitude
bhavan – building intended and used for a special purpose
bij mantra – seed or short sound for a mantra
brahmachari – one who has taken a vow of brahmacharya or abstinence
brahmacharya – the state of celibacy in student life; the initial stage of the Brahmanic ashramas in the Vedic culture.
Brahman – God
chapatti – roti, flat bread

darshan – vision, sight (of a divine being)
diksha – initiation
Durga – Goddess riding a tiger, destroyer of delusion
ekadasi – eleventh day of the lunar fortnight; often a day of fasting
ganja – marijuana
gerua – orange color of dyed cloth, used for the order of sannyas
ghat – broad steps leading down to a river where bathing and worship take place.
ghee – clarified butter
gopis – cowherd maidens, devotees of Krishna
grihasta – householder, second of the four stages of life in the Vedic culture
guha – cave
guna – a force or quality of nature, as in tamoguna, rajoguna and sattvoguna
guru stotras – verses giving thanks and praise to the guru
idli – a South Indian steamed cake of rice, usually served with a tasty sauce.
ishta devata – aspect of God to which one feels closest, chosen ideal, or favorite deity
japa – repetition of a mantra, either audibly or silently
jnani – one following the path of wisdom and self-enquiry
Kartikeya – (also Subrahmanya), Siva and Parvati's son
khadi – homespun cotton cloth
kicheri – dhal and rice cooked together
kirtan – devotional singing, lead by one singer and followed by all
kundalini – the primordial cosmic energy located in the individual
kurta – knee length dress, or cotton shirt worn over pants
kutir – room or building with multiple rooms
likhit japa – writing of the mantra
mahamantra – the great mantra

GLOSSARY/DICTIONARY

maha samadhi – the highest state of super consciousness, attended with all knowledge and joy; when a realized saint leaves his body

mala – string of 108 beads used for doing jape; rosary

mantra – sacred syllable or word, or set of words through the repetition and reflection of which one attains realization of the Self.

mantra diksha – mantra initiation, given by the guru to the disciple

mataji – Mother, affectionate form

maya – illusion; the sense-world of manifold phenomena held in Vedanta to conceal the unity of absolute being.

mouna – silence

mumukshutva – intense aspiration for liberation

Muni-ki-reti – Beach of the Sages, location of Sivananda Ashram

murti – statue of a deity

muth – holy ashram or temple

nada – divine sound

Navaratri – nine nights, worship of the Divine Mother

Neelkanth – a temple to Siva in Pauri Garhwal

pukka – genuine (Hindi)

Parvati – Siva's consort, an aspect of the Divine Mother

panchakshari mantra – five syllabled mantra: (Om) Na-ma Si-va-ya

pandal – large outdoor tent or marquee, used for satsangs, weddings, etc.

poornima – full moon

prakriti – the prime material energy, of which all matter is composed, Nature

prana – vital energy, subtle life force

pranam – The traditional Indian greeting of respect, bowing, with palms together, often touching the feet of the person being greeted.

prasad – blessed food, offered to God and given to devotees by a holy person

preyo marga – easy, pleasant path

puja – ritualistic worship of the deity

pujari – man or priest who performs the puja

raja – king

rajas, rajo guna – One of the three aspects of cosmic energy; brings about change, dynamism; generates restlessness and passion; rajasic – adjective

Rama – An incarnation of God, the upholder of dharma, the ideal man.

Ramacharitamanas – a scripture, the story of Lord Rama

rishi – sage

roti – flat bread, chapatti

rudraksha – beads made from rudraksha seeds, used in japa malas especially to worship Lord Siva

sadhak – spiritual seeker

sadhana – spiritual practice

sadhu – a wandering monk, or ascetic

samadhi – the state of super-consciousness achieved through intense concentration, where the meditator becomes one with the object of meditation. In yoga this is regarded as the final stage when union with the Divine is reached.

sannyasa – the fourth stage of life in the Brahmanic ashramas of the Vedic culture

sannyasin – a monk, one who has embraced the life of renunciation

Saraswati – Goddess of wisdom, arts and learning

sattva – element or state associated with purity, wholeness, and light

sattvic – pure, denoting foods that are fresh, juicy light and nourishing

satya(m) – truth

shaivites – worshippers of Lord Siva

shakti-pat – transmission of energy from guru to disciple

shanti mantras – peace chants

Shivanandanagar – the post office name for Sivananda Ashram

siddhi – occult spiritual power

sreyo marga – path of righteousness, leading to the good

stotra – Sanskrit verse or hymn

subji – vegetable soup

GLOSSARY/DICTIONARY

swastir – auspiciousness

tabla – a pair of Indian drums

tamas, tamo guna – the dark forces; ignorance, lethargy, laziness; tamasic, adjective

tiffin carrier – stainless steel stacking dishes used to carry food

tonga – a horse drawn carriage, big enough for two passengers and the driver

trikuta – third eye, space between the eyebrows

Uttarpradesh – northern province of India, now Uttarakhand

vairagya – dispassion, indifference towards sensual objects

vanaprasta – retirement, third of the four stages of life in the Vedic culture

veena – musical stringed instrument with a large gourd on either end

Veda – the most ancient, authentic scripture of the Hindus

Vedanta – the end of the Vedas; the Upanishads; the school of Hindu thought upholding the doctrine of non-dualism.

Vishwanath Mandir – Sivananda Ashram temple, dedicated to Lord Viswanath

yajna – a ritual sacrifice with a specific objective

yajna shala – the room where the fire ceremony and other sacrificial events are performed

yantra – a geometric form denoting different kinds of spiritual energy, used as an aid in meditation

CPSIA information can be obtained
at www.ICGtesting.com
Printed in the USA
BVHW031339280419
546721BV00001B/130/P